Diary And Correspondence Of Count Axel Fersen, Grand-marshal Of Sweden, Relating To The Court Of France;

Fersen, Hans Axel von, greve, 1755-1810

IARY AND CORRESPONDENCE

OF

COUNT AXEL FERSEN

Count Axel Fersen

DIARY AND CORRESPONDENCE

OF

COUNT AXEL FERSEN

GRAND-MARSHAL OF SWEDEN

RELATING TO

THE COURT OF FRANCE

TRANSLATED BY

KATHARINE PRESCOTT WORMELEY.

ILLUSTRATED WITH PORTRAITS FROM THE ORIGINAL

BOSTON:

HARDY, PRATT & COMPANY.

1902.

Copyright 1902,
BY HARDY, PRATT & COMPANY.

———

𝔘niversity 𝔓ress
JOHN WILSON AND SON, CAMBRIDGE, U.S.A.

CONTENTS.

CHAPTER I. — 1755–1780.

CHAPTER II. — 1780–1782.

CHAPTER III. — 1783–1791.

CHAPTER IV. — 1791.

CHAPTER V — 1791.

CHAPTER XI. — 1792.

APPENDIXES

LIST OF

PHOTOGRAVURE ILLUSTRATIONS.

FAC–SIMILE LETTERS

DIARY AND CORRESPONDENCE

OF

COUNT AXEL FERSEN.

———•———

CHAPTER I.

1755–1780   Introductory — Count Fersen's first and second Visit to the
French Court — The Dauphine and Queen, Marie-Antoinette —Fersen
joins the French Expedition to America as Aide-de-camp to the Comte
de Rochambeau

THE Diary of Count Axel Fersen was not intended for
publication.   It is a collection of notes written daily to aid
his memory from 1780 to 1810, the year of his death.   He
mentions with deep regret, in a letter to his intimate friend
Baron Taube, that the portion from 1780 to 1791, was
destroyed in Paris in 1791, as a matter of precaution, by the
friend in whose care he had left it at the time of the flight
to Varennes.   A precious record was thus lost of Louis XVI.
and Marie-Antoinette during their last years of peace and
the first years of the Revolution, written by one who judged
them nobly, and apart from the vile prejudices and jealousies
of their Court.   But enough remains to form a connecting
thread for his valuable and interesting Correspondence.

These letters, papers, and documents are in the possession
of Count Fersen's family, and the parts concerning his con-
nection with the Court of France were published by his

great-nephew, Baron Klinckowström, in 1878 (Paris, Firmin-Didot and Co), from which edition this translation is made. The sketch of Count Fersen's life, which begins the present volume and is continued now and then through the course of it for the purpose of elucidating the diary and correspondence, is taken chiefly from the anonymous Introduction to the French edition, with a few comments from other sources which will be named as they occur.

Count Jean Axel Fersen was born September 4, 1755, of a noble Swedish family distinguished in war by three field-marshals. He was the son of Field-marshal Frederick Axel Fersen, the eloquent leader of the political party called " Les Chapeaux," which, in harmony with France, followed a steady course of liberal opposition. Count Fersen, the father, battled, under support of fundamental laws, for the liberty of citizens against the assumptions of royal power tending to despotism. In this struggle King Gustavus III. was the chief actor on one side, on the other were the nobles, defending the cause of national liberty and the maintenance of laws against despotism, and always inclining to oppose or ignore the sacred right of kings.

Gustavus III played an important part in the affairs of France at the beginning of the Revolution. No other king has been so variously judged by his contemporaries and by posterity. He has been lauded beyond measure by his admirers, and regarded by them as the saviour of the country, the founder of a new era, a great statesman, a hero, a conqueror, the promoter of religious liberty, a literary man, a dramatist, devoid of vanity as a man and as a king.

His political antagonists, on the other hand, charged him with all the worst propensities and faults of kings, and even with the foibles and vices of humanity, — levity, falsehood, prodigality, indifference to the welfare of his people; they called him tyrannical, despotic, perjured; attributing great crimes and evil-doings to him The truth lies, as usual, between the two extremes. The reason is that the life and actions of this king have never been sufficiently made known to warrant an impartial judgment. Gustavus III. was not the same man, the same king, at the beginning of his life that he was at the close of it : principles, views, will, plans, resolutions, all were changed in his versatile and fluctuating mind. The object of his actions also varied much. And yet, he began his reign by an act of great importance to his country, — the revolution of 1772, which crushed anarchy, and freed Sweden from dependence on foreign powers and from the evil effects of degrading corruption. That is one of the finest pages in the king's history. The ball of an infamous assassin put an end to his life, March 6, 1792, made a martyr of him, and drew a veil over his faults and his foibles.

When young Axel Fersen was sixteen years old he was sent by his father, in charge of a tutor, to study the art and profession of arms in foreign countries and thus complete his education. During this journey, which lasted four years, he studied in the military schools of Brunswick, Turin, and Strasburg A journal which he kept very punctually during those years gives a picture of his youthful mind and his way of looking at what he saw.

Basle, October 17, 1771. I find here all sorts of extraordinary customs which divert me much. For instance, the town clock is always one hour in advance of the clocks of other countries. This difference, they tell me, goes back to a remote period when the inhabitants resolved to kill their chief magistrate, who, warned of the plot, foiled the conspirators by putting on the hands of the clock. — It is not permissible to dance in Basle unless the master of the house plays the violin himself; and you can drive in a carriage only up to ten o'clock at night, without servants behind, and in a plain carriage of one colour only and no gilding. It is forbidden to have silk fringes in the carriage or on the harness when you drive to church, and the ladies must wear black, not gowns but dishabilles. Diamonds, pearls, laces, and pretty things of all kinds are forbidden. It is good taste not to go out before five o'clock; at that hour visits are made to family circles.

One of my acquaintances offered to take me to the *Assemblée du Printemps* [assembly of Spring-buds]; he presented me first to his sister and she introduced me to this assembly, which is entirely composed of young girls. What surprised me extremely was to see these young ladies arriving alone, or with a gentleman, and no maid or man-servant They played cards and talked with foreigners or with the young men of the town who had the honour to be admitted. They go to walk in the promenades all alone

Geneva, October 30, 1771. We had a letter to M Constant, an intimate friend of M. de Voltaire. He took us the next day to the country-house of Mme Jennigs, a very agreeable woman, who talked to us much about Sweden. From there we went to see M de Voltaire at Ferney, a very pretty house which he built himself on French soil. But he did not receive us, he had taken, they told us, a purgative; which is the pretext he gives when he does not wish to see people, he appointed for us to come on the following day, which obliged us to stay longer than we intended. We were received at the appointed time and talked with him for two hours. He was dressed in a scarlet waistcoat with old embroidered buttonholes, which his father and his grandfather had doubtless worn before him. An old wig, not curled, old-fashioned shoes, woollen stockings, pulled on over his drawers, and an old dressing-gown completed his toilet, admirably in keeping with his wrinkled face, but we were struck with the beauty of his eyes and the liveliness of his glance. The whole air of the face was very satirical.

He had with him Père Adam, a Jesuit, and a *valet de chambre* who knows the whole library of his master by heart. M. de Voltaire does much good in his village, he has collected all the watch-makers of Geneva and makes them work at his house, the part of his house where he once had a theatre he has now converted into lodging-rooms which he puts at their disposal, and he provides for their wants

Turin, November 11, 1771. While we were at the Academy the governor presented us to the king [Charles-Emmanuel III.], a little wrinkled old fellow walking with the help of a cane. After several compliments he gave me a lecture, saying that I ought to diligently profit by the teachings of the Academy in order to defer to the wishes of my relatives who had sent me to Turin. His son, the Duc de Savoie, was very polite, and so were all the family.

Paris, January 1, 1774. New Year's day, as they call it here I had to go to Versailles to pay my court to the king [Louis XV.] and see the ceremony of the Order of the Saint-Esprit By ten o'clock I was at Versailles. The ceremony consists of a mass at which the king and all the chevaliers of the Order are present in full dress. After having dined, I went with Count Creutz[1] to pay a visit to Mme. du Barry She spoke to me then for the first time. Leaving her, we returned to Paris.

January 3. I went to pay a visit to the Spanish am-

[1] Swedish ambassador to the French Court, often mentioned by Mlle. de Lespinasse See preceding volume of this Hist Series — Tr.

bassador; Count Creutz took me later to see the Comtesse de Brionne, who received us in her dressing-room   I thought her very good-looking, although of a certain age. she is tall, well-made, pretty in face, amiable, and very gay   I saw a part of her toilet which amused me very much.   After having powdered herself, she took a little silver knife, about a finger long, and carefully removed the powder, going over her face several times.   Then one of her women, of whom she had three, brought a large box, which she opened, in it were six pots of rouge, and another box, small, which was full of a pommade that seemed to me black.   The Comtesse took some rouge on her finger and daubed it on her cheek, it was the prettiest rouge that ever was, she increased it by taking more from all the six pots, two and two.   Then she rose, and went into her bedchamber, where her daughter, Mlle. de Lorraine, came and joined her; the latter did not seem to me as handsome as they said she was, but she has a very lively and piquant face.

January 10.   I went at three o'clock to the ball of Madame la Dauphine [Marie-Antoinette].   The ball began, as usual, at five o'clock, and lasted till half-past nine; I then returned to Paris.

January 30.   I dined with M Bloome, Danish minister; thence I went to Mme d'Arville, and, after talking with her half an hour, I went to the assembly at the Spanish ambassador's, where Count Creutz took me up and drove me to the house of the Princesse de Beauvau, and then to a concert of Stroganoff.   At nine o'clock we all went together to sup with Mme d'Arville, whence I started at one o'clock for the masked ball at the opera.   It was crowded: Mme. la Dauphine, M le Dauphin, and the Comte de Provence came and spent half an hour there without their presence being noticed.   Mme. la Dauphine talked to me a long time with-

out my recognizing her.   At last she let it be known who
she was, and then every one crowded round and she retired
into a box.   At three o'clock I left the ball.

January 31.   Went to Versailles at three o'clock.   Returned to dress and was, by a quarter past nine, with Mme.
d'Arville, who had invited me to supper the evening before.
We were five, and the supper was very gay.   At one o'clock
we separated.

Wednesday, February 2.   Had to get up at eight o'clock
to go and order a suit to be ready at midnight for the ball at
the Palais-Royal.   In the afternoon I paid visits to the
Duchesse d'Arville, Mme du Deffand, and the Comtesse de
La Marck, the latter of whom loaded me with civilities.
She had been so good as to write me a note, a few days
earlier, excusing herself because I had made frequent visits
at her house without finding her: she now reiterated the
same excuses and said she hoped I should not feel discouraged; in short, I was enchanted with her politeness and her
gracious manners.   It was a quarter past nine when I left
her.   I then went to see de Géer, where Poniatowski came
at midnight.   They went off together to the Palais-Royal.
I had waited impatiently all the evening for my suit, and I
felt myself getting angry, when they brought it just as de
Géer went off.   I dressed in haste and went to the Palais-
Royal.   On entering, I was much surprised to see all the
women dressed as shepherdesses, in gauze and taffeta gowns,
and all the men in rich suits embroidered along the seams.
The ball had begun; I thought at first it was a public ball
and that the girls who were dancing were wantons, I
imagined that ladies always wore rich costumes.   There
were only twenty women present, and the ball was not very
lively and only lasted till six o'clock; I then escaped, for no
one remained but the Duchesse de Chartres, the Duchesse

de Bourbon, Mme. de Laval, and Mme. de Holstein, who is, beyond contradiction, the best and prettiest dancer in Paris. As I went away I reflected that the French do not know how to amuse themselves, they have the bad habit of saying, " I am ennuyèd," and that poisons all their pleasures.

February 15, *Mardi gras.* Ball at Versailles. I went towards the end of it. Mme. la Dauphine, Mme. de Provence, Mme. d'Artois, Mme. de Lamballe, and two other ladies came with the Dauphin, M. de Provence, M. d'Artois, MM. de Ségur, de Coigny, and one other, all wearing the costume of Henri IV., which is the old French style They danced different *entrées,* some of them very badly, especially the Dauphin and M. de Provence; the others pretty well. The *coup-d'œil* was charming.[1]   I returned from there to sup with de Géer, then at one o'clock I went to a ball given by the ambassador of Malta.

Sunday, February 20   Supped with the Duchesse d'Arville, who, as usual, overwhelmed me with kindness and civilities, and so did her sister, the Duchesse d Estisac.

I paid visits pretty regularly, and often went to the theatre.

---

[1] Description of Marie-Antoinette as Dauphine in the " Mémoires Secrets " by Bachaumont   " Here is the exact portrait of Madame la Dauphine. This princess is of a height proportioned to her age, thin, without being emaciated, and such as a young girl is when not fully formed. She is very well-made, well-proportioned in all her limbs   Her hair is a beautiful blond, I judge it will some day be a golden chestnut, it is well planted on her head   Her forehead is fine, the shape of her face a handsome oval, but a little long, the eyebrows are as well marked as a blonde can have them   Her eyes are blue, but not insipid ; they sparkle with a vivacity full of intelligence   Her nose is aquiline, a little sharp at the tip, her mouth is small, the lips full, especially the lower one, which every one knows to be the Austrian lip   The whiteness of her skin is dazzling, and she has a natural colour which dispenses her from putting on rouge   Her carriage and bearing is that of an archduchess , but her dignity is tempered by gentleness, and it is difficult on seeing this princess to refuse her a respect mingled with tenderness " —Tr

Marie Antoinette
Dauphine

Count Creutz took me to the house of the Marquis de Brancas, where much politeness was shown to me. I supped there several times, and on Friday, March 4, they gave a charming little ball, five gentlemen and six ladies danced from eight in the evening till six in the morning. We only left off one hour for supper These dancing-suppers are often given during Lent in Paris, where times of abstinence are not so strictly kept as in Italy, where people would think themselves excommunicated if they danced at this season, and a woman who committed such a fault would hurry the next morning to confess it and obtain absolution.

[It was at this time that the Swedish ambassador, Count Creutz, wrote to King Gustavus III, May 20, 1774, in praise of the youth as follows: —

"The young Count Fersen has just departed for London. Of all the Swedes who have been here in my time he is the one who has been the most welcomed by the great world. The royal family have treated him remarkably well. It is not possible to have shown a more discreet and becoming conduct than he has maintained With the handsomest face and much intelligence he could not fail to succeed in society, and he has done so completely. Your Majesty may certainly be content with him; but what makes Count Fersen even more worthy of Your Majesty's kindness is that he thinks nobly and with singular loftiness"

Count Axel arrived in London May 15, 1774, and stayed there four months; amusements of all kinds interfered with the regularity of his journal, but some of his notes are of permanent interest.]

Monday, May 16, 1774. At eight o'clock we went to Ranelagh. I was struck, on entering, with the magnificence of the *coup-d'œil*, and the beauty of the hall, built in a circle and of great height. In the centre is a species of altar, very large, and the seats surround it; it is there that they heat the water for the tea. The seats, as well as the boxes, which are built round the outer wall, are filled from seven o'clock till midnight, at which hour every one withdraws. Above the boxes are galleries where people promenade, and nothing is more agreeable than to sit there and watch them as they circulate about. The illumination is very fine. The men are not allowed to give their arm to the women, unless they are married to them. They leave them to walk about alone and come and speak to them only occasionally.

Wednesday, May 18. At midday I went to Court with Baron Nolcken. The apartments are neither large nor magnificently furnished; nothing about them bespeaks the grandeur of a king. The chandeliers are of wood, gilt or silvered according to the importance of the room. When the king was dressed we entered his chamber, where we saw an old bed of red velvet, blackened by smoke and shiny with grease, before which was a sort of railing of silver wire. The king [George III.] is obliged to speak to every one, and when he came to Baron Nolcken I was presented. He spoke to me, but in a very low voice, for that is his way. As his conversation is limited to three or four topics, he is afraid the others shall hear that he asks the same questions of everybody.

Thursday, May 19. I have been presented to Queen Charlotte, who is very gracious and amiable, but not at all pretty. In the evening I was taken by the Earl of . . . to Almack's, a ball which is given by subscription throughout the winter. The hall where they danced was well-arranged and brilliantly lighted. The dancing ought to begin at ten o'clock, but the men stay at their clubs till half-past eleven,

during the interval the women wait, sitting on benches to
right and left of the long gallery in great ceremony; one
would think they were at church; they are all sad and
serious, and never even speak to each other. The supper,
which takes place at midnight, is very well served and is a
little less sad than the rest. I was placed beside Lady Car-
penter, one of the handsomest young girls in London; she
was very agreeable and talked much I had occasion to see
her a few days later, and addressed a few polite words to
her, which she did not even answer. I was much surprised
to see the young ladies talking tête-à-tête with men, and going about by themselves. It reminded me of Lausaunne
where they enjoy entire liberty.

[The young count returned to Sweden at the beginning of
the year 1775. He was already a lieutenant, unattached, in
the Royal-Bavière regiment of the French army, he was
now made a captain, unattached, of the light-horse cavalry of
the King of Sweden. He took part in all the amusements
of the Court of Gustavus III., then considered the gayest in
Europe; but the desire to follow the example of his ances-
tors on the battle-field pursued him. Sweden being at peace
without prospect of war, he had to seek a military career in
foreign countries. He went first to London in 1778, where
he stayed three months. Thence he went to Paris, arriving
there during the dull season, when the great world had
scattered into the country.]

Paris, August 25, 1778. I had to begin by being presented to the persons who were still in Paris, of whom there
were but few. Creutz took me to call on Mme. de Boufflers,
a charming woman and one of the most renowned in Paris
for her wit. She is in close correspondence with the king

[Gustavus III.]. I was perfectly well received. She has a daughter-in-law whom she loves to adoration, who is beautiful as an angel, but capricious to the last degree. I saw Mme. Dusson, the wife of our ambassador, she is a good, fat Dutchwoman, malicious and caustic as a demon when she takes a dislike to any one; but otherwise very polite She has always overwhelmed me with civilities and friendship. Mme. du Deffand is still blind.

August 26, 1778 Last Tuesday I went to Versailles to be presented to the royal family. The queen, who is charming, said when she saw me, " Ah ! here is an old acquaintance." The rest of the family did not say a word to me.

September 8, 1778 The queen, who is the prettiest and most amiable princess that I know, has had the kindness to inquire about me often, she asked Creutz why I did not go to her card parties on Sundays; and hearing that I did go one Sunday when there was none, she sent me a sort of excuse. Her pregnancy advances and is quite visible.

November 19, 1778. The queen treats me with great kindness; I often pay her my court at her card-games, and each time she makes to me little speeches that are full of good-will. As some one had told her of my Swedish uniform, she expressed a wish to see me in it, I am to go Thursday thus dressed, not to Court, but to the queen's apartments. She is the most amiable princess that I know.

In a letter to his father, dated November 19, 1778, he says : —

" My stay here becomes every day more and more agreeable I make new acquaintances all the time, and I think I can soon, without incommoding myself, cultivate them all. I have not yet seen the Duc de Choiseul; he is in Paris, but his house is not open. All the persons whom I knew on my first visit seem to see me again with pleasure. In short, it

is a charming place, where nothing is lacking to me to be
perfectly happy but the satisfaction of seeing you, my dear
father."

[During this time, however, the jealousy of the courtiers
was roused. Fersen was received into the queen's most private circle ; much was said about the little fêtes given by
Mmes. de Lamballe and de Polignac to which very few were
admitted, but Fersen was among them. The malice of dis-
appointed courtiers was the origin of the calumnies against
Marie-Antoinette, and it was convenient to publicly connect
them with the name of the young foreigner. An allusion to
these tales appears in a private despatch of Count Creutz
addressed to Gustavus III., April 10, 1779.—

" I ought to confide to Your Majesty that the young Count
Fersen has been so well received by the queen that this has
given umbrage to several persons. I own that I cannot help
thinking that she had a liking for him ; I have seen too
many indications to doubt it. The conduct of the young
count has been admirable on this occasion for its modesty
and its reserve, but above all, in the decision he made to go
to America. By thus departing he avoided all dangers, but
it needed, evidently, a firmness beyond his years, to surmount that seduction The queen's eyes could not leave
him, during the last days, and they often filled with tears.
I entreat Your Majesty to keep this secret, for her sake and
that of Senator Fersen. When the courtiers heard of Count
Fersen's departure they were delighted. The Duchesse de
Fitz-James said to him, ' Why! monsieur, is this the way
you abandon your conquest?' 'If I had made one, I should
not abandon it,' he replied. 'I go with freedom, and, unfortunately, I leave no regrets behind me.' Your Majesty
will agree that that answer shows a wisdom and prudence

beyond his years. In other respects the queen behaves with much more reserve and wisdom than formerly. The king is not only quite submissive to her will, but he shares her tastes and her pleasures."

These mischievous rumours had and could have had no real foundation, because young Fersen was at this time meditating a marriage with Mlle. de Leijel, of a noble Swedish family, whose father was naturalized in England, where he had inherited an immense fortune from two unmarried uncles, members of the East India Company of London, where the family resided. Many letters from Count Axel communicated this project to his father, who highly approved of it. The war in North America and an absence of five years caused the young people to forget their first attachment, and Mlle. de Leijel married, in 1783, John Richard West, fourth Earl of Delawarr.

Perhaps, the most cruel fact in the history of Marie-Antoinette is that the calumnies against her began in the circle of her friends, whom she unwisely trusted. What wonder if her heart were touched by the youth who was destined (as we shall presently see) to give her, from first to last, the chivalrous devotion of a knight of old, high above all personal considerations. Two men have spoken of Marie-Antoinette in words that should never be forgotten. one is the gay, light-hearted Prince de Ligne, who knew her intimately during these very years.[1] the other is M de Sainte-Beuve, whose words are as follows : —]

" There is a way of considering Marie-Antoinette which seems to me the true way, and I would fain define it, because it is in this direction that, as I believe, the definitive

[1] See the " Memoirs of the Prince de Ligne," of the present Hist. Series — Tr.

judgment of history will go. Some persons may, from a
lofty feeling of compassion, fall in love with the ideal interest attaching to her, endeavour to defend her at all points,
make themselves her advocates, her knights toward and against
all comers, and resent the mere idea of stains and foibles
that others think they have discovered in her life. The
rôle of such defenders is to be respected when it is sincere ;
and we can well understand it in those who worship the
traditions of the old royalty ; but it moves me far less in
others with whom it is merely a chosen view That point
of view is not mine, and it is difficult that it should be that
of men who were not brought up in the religion of the
ancient monarchy.

"What seems to me safer, more desirable for the tender
memory of Marie-Antoinette is to see that it is possible to
disengage from the multitude of writings and testimonies
of which she has been the object a noble, beautiful, and
gracious figure, — with its weaknesses, its frivolities, its
frailties perhaps, but with the essential qualities, preserved
in all their integrity, of woman, mother, and, at moments,
queen ; with kindness ever generous, and, in the final hours,
with the virtues of resignation, courage, and gentleness
that crown a vast misfortune. It is thus that, once established historically on that plane, which is noble indeed,
she will continue in future ages to interest all those who,
indifferent to the politics of the past, treasure the delicate
human sentiments which form part of civilization as of
nature, — all those who weep over the sorrows of Hecuba and
of Andromache, and who, reading the tale of sorrows like
theirs, but greater still, will mourn them in reality.

"But there is this difference, that poesy alone presents the
traditions of Andromache and Hecuba , we have no memoirs
of the Court of Priam ; whereas we have those of the Court of

Louis XVI., and there is no way to avoid taking account of them.   What say these memoirs about Marie-Antoinette ? I speak of the true memoirs, not the libellous ones.   What says the Comte de La Marck, who presents so well the spirit of that first epoch of the young dauphine's life.   Arriving in France when fifteen years of age, she was not nineteen when she found herself a queen beside Louis XVI   That prince, furnished with a solid education and endowed with the moral qualities which we know, but feeble, timid, brusque, rough, and particularly ungainly towards women, had nothing of what was needful to guide his young wife She, the daughter of an illustrious mother, was not brought up by Maria Theresa, — too busy with the affairs of State to attend to the affairs of family, — so that her early education in Vienna had been much neglected   No one had given her a taste for, or even the idea of serious reading.   Her mind, by nature quick and honest, 'seized and rapidly comprehended the things that were said to her,' but it had neither a wide range nor great capacity, — nothing, in short, that could repair the want of education, or take the place of experience. Amiable, gay, and innocently merry, she had, above all, 'great kindness of heart and a persistent desire to oblige the persons who surrounded her.'   She had also a great need of friendship and intimacy, and she at once sought for some one with whom to ally herself in a manner that was not customary at Court.   Her ideal of happiness (every one has his or her ideal) was, evidently, that of escaping from ceremonies which bored her, to find an agreeable, merry, devoted, chosen society, in the bosom of which she could forget she was queen — all the while remembering it very well in her heart.   She delighted in giving herself the pleasure of this forgetfulness, and in recalling what she was only in shedding kind favours around her   We have seen,

in comic operas and pastorals, disguised queens who thus
made the joy and charm of all around them Marie-
Antoinette had precisely this ideal of a happy life, which
she might have realized without impropriety had she remained a mere archduchess in Vienna, or reigned a simple
sovereign in some Tuscany or Lorraine.   But in France she
could not lead that life with impunity; her little Trianon,
with its dairies, its shepherdesses, and its comedies, was too
near Versailles.   Envy prowled about those too exclusive
regions, — Envy, beckoning to stupidity and calumny.

"M. de La Marck, in a brief Notice inserted in the Introduction to a work lately published on Mirabeau, has very
well shown the injury it was to the queen to confine herself at first so exclusively to the circle of the Comtesse Jules
de Polignac, giving to the latter with the name of friend
the attitude of a favourite, and to all the men of that coterie
(the Vaudreuils, Besenvals, and Adhémars) pretensions and
rights which they speedily abused, each in the line of his
own temper and his own ambition.   Although she never
knew the extent of this injury she nevertheless perceived
some part of it, she felt that where she had looked for re-
pose and relief from high rank, she found only selfish
besetments; and when some one said to her that she
showed too much preference to foreigners of distinction who
passed through France, and that this might do her injury
with Frenchmen, she answered sadly, 'You are right, but
they at least ask nothing of me.'

"Some of the men who, admitted into this intimacy and
favour of the queen, were the most bound to gratitude and
respect, were the first to speak of her disrespectfully, because they did not find her sufficiently docile to their wishes.
Once, when she seemed to separate herself a little from the
Polignac circle, 'a frequenter of that circle' (whom M. de

La Marck does not name, but who seems to have been one
of the most important men of it) 'wrote a very malignant
couplet against the queen; and that couplet, founded on an
infamous lie, circulated through Paris' It was thus that
the Court itself and the private circle of the queen supplied
the first leaven that mingled with the scurrilities and in-
famies of the outside public.   She herself was ignorant of
all this, she did not suspect what influenced people against
her at Versailles, any more than what alienated the public
of Paris.

"To-day, even, when testimony is quoted in reference to
Marie-Antoinette — testimony of some one of note — it is from
the 'Memoirs of the Baron de Besenval' that it is usually
taken.   She sends for Besenval in 1778 on the occasion
of the duel between the Comte d'Artois and the Duc de
Bourbon ; he is introduced by Mme Campan (her secretary)
into a private room which he did not know, 'simply, but com-
modiously furnished. — I was astonished,' he adds in passing, 'not that the queen should have desired such facilities,
but that she dared to procure them.'   That single sentence,
dropped by the way, as it were, is full of insinuations, on
which the queen's enemies have not failed to fasten.

"Here I shall not affect more reserve than is proper;
neither shall I fear to touch on the delicate point of all this.
There are persons whose prepossessions deny absolutely all
levity and all weakness in the heart of the queen (supposing
always that such persons still exist at this period).   For
myself, I boldly think that the interest which attaches to
her memory, the pity excited by her misfortunes and the
noble manner in which she bore them, the execration that
her judges and executioners deserve, do not in any way depend on anterior discovery of some frailty of womanhood, and
cannot in the slightest degree be invalidated by it.   And now,

in the present state of historical information about Marie-
Antoinette, taking into account all true testimony, remembering also what we have heard related by contemporaries who
were sufficiently well-informed, it is very permissible to think
that this affectionate and eager woman, wholly given to impres-
sions, loving elegant manners and chivalrous forms, needing,
simply enough, expansion and protection, may have had,
during those fifteen years of her youth, some preference of
the heart, indeed, it would be strange had it been otherwise.
Many ambitious men, many fatuous men had pretensions
and failed; attempts were made, beginnings without number.
Lauzun in his Memoirs tells of his, and explains it after his
fashion, but the fact remains that, in one way or another,
he failed.

"The Prince de Ligne, who was often in France at this
period, and was one of those foreigners wholly French and
charming who particularly pleased the queen, speaks of her
thus: 'Her so-called gallantry was never anything but a
deep sense of friendship, which, perhaps, distinguished one
or two persons, and a general coquetry of woman and queen
which sought to please every one.' This impression, or conjecture, which I find in other good observers who were near to
Marie-Antoinette is, and will remain, I think, the probable
truth. These 'two persons' whom she particularly distinguished at different periods appear to have been the Duc
de Coigny, a prudent man already mature, and, later, Count
Fersen, colonel of the Royal-Swedish regiment in the service
of France, a man of lofty and chivalrous nature, who, in
the days of misfortune, proved himself such by an absolute
devotion."

[From the beginning of the year 1779 Count Axel Fersen,
liberal in opinion through family tradition and parental ex-

ample, and inspired by the new enthusiasm then reigning in
France, demanded earnestly to be allowed to take part in the
expedition of French troops to the war of independence then
going on in North America At last, thanks to the recommendation of the King of Sweden [Gustavus III.] and to the
exertions of his ambassador, Count Creutz, thanks also to
the friendship of the Comte de Vergennes for his father, young
Fersen was appointed aide-de-camp to the Comte de Vaux,
who had just been made commander of the first expedition,
which was to have sailed from Havre-de-Grâce, where the
troops assembled, but never did so.

It was not until the spring of 1780 that young Fersen
embarked at Brest, as aide-de-camp to the Comte de Rochambeau, commanding the expeditionary corps of the French
army to aid the Americans in their war of independence
against England. His letters to his father, from that period
until 1783, extracts from which here follow, are of very
great interest from their contents during three campaigns.
After taking part in the expedition to Rhode Island, Count
Fersen was present at the siege and capitulation of Yorktown when the English general, Cornwallis was made prisoner
with all his troops, October 19, 1781, which contributed in a
great measure to put an end to the war. Young Fersen had
been employed by General Comte de Rochambeau, in preference to the other aides-de-camp, during the conferences
with General Washington and the other leaders of the
American army, and it was he who conducted the negotiations, — a preference founded as much on his personal qualities as on his knowledge of the English language]

CHAPTER II.

1780–1783   Letters of Count Axel Fersen to his Father, Field-Marshal Fersen, during the French War in North America in aid of the Independence of the United States

PARIS, March 2, 1780

YOU see me, my dear father, at the summit of my wishes. A great expedition of 12,000 men is being fitted out, but they assure me it will mount up to 20,000. I have obtained permission to belong to it as aide-de-camp to the general, who is M. de Rochambeau; but I am told to keep this secret, for it has been refused to many others. Every one wishes to go, so they have taken a firm resolution not to send any but the officers belonging to the marching regiments. I owe this obligation to M de Vergennes, he took charge of the affair. I am in a state of joy that cannot be expressed.

When I spoke to M de Rochambeau, he said all sorts of civil things to me, and talked to me a long time of you, father; he ended by saying he was charmed to have me with him, and be able to show how much he esteemed you and how sincerely he was attached to you   The generals who are with him are· the Marquis de Jaucourt, the Comte de Caraman, and the Marquis de Viomesnil; the last two have much reputation, that of M de Rochambeau is already secure, it is, in general, the best choice that could have been made. There are three German regiments: Anhalt, Royal-Deux-Ponts, and Royal-Corsican. I have not yet seen the list of the French regiments, but their colonels have orders to be at Brest on the 15th, — we on the 25th, to sail April 1st to 4th. The convoy will be escorted by twelve ships of the

line and a sufficient number of frigates   Our fleet is commanded by M. Duchaffaud, and Comte d'Estaing commands
that of observation, which is to remain in the Channel all
winter.   The navy will burst with vexation , but I think it
is for the good of the thing.

BREST, April 4, 1780.

Our embarkation is getting on , the artillery, munitions,
and commissariat are already on board, and we shall be busy
now with that of the troops   The first regiment arrives to-
day, and all will be embarked by the 8th.   M. de Rochambeau wants to be in the roadstead by the 10th so as to set
sail the 12th or 13th.   I am so glad I do not know what to
do with myself, but my joy will not be perfect till we are
off Cape Finisterre.

I wrote you, my dear father, that our division (for it cannot yet be called an army) was of 7,683 men ; that number
has been reduced to 5000 by the negligence and inefficiency
with which everything is now done in this country.   You
shall judge : when it was first a question of this expedition,
the number of men was fixed at 4000   M. de Rochambeau
refused to take charge of it in view of that small number , he
said that he could not accept the command if there were
less than 7000 men , on which every one blamed him for the
modesty of that number ; he replied that he was sure of
having more than he could carry with him.   The event justi-
fied his speech ; for instead of a tonnage of 30,000 which M.
de Sartine [minister of the navy] promised him, there proved
to be in all the transports collected at Brest only 10,000
tons, the allowance being a man to each two tons, — the third
of what was promised ! However, by dint of management
we found means to leave only 2595 men behind us and to
sail with 5088.

This puts us in despair, and we cannot help being surprised and indignant that they never thought of sending the ships from Havre and Saint-Malo to Brest during the winter, instead of waiting till spring, when the pirates of Jersey prevent communication between the three ports. This is happening now, we had counted on ten or twelve large ships from Havre and Saint-Malo, but they had to return to port for fear of being taken, and we have written to Bordeaux to get others. We expect them daily; but if they do not come before the 12th we shall sail without them, and the rest of our little army must join us when it can. I have reason to think it will be increased by 4000 men; this is very necessary.

We have four general officers the Chevalier de Chastellux, the Chevalier and the Baron de Viomesnil (two brothers), and M. de Wichtenstein, formerly colonel of the Anhalt regiment; all four are brigadier-generals We are taking much artillery, the siege train is very considerable. We have provisions for four months at sea, and three months ashore. We shall be escorted by seven vessels of the line. the " Duc de Bourgogne," 80 guns, the " Neptune," 74, the " Conquerant," 74, the " Jason," 64, the " Eveillé," 64, the " Provence," 64, the " Ardent," 64 (that is the one that was taken by the English last year), and two frigates The convoy is of 24 transports

> At sea, May 16 (Monday), 1780, on board
> the " Jason " off Finisterre

I have only time to write you two words to tell you I am well. I have not suffered from seasickness. We have already had rough weather, which dismasted one of our ships. The wind is fair, and I think that in forty days we may reach America. We have sighted a large vessel in the distance, and do not know whether it is friend or enemy. I have no time to write more.

August 5, 1780. NEWPORT, in Rhode Island

The letter I wrote you on July 16, which returned to Newport on the 23d on account of the appearance of the English fleet, is now at the bottom of the sea. The ship that carried it sank as it left the harbour July 30, having struck a rock. In it I sent you an account of a naval fight we had, also a plan, and a short account from my journal of our voyage. I have no time to rewrite the fight, or sketch the plan; as for the journal, here it is · —

May 4, left Brest; met a gale in the bay of Biscay 11th; 17th, doubled Cape Finisterie; went southward to the 27th degree of longitude; then steered west, June 20, off the Bermudas, met five English vessels and fought them two hours without doing ourselves much damage. In the darkness they disappeared; our escort would not let us follow them. We intended to anchor in the bay of the Chesapeake, but July 4, when we were only thirteen leagues distant, we sighted eleven vessels which we took to be men-of-war; this induced us to change our course and sail for Rhode Island, where we arrived safely on the evening of the 11th and anchored in the roadstead. It was not without strong fears of meeting the English fleet on our way from the Chesapeake here, which were well-founded, for Admiral Graves, despatched from England to intercept and fight us if possible, reached New York on the 13th, shipped more sailors, and appeared before our roadstead on the 17th. Had he got here before us he would have occupied Rhode Island, and we could have entered it only after a fight in which we should certainly have lost our convoy, whatever gains we might otherwise have made.

I can tell you nothing, my dear father, about our campaign, for I know nothing. We wish to join General Washington, who is only 25 miles from New York, because we

think that is the only means of operating and doing something
I do not know if this junction can be made. Meantime we
are blockaded by twenty sail, ten of which are ships of the
line. They come in daily very near the coast; it is said
they will do nothing, and I believe it. We are expecting
General Clinton at any moment; he sailed from New York
with 10,000 men; we are ready to receive him, all dispositions are made; I hope he may come, but I can hardly
believe he would commit such folly.

NEWPORT, September 8, 1780.

No event since my last. We have not left our island;
we occupy it peacefully, and with the best order, in a very
healthy camp, well placed and perfectly well trenched , the
works are not yet finished, but they are going on The
strictest discipline is maintained; nothing is taken from the
inhabitants except by their free will and for ready money;
we have not yet had a single complaint against the troops.
Such discipline is admirable and astonishes the inhabitants,
who are accustomed to the pillage of the English and even
of their own troops The greatest confidence and the best
harmony are established between the two nations , if that
could suffice for the success of our expedition we might feel
sure of it.

For the last four or five days we are no longer blockaded.
We are expecting every moment news from Jamaica ; if that
is taken I fear we shall not have much to do here. General
Sir George Clinton, who commands in New York, is still in
Long Island with twenty thousand men, where he has made
a great provision of wood and commissariat supplies. He
seems determined to pass the winter there. I fear much
that we shall pass ours here; I shall be consoled if we begin a campaign in the spring. Our army is in the best con-

dition; officers and soldiers, all are full of good-will, and ardour for the common cause. From time to time there are trifling squabbles,—that is inevitable; but the order and discipline which reign are admirable, especially among the French troops That proves that they only need a good leader. We have not yet begun to manœuvre, but we shall begin in a few days.

You know Frenchmen, my dear father, and what are called courtiers enough to judge of the despair of our young men of that class, who see themselves obliged to pass the winter tranquilly in Newport far from their mistresses and the pleasures of Paris, no suppers, no theatres, no balls; they are in despair, nothing but an order to march on the enemy could console them. We have had excessive heat throughout the month of August; I have never felt the like in Italy. Now the air is cooler; the climate is superb, and the country charming.

The general went upon the mainland a week ago. I was the only one of the aides-de-camp who accompanied him We stayed two days and saw one of the finest regions in the world, — well-cultivated, situations charming, inhabitants prosperous, but without luxury or display; they content themselves with mere necessaries, which, in other lands, is the lot of the lower classes; their clothes are simple, but good, and their morals have not yet been spoiled by the luxury of Europeans. It is a country which will surely be very happy if it can enjoy a long peace, and if the two political parties which now divide it do not make it suffer the fate of Poland and so many other republics. These two parties are called " Whig " and " Tory·" the first is wholly for freedom and independence, it is composed of men of low extraction who own no property; the greater part of the inhabitants of the country belong to it. The " Tories " are for the English, or, to be more correct, for peace, without caring much about freedom or independence. These are persons of a more distinguished class, the only ones who own property in America ; some have relatives and property in England, others, to preserve what they have in this country, take the English side, which is the stronger. When the Whigs are the stronger they pillage the others as much as they can. That excites between them a hatred and animosity which can be extinguished only with much difficulty, and will always be the germ of great trouble.

NEWPORT, September 14, 1780.

I have no news that is very interesting or very good for us to send you. There is some that is very grievous to us : the defeat of General Gates by Lord Cornwallis in South Carolina on the 10th of August. The American general had advanced imprudently; he was attacked; half his troops were killed, the other half captured; he himself escaped with one aide-de-camp As yet we have no details of the affair. M de Rochambeau received the news by express the day before yesterday, but he has not yet made the matter public; he does not speak of it; yet all the town knows it. An American, with whom I talked this morning, told me he had seen a letter written to a member of the council, in which the writer said that the militia under General Gates all went over to the English at the beginning of the action. If that is true, what reliance can be placed on such troops ? a brave man is much to be pitied for having to command them.

This, my dear father, is our present situation, it is not gay, we must hope it will change before the arrival of our second division, which we are expecting with the greatest impatience The garrison of Newport is becoming very melancholy.

NEWPORT, October 16, 1780

This is the first safe opportunity I have had for a long time to write to you, my dear father. I am certain this letter will reach you, and without being read, it goes by a frigate that M. de Rochambeau is sending to Europe. The Duc de Lauzun sends one of his servants in it, who promises to deliver my letter to Count Creutz, to whom I write by the same opportunity An officer is to be sent to France in this frigate to give an account of the state and situation of the army and of our dear allies, both of which are bad enough. We do not know who will be charged with this commission; every one names me; several of the general officers, M de Chastellux and the Baron de Viomesnil have spoken of me as one who could carry out the intentions of the general in this respect. I do not know what will be the result; I shall take no steps to obtain the appointment, neither should I refuse it if the general were to offer it to me. Nevertheless, I would much rather not be selected for this service. Something interesting might happen during my absence, and I should be in despair at having missed it.

Our position here is very disagreeable. We vegetate at the gate of the enemy, in the saddest and most dreadful idleness and inactivity, we are compelled to take, owing to our small numbers, the wearisome rôle of the defensive; we are of no use whatever to our allies; we cannot quit our island without exposing our fleet to be taken or destroyed, in fact, our fleet could not get out without delivering us up to the enemy, who, vastly superior in vessels and men, would not fail to attack us and cut off our retreat to the continent. English vessels, more or less large, continue to reconnoitre us closely; we dare not attack them, for they have other vessels stationed at Gardner's Island, twenty miles to the southwest, and we can nearly always count fifteen or twenty sail of the English fleet in the offing   So long as we are not the stronger of the two we shall be obliged to stay where we are, unless we decide to send away the fleet and abandon Rhode Island to the English.   The one would follow the other.

Far from being useful to the Americans we are only a burden upon them; we do not reinforce their army, for we are twelve days' march away from it, and separated by arms of the sea which cannot be crossed in winter on account of the drifting ice.   We are even an expense to them, because, in consuming so much we make provisions scarce, and by paying ready money we bring down the value of paper and thus deprive the army of General Washington of its facilities for subsistence, which the dealers now refuse to sell for paper money.   Our condition as to money is not any better than our military position.   We brought with us two million six hundred thousand francs, half of which is in ready money, and the remainder is in letters of exchange on a banker in Philadelphia, M. Holcher.   We ought to have brought the double of this.   This want of specie, in a nation where one always needs to have money in hand, forces us to great economy; whereas what is needed is magnificence and profusion.   This ruins our credit.   The forage department has been neglected and left in the hands of a commissary, who relied on the contractors, the latter did not view the matter in a military way; they consulted their own interests solely, and instead of storing the forage of the island and for thirty or forty miles round it, which is easy to transport, they used that first, and kept the more distant supplies for winter. God knows how we shall get them, we have twice been two days without forage, obliged, each of us, to buy it where we could.

The generals are not agreed among themselves.   The whole army is discouraged at staying here so long with nothing to do. The second division has not arrived; without it we can do nothing, or at least not much. M. de Rocham-beau has sent a report of his condition to France with a re-quest for the increase of his forces, both in men and money. We shall see what will be the result.

I went with M. de Rochambeau, about two weeks ago, to Hartford, which is forty leagues from here. We were six in party: the general, the admiral, the chief of the engineers, the Vicomte de Rochambeau the (general's son), and two aides-de-camp, of whom I was one. An interview was to take place with General Washington. M. de Rochambeau sent me in advance to announce his arrival, and I had time to see that illustrious, not to say unique, man of our era. His noble and majestic, but at the same time gentle and honest face agrees perfectly with his moral qualities, he has the air of a hero; he is very cold, speaks little, but is polite and civil. An air of sadness pervades his whole countenance, which is not unbecoming to him, and makes him the more interesting. His suite was more numerous than ours: the Marquis de Lafayette, General Knox, chief of artillery, M. de Gouvion, a Frenchman, chief of engineers, and six aides-de-camp in attendance. He had, besides, an escort of twenty dragoons, which was necessary, for he had to cross a region full of the enemy, and as there are no post-houses in this country one is obliged to travel with one's own horses, and nearly always on horseback on account of the bad roads. However, on this occasion, all were in carriages, except the two aides-de-camp. It took us three days to reach Hartford; General Washington the same. On the way we heard of the arrival of Rodney's fleet at New York, but we continued our journey. The two generals and the admiral were shut up together during the whole day we stayed at Hartford. The Marquis de Lafayette was called in as interpreter, for Gen-

eral Washington can neither speak French nor understand
it. They separated very well pleased with one another, at
least they said so.

It was on his way back from there that General Washington heard of General Arnold's treachery. The latter was
one of his best generals, he had two balls through his body
and his conduct was always excellent   General Clinton had
bribed him, he agreed to deliver up West Point, where he
commanded. Major André, chief aide-de-camp to General
Clinton, went to West Point, disguised as a countryman, to
examine the fortifications, and agree as to the manner of
attacking and the way by which General Arnold should
retreat in order to cause no suspicion.   A frigate was waiting
for the aide-de-camp in the Hudson River, and a boat was to
be at a spot agreed upon. After arranging everything with
General Arnold, Major André went to take the boat, but
could not find it.   The frigate had been obliged to change
her position as the guns of West Point fired upon her   She
was now lying five miles farther down the river.   Major
André, ignorant of this, fancied he could reach New York
by land.   He was arrested by a party of countrymen, who
were patrolling that region very carefully, on account of the
passing of General Washington   He (André) showed his
passport, given him by General Arnold, they doubted its
authenticity and, in spite of all the offers he made to them,
they took him to the army.

At this same moment General Washington arrived at
West Point from Hartford.   He sent his aides-de-camp to
General Arnold to say that he would dine with him, and
meantime was going himself to inspect the forts   The aides-
de-camp found Arnold at breakfast with his wife.   A moment after they were seated some one came and whispered
into the general's ear, on which he rose, said a word in

a low voice to his wife, and went out. The words were,
"Good-bye forever." The wife fainted   The aides-de-camp
succoured her without knowing what was the matter,
but a few moments later a courier arrived with the news
for General Washington. They pursued the traitor, but it
was then too late. If the English had succeeded in seizing
West Point they would have been masters of the whole Hudson River, they could have prevented all communication and
junction of our forces with those of the Americans (unless
by a very great détour) and Washington, who is camped at
Orange-town, between West Point and New York, would
have been between two fires and certainly destroyed before
we could get to his assistance. It might, perhaps, have been
all over for America, and we, ourselves, would have had the
shame of coming here to be mere spectators of the ruin of
our allies. Our own position would have been no better, for
the English, no longer fearing the Americans, would have
turned all their forces against us, and we are not strong
enough to resist them. Happily, the thing failed. They say
that Major André has been hanged   That is a pity ; he was
a young man twenty-four years of age, with great talent.
The general has no news of this, and I hope it is false.

I have already told you, my dear father, that I am particularly intimate with the Duc de Lauzun   Opinions are divided about him. You will hear both good and harm, the
first is right, the second is wrong, if people knew him, they
would change their ideas and do justice to his heart. He
has taken a friendship for me, and proposes, in the most
courteous manner in the world, that I shall accept the place
of colonel, commanding his legion, which is vacant; and he
wishes to cede the proprietorship to me a year hence, at
which time he intends to retire from service   His legion
has one thousand infantry and three hundred hussars, with a

few small pieces of artillery. The proposal is too agreeable
and too advantageous to me to be refused. The Duc de
Lauzun has written about it to the queen, who has much
kindness for him, she has a little for me also, and I have
written to her, I hope that the frigate which brings back
her answer will bring me also my brevet. Lauzun assures
me there can be no difficulty.

NEWPORT, October 26, 1780.

You have already heard of General Gates' defeat in the
South   I wrote you about it.   Congress has just recalled him
to Philadelphia and has given the command of his corps to
General Greene.   He is suspected, because he was closely
allied with Arnold.   It seems that his defeat has had no
further results.   All is quiet.   Two battalions of grenadiers
and chasseurs, with detachments from other regiments, have
just been embarked, to the number of four thousand, at New
York for service in the South.   A fleet has arrived at New
York from Cork in Ireland, laden with provisions, of which
they were beginning to be in great want.   The same fleet
brings four thousand recruits, both English and Hessians.
What a war this is for the English ! — obliged to bring everything, even subsistence !   That Power must have great resources to be able to maintain the war so long

NEWPORT, November 13, 1780.

The frigate that carried our letters sailed on the 28th
of last month ; on the 27th we had seen a fleet of thirteen
vessels of war, but not seeing them the next morning, and
hearing that they had steered east, three of our frigates left
port ; I do not know the destination of the two others.

The affair of Arnold has had no results.   Poor Major
André, a young man twenty-eight years of age, of the
highest promise, a friend of General Clinton, has been

3

hanged. The sight touched the whole army; and the two officers whom General Washington gave him as a guard of honour to attend his execution had not the strength to follow him.

General Gates, of whose defeat you have read in the gazette, was recalled to Philadelphia; they say that Congress suspects him, because of his intimate relations with Arnold, and that this is the cause of his recall The three States of New York, Connecticut, and Massachusetts have just named General Washington dictator, with absolute power over military affairs It is thought that the ten other States will do the same. This determination will give vigour to affairs, by changing their aspect and rousing the sluggish indolence of the Americans Fourteen Spanish and nine French vessels have just captured in the neighbourhood of Madeira a convoy of fifty ships, coming partly from the Indies and partly from the Isles, and richly laden.

Our war is not more active than it has been. There is talk of a little advantage gained by the Americans over the English; the news is not sure, and I doubt it Of the six thousand men embarked at New York (nearly all grenadiers and chasseurs), three thousand have already been landed in the Chesapeake Bay. It is said that General Clinton goes with the rest. This is undoubtedly an expedition to the South, either to seize North Carolina and Virginia or do them as much injury as possible. It will meet with little resistance. The American *corps d'armée* stationed there is only four thousand strong, with a few militia who cannot be relied on. Half, or perhaps three-fourths, of the four thousand finish their time of service in January, which reduces that army to nothing General Washington cannot quit the position he has taken without abandoning to the English the whole course of the Hudson River and its adjacent territory;

and we, for want of sufficient means, cannot quit our island, where we are forced to stay like an oyster in its shell. The English will therefore have full liberty to act as they please in the South; they have a garrison of six thousand men in Charleston, from which they can reinforce their army, and one-half of the country is for them Their position is a fine one, if they know how to profit by it, ours is disheartening if it does not change.

M. de Rochambeau has just sent the Lauzun legion into quarters on the main land twenty-nine miles from here. The lack of forage made this necessary. The Duc de Lauzun treats me with the same friendship, he talks to me incessantly of my affair, and says how happy he shall be when he can hand over to me the proprietorship of his legion, he wants no money for it, and when I spoke of it he replied "I do not sell men — though I have bought them sometimes; besides, I pay myself in finding a man to whom I can leave my corps, whom I love as my children, with the confidence that I place in you." His manner in saying this was perfect and shows the man The hope of the speedy success of this plan enchants me and makes me happy.

NEWPORT, December 7, 1780

You see, my dear father, that we are still in Newport; we do not even think of leaving it. We are living tranquilly in winter-quarters. Washington's army went into theirs two weeks ago. Admiral Rodney has returned to the Isles with his ten vessels; we now have Arbuthnot here with seven ships of the line and three or four frigates. Affairs at the South are going well, Colonel Ferguson has just been defeated by the Americans; his corps of fourteen hundred men was almost destroyed; this has obliged Lord Cornwallis, who commands the English troops in that region, to retire to Charleston, with his corps of four thousand men, most of whom are dying of fatigue and disease The English had sent Brigadier-general Leslie with twenty-five hundred men to join Cornwallis. By a letter from that officer to Lord Cornwallis, which was intercepted, we learn that he landed his troops at Portsmouth, Virginia, where he was awaiting orders for the junction. Apparently it will not be made, in view of the retreat of Cornwallis; it is even said that Leslie is returning to New York.

Before going into winter-quarters General Washington wished to make a descent on Staten Island; he wanted to draw the attention of the English to that side while he made a forage around Kingsbridge; but they were not misled by it; all their posts on Staten Island had been strengthened, and he therefore abandoned the project. M. de Rochambeau has just made a little journey of six days on the mainland. I went with him, we were only three, and we did not see a fine country or pleasant people; they were, as a rule, lazy and selfish; how is it possible with those two qualities, to make them useful in war ?

NEWPORT, January 9, 1781

Nothing new as to our military operations, my dear father. It seems that we are all, on both sides, on the defensive, and it is very difficult to know who will begin the next campaign; it will probably depend on the arrival of reinforcements from Europe : whoso receives the first will, it seems to me, profit by that advantage to attack the other. If the reinforcements which, they say, are intended for us in France, are really coming, we shall have, at any rate for a moment, the superiority at sea. That is the only means of operating and of ending a war both long and ruinous. As long as we are not masters of the sea we may prevent the English from penetrating into the interior, but nothing obliges them to leave the coast; their commerce will continue to flourish, and will furnish them means of subsistence, which they would lack without it. So long as they are masters of Quebec, Halifax, New York, Charleston, and Jamaica, they will not make peace, they will do so only when their commerce is ruined and one or two of those places are captured. We missed the chance of taking Jamaica this year, and I do not believe it will ever come again. The reinforcements which, they say, are preparing for us in France are eight ships of war, — one of one hundred and ten guns, three of eighty guns, three of seventy guns, and one of sixty-four guns. We do not know the number of troops This news reached us by a merchant ship which came from Nantes to Boston in thirty-eight days. Since we have been here we have had no letters. Such forgetfulness of the minister, or the ministry, is unpardonable.

The campaign in the South seems more active than ours at the North . . . It is said that Cornwallis's army is surrounded at Camden; that it suffers much from sickness and from hunger, being now reduced to eat its horses, this rumour needs confirmation. That of the embarkation of twenty-five hundred men from New York for the South is more certain. Their destination seems to be to join another corps of the same size off Cape Fear, march from there to Camden, relieve Cornwallis if he is hemmed in, join him, and begin operations. If this junction is effected, and it can scarcely fail, the South is lost; the Americans have no army there; the one they had was destroyed under General Gates, the little that remains of it does not deserve the name of army; the men are without coats, shoes, or arms, there is nothing to oppose well-disciplined and veteran troops but raw militia, who are assembled only when danger is imminent, and who run away when it becomes great.

That is the state of affairs at the South; ours are not much better. We are forced to be tranquil spectators of the loss of that part of America, and we cannot do otherwise. I have not yet travelled through the country; many officers of the army have done so, I await their return; what they have seen and the mistakes they have made will be useful to me, I await the month of March.

The different States of America have passed a resolution to raise an army of twenty thousand men for three years; the assessment to each State has been made, and minds are again excited. They hope to get the new recruits by March 1. I desire it, but I am not convinced it will be done. Some will be enlisted for three years, others for the whole war; but neither will serve for nothing; and it will be by very large pledges only that they will succeed in filling up the regiments. Money is scarce; in fact, there is none; the taxes do not suffice; no credit, no resources. This is the moment when we might be of some use to them, and redeem our idle and useless campaign by furnishing the money and clothes of which they are in need, but we ourselves are in danger of needing both if no supplies are sent from France, and of being reduced to the mortifying expedient of paying our troops with paper money

You see, my dear father, from this statement, which is strictly correct, the reasons which prevent the formation of an army, which can only be raised and maintained by force of money Add to this that the spirit of patriotism exists only in the leaders and principal people of the country, who are making the greatest sacrifices; the others, who form the greater number, think solely of their personal interests. Money is the prime mover of all their actions; they think

only of means to gain it; each is for himself, and none
are for the public good. The inhabitants along the coast,
even the best Whigs, carry provisions of all kinds to
the English fleet which is anchored in Gardner's Bay, and
that because the English pay them well. They fleece us
pitilessly; the price of everything is exorbitant; in all the
dealings that we have with them they treat us more like
enemies than friends Their cupidity is unequalled, money
is their god; virtue, honour, seem nothing to them compared
to the precious metal. I do not mean that there are no
estimable people whose character is equally noble and
generous, — there are many; but I speak of the nation in
general; I think it is derived more from the Dutch than
from the English.

That, my dear father, is my opinion on this country, on its
inhabitants, and on this war, it conforms to that of persons
who are more enlightened and in a better position to see and
to judge than I am. With more troops, ships, and much
money, all may be changed; but if the government does not
send us enough of the latter article for our needs and that
of our allies, nothing is repaired, and the French ministry
will have crowned its folly.

We have just received some very sad news, that of the
desertion of the Pennsylvania "line" — that is what they call
the twenty-five hundred men raised in that State'; they went
over to the English because of their discontent at lacking
everything. They had neither coats nor shoes; and they
were left without food for four days There is a rumour that
on the way they thought better of it and returned to their
duty, sending six sergeants to negotiate with Congress the
terms on which they were willing to do their duty, this last
rumour lacks confirmation. However it may be, this desertion sets a very dangerous example; it proves how little

reliance can be placed on such troops. We have no fresh news from the South, and are ignorant of what is going on there.

NEWPORT, January 14, 1781.

We have received details of two little affairs at the South in which the Americans had the advantage It was only the repulse of small detachments. The Pennsylvania " line " did not go over to the English , it has taken up a very strong position at Morristown.   All has been done in the greatest order. Sergeants are the leaders ; they have no officers. They keep guard perfectly ; they send about the country to get the supplies they want, giving receipts, which they say that Congress will pay.   General Clinton sent two spies to them with a letter in which he offered to give them the fourteen months' pay now due to them, a present of money besides, also new clothes, and pay them in future the same that the English soldiers receive.   He promised to keep them a corps apart in the British army, commanded by their own officers , and to their leaders he promised ranks and considerable rewards.   In spite of all these promises they arrested his spies and hanged them.   Congress has just sent three of its members to treat with them, and they have appointed six of their sergeants charged with powers to negotiate.   They demand the fourteen months' pay which is due to them, with clothes and their future subsistence.   These demands will certainly be granted , but the difficulty is to find the money ; it can only be found with difficulty.   This is the moment when we ought to furnish it and secure to the Americans all that is needed to suppress this mutiny , but we have nothing, and unless we receive immediate succour from France we shall not have enough a month hence to pay our own army.

There is a coolness between General Washington and M. de Rochambeau ; the displeasure is on the side of the

American general; ours is ignorant of the cause of it. He has charged me with a letter to take to General Washington; I am also to inform myself as to the causes of this displeasure, and remove them if possible, or, if the matter is more serious, to send him an immediate report So you see, my dear father, I am entering diplomacy; it is my first attempt, and I shall try to come well out of it.

NEWPORT, April 3, 1781.

It is impossible to judge of the campaign we are about to make here, I cannot even form a plan without first seeing the turn that affairs are likely to take after it. The war cannot be a long one, — not more than one, or two campaigns at the most I even think that if the present one is vigorous, as it seems likely to be, it will be the last. This country is not in a state to support a long war. It is ruined; no money, no men; if France does not succour it vigorously, it must make peace. Up to the present moment we have not made great efforts. Here we are for the last ten months a handful of men on this little island; we have been of no use whatever, the South has been devastated by the English, we can take no troops there on account of our small number, and if the English conduct themselves well the whole South will be captured; discouragement will be the result of such a loss, and peace is a sure consequence.

We are now expecting news from that region; Lord Cornwallis, who commands the English troops there, having made an imprudent advance, was obliged to retreat. It is said that he had taken a very favourable position, but that he is surrounded by the militia of the region, and that, according to all appearance, he may be furiously attacked, or mauled during his retreat. But it is now a whole month that we lack confirmation of this news, and I find it hard to believe it.   The first news that reaches us will be very interesting.

I wrote you, my dear father, that Arnold had been sent to the bay of the Chesapeake to do all the damage he possibly could   He is there since the month of January.   It was resolved to send down a detachment and try to take him, by a combined operation with fifteen hundred Americans under the orders of M. de Lafayette.   Seventeen hundred men were embarked in the fleet, under the command of the Baron de Viomesnil; they started the 8th of March.   I join to this letter a report of what took place, and of the fight there, you will see that it was not to our disadvantage, we say that we won it, but we did not win our object, for the English are where we ought to be, and we are forced to return here.   Until now I had always believed that in war a detachment was not victorious unless it amply performed the purpose for which it was sent.   Two of our vessels were so battered that when M. Destouches made the signal to renew the battle, those two vessels signalled that they were considerably disabled.   Only four of the English vessels were closely engaged; the others fired from a distance. The number of our dead and wounded amounts to about three hundred; only two hundred are mentioned in the report.   I have corrected the gross blunders in one of the copies which I send you; if one tried to correct all it would have to be rewritten.

NEWPORT, April 11, 1781.

In the South, the English, under Lord Cornwallis, have just won a very considerable advantage over General Greene, who commands the American army in those parts.   We do not know what results may come from this advantage; I believe, myself, there will be none, except that of rendering Cornwallis's retreat very safe.   He advanced too far into the

country, and supplies began to fail him If he gets no
other fruit than this victory it is still a great thing I hear
him taxed by every one with heedlessness and incapacity;
but I cannot bring myself to regard as a bad general a man
who, up to the present moment, has always been successful,
and who, having advanced too far into an enemy's country,
surrounded, they say, on all sides, and certain of being taken,
begins a retreat in face of the enemy, halts in a very advantageous position, beats the enemy, forces him to retire twenty
miles from the battle-field, and procures by doing so an easy
retreat. This war does honour to the English, although
their generals behave badly in America. I fear the war
will not be equally to our credit.

It seems that our winter is quite over here: we are now
enjoying the finest weather in the world; it is even very hot
at times.

NEWPORT, May 13, 1781.

Since my last, nothing has happened here. We are still
tranquilly in Newport, the English in New York, and General
Washington at New Windsor on the Hudson River. God
knows when we shall get out of this position; it is very long
since we got into it   The campaign at the South is ending;
summer is approaching, and at that season all military operations are impossible without a very considerable loss of men
from heat and malaria. As I have already told you, Lord
Cornwallis advanced too far into the enemy's territory and
was forced to retire. General Greene, with four thousand
soldiers and as many more militia, harassed his retreat.
Lord Cornwallis took up a good position, waited for General
Greene, and fought him. All the militia, after the first dis-
charge, gave way and went home; not one of them stopped
until he reached his own house. The rest were repulsed
and forced back twelve miles. Lord Cornwallis then con-

tinued his retreat to Camden, and thence, I suppose, to Charleston, where he will spend the hot season and renew the campaign in the autumn.

We are making all our preparations to march; every one is getting ready his equipments. I have already told you, my dear father, of what mine consist. My comrades have canteens — supply-boxes; but I thought that expense very great and useless. Possibly I shall be less comfortable, but no matter, it involved too much expense

NEWPORT, May 17, 1781.

It is impossible to form any conjecture about the campaign on which we are entering; nothing has transpired as to the news which our general has received from France, so that we do not know what reinforcements have been sent to us; some say 650, others 1500 men; others again declare that M. de Grasse, who went to the West India Islands with 21 ships and 10,000 troops, will come here with part of them when the wet season renders all operations impossible in that region, that is to say, in the months of July and August. If that were so, we should at once begin the siege of New York, and we might reasonably hope for success. Without it the whole thing is a chimera and an impossibility, to which we have sacrificed much. If supports as considerable as those I speak of do not arrive we shall evacuate this island; we shall establish our storehouses in Providence, where we have already sent part of our artillery and army waggons. We should then march along the North River and approach New York to threaten it and prevent General Clinton from sending away detachments. This would give General Washington the time to go into Virginia, drive out Arnold, and destroy the settlement that the English seem inclined to make there. Perhaps the Americans will remain before

New York and we shall be charged with the expedition to
Virginia, I should prefer that.

This was our general's plan of campaign before the arrival
of the frigate which brought out the new admiral and de-
spatches from Court.	Since then I do not know what changes
may have been made; but I think that, unless M. de Grasse
arrives, there will be none.	There is to be a conference
shortly between General Washington and M. de Rochambeau
at the same place as that of last year, namely, Hartford, forty
leagues from here.	There they will probably decide on the
plan of campaign.	Provided it is active, and something is
done, that is all I desire.	We have had too much inaction,
mortifying inaction.	It would have been more useful to
America had we sent her the money we are costing the king
here, the Americans would have employed it better.	We
ought to have had here an army of 15,000 men; only 5000
were sent, who have been a year in garrison in Newport and
of no use whatsoever, except to eat up provisions and make
them dearer.	I hope we shall soon get out of this sloth and
be active.

I say nothing to you about my own affair, my dear father:
since my last letter, in which I spoke of it, nothing new has
taken place, or rather I have heard no news of it.	I desire
it much, for I begin to be tired of being with M. de Rocham-
beau.	He treats me with distinction, it is true, and I feel
it: but he is distrustful in a very disagreeable and sometimes
insulting manner.	He has more confidence in me than in
my comrades, but even that is paltry; nor does he show
more to his general officers, who are much displeased, and so
are the superior officers of the army.	They have, however,
the good sense to conceal it, and to concur for the good of
the cause.

We push economy to such an extent that we have not

even one spy in New York, because it would cost us perhaps
fifty louis a month; we prefer to receive news from General
Washington, and to leave to the Americans, who have no
money to pay for news, the duty of obtaining it. The spies
who are there do it from love of country. For this reason
we get our information very late, and we shall end by having
none at all, for men soon weary of doing gratis a business
which leads to the gallows.

We are preparing to march, but I do not know when we
shall really do so   Part of the artillery munitions and the
heavy baggage of the army are already stored in Providence.
The general officers are now getting ready their own equipments   Our army is just as little disciplined as a French
army usually is. Nevertheless the leaders are very severe:
there is seldom a day when two or three officers are not
under arrest; I have seen indecent scenes when a whole
corps deserved to be cashiered, but we are only 5000 strong
and we cannot spare a man.

The fleet received orders yesterday to sail, and we supply
500 men to complete the crews of the ships; they have
scarcely any sailors left, so landsmen have to be supplied.
This puts the colonels in very bad humour, and with reason;
it gives me pain, — 500 men less, when we have need of all
our soldiers! I think the squadron is going to meet the
convoy which they say is on its way to us.

NEWPORT, June 3, 1781.

At last we depart; in eight or ten days the army will be
on the march. This is the result of the conference between
the two generals. What the plan of campaign is and where
we are going is a secret, and ought to be one. I hope we
shall be in active service, and that they will not make us
quit Newport only to put us in garrison in some other little

town. Our fleet stays here, guarded by American militia
and 400 of our own troops. I pity those who are selected
for this detachment. The whole army is enchanted to
depart.

Nothing has happened in these parts since my last. The
English are making progress in the South; they burn or
plunder everything; but they spend money and that makes
them friends, before long the whole of that part of America
will be conquered; then the English will recognize the
independence of the Northern States, or at least, will treat
them as independent, and will keep the South for themselves. Imagine how glorious this will be for the arms of
France! What confirms me in this idea is that all things
indicate the total evacuation of New York, they have already sent away several detachments, the last, within a few
days, of twenty-five hundred men. Moreover, they are shipping a great many things at night, after taps, when the
inhabitants of the town are not allowed to be out. If they
totally evacuate New York to take their forces south, they
do well. — I am obliged to finish.

YORKTOWN, October 23, 1781.

As I have had no time to write you the slightest detail of
the siege I annex here a little diary of our operations. They
are over for this year, and we are going into winter-quarters
in the neighbourhood, headquarters will be at Williamsburg,
a villanous little town that looks more like a village.

Journal of Operations during the Siege and Surrender of Yorktown.

After spending eleven months at Newport in total inaction, our army started from there June 12, 1781, leaving
six hundred troops, and one thousand militia, under com-

mand of M. de Choisy, brigadier-general, to defend the works
we had made there, protect our little squadron of eight
vessels, and cover our storehouses in Providence, where we
had placed our siege artillery. The army went by water
from Newport to Providence, and then marched by land to
Philipsburg, fifteen miles from King's-Bridge, where it arrived July 6, and went into camp on the left of the Americans The Lauzun legion had all along covered our left
flank, marching eight or ten miles apart from us on the sea
side. Our army was about five thousand strong; that of the
Americans three thousand.

During our stay at Philipsburg we made several great
forages and reconnoitrings about King's-Bridge. August
14 we received news of the arrival of M. de Grasse. He left
the Isles July 24. I was sent back to Newport to hasten the
departure of the fleet and the embarkation of our artillery at
Providence. On the 17th the army left Philipsburg and
arrived on the 21st at King's-ferry, on the banks of the
North, or Hudson, River. It was four days in crossing; on
the 25th we began our march, two thousand Americans
were with us; three thousand had been left to guard the
defiles near Philipsburg. All things seemed to announce
the siege of New York. The setting-up of a bakery and
storehouses at Chatham, four miles from Staten Island; our
crossing of the North River and the march we made to
Morristown seemed to indicate that we intended to attack
Sandy Hook, in order to facilitate the entrance of our vessels.
We were not long, however, in perceiving that New York
was not our object, but General Clinton was completely
duped and that was what we wanted.

We crossed Jersey, one of the finest and best cultivated
provinces in America, and the army arrived at Philadelphia,
September 3. It crossed the city on parade, and won the

admiration of the inhabitants, who had never before seen so many men armed and clothed uniformly, and so well-disciplined. After staying there two days, it marched for the head of Elk River at the upper end of the Chesapeake Bay. On the 6th we heard that M. de Grasse had arrived in that bay on the 3d with twenty-eight vessels, and that three thousand troops under command of M. de Saint-Simon, brigadier-general, had disembarked and joined the eighteen hundred under the Marquis de Lafayette at Williamsburg. The march of the army was therefore hastened, and on the 7th the whole army arrived at the head of Elk River. It was there decided to embark the army, but the lack of boats, which the English had either taken or destroyed during the five months when they were masters of the bay, prevented us from shipping more than our grenadiers and chasseurs (eight hundred men) and seven hundred Americans. The rest, with the baggage and equipments, marched to Annapolis, and were there embarked on the frigates. The whole arrived and were in camp at Williamsburg about the 26th. Two days after M. de Grasse entered the Chesapeake he descried a large English fleet of twenty vessels. Admiral Hood with twelve ships had joined the eight of Admiral Graves. M. de Grasse at once went out with twenty-four vessels, leaving four to guard the New York and the James Rivers; and after a fight, which was not very sharp, the English retired M. de Barras with eight ships joined M de Grasse, and on the 8th they were all in the bay

As soon as we reached Williamsburg, they went to work to land the field artillery and the equipments; all was ready by the 28th [of September], and the army marched to invest Yorktown, where Lord Cornwallis was. He occupied Yorktown, which is on the right bank of the river, and Gloucester, which is on the left bank The river is one mile wide, that is to say, the third of a French league. We began our investment the same day, but the Americans could not finish theirs till the day after. They had a marsh to cross, the bridge was broken, and they were forced to make another. On the 29th the investment was complete and we went to work to land our siege guns and make the quantity of fascines, *saucissons* [bundles of faggots], hurdles, and gabions necessary for the siege. On the 30th the enemy evacuated their advanced works and retreated within the body of the place The works consisted of two large redoubts, and a battery of two cannon, which were separated from the town by a deep ravine of twelve hundred yards We took possession; and this advanced our own work very much, leaving us the ability to put our first parallel on the other side of the ravine. Though that was a blunder made by Lord Cornwallis, it is, perhaps, excusable, because he had express orders from General Clinton to retire within the place, and a promise that he (Clinton) would relieve him.

October 6, at eight in the evening, we opened the trench at nine hundred yards from the works. The right rested on the river, the left on a great ravine which falls perpendicularly on the town to the right of the works, and thence to the river on the right of the town. Our trench had twenty-one hundred yards of development, and it was defended by four palisaded redoubts and five batteries. The ground, which is much intersected by little ravines, facilitated our approach and enabled us to reach our trench under cover without being obliged to make a branch way On our right we opened another trench, resting its left on the river and its right on a wood. There we had a battery of four mortars, two howitzers, and two pieces of twenty-four which commanded the river, making communication between Yorktown and Gloucester insecure and rendering the ships in the river very uneasy. The enemy did not fire much during the night.

On the following days we worked at perfecting the trench, palisading the redoubts, and putting the batteries into condition. On the 10th, they all fired during the day. We had forty-one guns, either cannon, mortars, or howitzers. Our artillery was marvellously well-served, the quality of the works, which were of sand, did not allow our cannon, though so well directed, to have all the effect they would have had on other ground, but we learned by deserters that our bombs had great effect and that the number of dead and wounded was increasing The besieged fired little, they had none but small cannon, — the largest was of eighteen; their mortars were only of six or eight inches, while ours were of twelve During the day we sent in many bombs and royal-grenades; at night the enemy established flying batteries. In the daytime they usually withdrew their cannon and put them behind the parapet

On the night of the 11th and 12th the second parallel of 360 yards was opened, the left resting, like the first, on the ravine, the right on a redoubt. We could not push the parallel to the river, on account of two redoubts belonging to the English, which were half a musket-shot in advance of our right. It was resolved to attack them first and then finish the parallel. On the 14th, at eight o'clock in the evening, four hundred grenadiers and chasseurs, supported by one thousand men, attacked the redoubt and carried it sword in hand There were one hundred and fifty men in it, half English, half Germans, we took only thirty-four prisoners and three officers. The Americans carried the other redoubt, they worked all night to continue the trench, and by morning on the 15th it was well covered. The English plied us with bombs all night and the next day.

On the 16th, our batteries were finished, and they worked at mounting the guns. Next morning at five o'clock the enemy made a sortie of six hundred men, entered a battery, and spiked four cannon. They were repulsed at once, and we had about twenty men killed and wounded. They made seventeen prisoners, of whom one was an officer. Our soldiers, who have been extremely tired since the beginning of the siege, were asleep and surprised

On the 17th, the enemy sent in a flag of truce, and Lord Cornwallis asked to capitulate. They were occupied the whole of the 18th in settling the articles; on the 19th the capitulation was signed and the troops laid down their arms. There were but ten cannon-balls and one bombshell left in the place. We had in our second parallel six batteries and sixty cannon, which would have opened fire on the 17th, and on the 18th or 19th we hoped to be in a condition to assault.

The legion of Lauzun, eight hundred troops, vessels, and one thousand militia were on the Gloucester side, to prevent any passing out in that direction. On the night of the 14th and 15th Lord Cornwallis sent two thousand men to Gloucester to force a way through for him, intending to march two hundred leagues through an enemy's country to reach [New ?] York. The enterprise was bold, but crazy, it might have succeeded with two hundred men. The only fault committed by Lord Cornwallis was that of having stopped at Yorktown; that fault, however, was not his, it was that of General Clinton, who ordered him to stay there, and he could only obey.

We have taken seventy-six hundred men in Yorktown, of whom two thousand are sick and four hundred wounded, four hundred fine dragoon horses, and one hundred and seventy-four cannon, seventy-four of them being of bronze.

Most of these guns are small mortars of four to six inches. There are also some forty vessels, the greater part of which are sinking or damaged. There was one fifty-gun ship, which our left battery set on fire with red-hot shot and burned.

Our army was composed of eight thousand men, that of the Americans had about the same number; in all, fifteen to sixteen thousand men We had two hundred and seventy-four killed or wounded, and ten officers.

YORKTOWN, October 23, 1781

There is every appearance that we shall make our campaign of next year towards Charleston and end by besieging that place The English will not fail now to send troops from New York to this part of America, so I think we may have an active war. It seems as if General Clinton would have nothing else to do. M. de Rochambeau has asked for reinforcements, and I think that M. de Grasse will return here from the Antilles with his twenty-eight ships. If they leave him in command he will bring troops with him. With his forces and ours united we shall be in a state to make a pretty campaign, and the taking of Savannah, where M. d'Estaing has failed, and that of Charleston, may well be the result of the campaign and crown the work we have now so well begun.

I have no doubt they will send M. de Rochambeau the troops for which he asks. He knows too well how to use them, and has just done too great a service to have so just a demand refused at such a moment. I fear peace only, and I offer prayers that it may not yet be made.

All our young colonels belonging to the French Court are departing to spend their winter in Paris. Some will return, others will stay there and will be much surprised if they are not all made brigadier-generals after being at the siege of Yorktown, they think they have done the finest thing in the world I shall stay here, having no other reason to go to Paris than my amusement and pleasure, and those I must sacrifice My affairs can get on without me; I should spend a great deal of money, and I ought to be careful of it. I prefer to employ it in making another campaign here and in achieving what I have begun When I took the resolution to come here I foresaw the annoyances I should have to put up with; it is fair that the instruction I have acquired should cost me something.

WILLIAMSBURG, March 25, 1782.

The last letter I had the honour to write to you, my dear father, was dated March 4 from Philadelphia. I left there on the 9th with the Chevalier de Luzerne, and we arrived here on the 17th. We made a charming journey and the *cantines* [provision boxes] he took with him, which were well furnished with pâtés, hams, wine, and bread, prevented our feeling the misery that reigns in the inns, where nothing is found but salt pork and no bread In Virginia the people eat nothing but cakes made of the flour of Indian corn, which they bake before the fire; that hardens the outside a little, but the inside is only dough not cooked. They drink nothing but *rum* (a brandy made from sugar) mixed with water, they call it "grog." The apples have failed this year, and that prevents them from having cider. At 250 miles from here, in a part of Virginia which they call "the mountains," all this is quite different. The country is richer, and it is there they cultivate tobacco; the soil also produces wheat and all sorts of fruits. But in the part of the country near the sea, called "the plains," where we are, they grow nothing but Indian corn.

The principal product of Virginia is tobacco; not that this

State, which is the largest of the thirteen, is not capable of other cultivation, but the laziness of the inhabitants and their conceit are great obstacles to industry. It really seems as if the Virginians were another race of men; instead of occupying themselves with their farms and making them profitable, each land-owner wants to be a lord. No white man ever works, but, as in the West India islands, all the work is done by negro slaves, who are ordered by the whites, and by overseers under them.

There are, in Virginia, at least twenty negroes to one white man, so that this State has sent but few soldiers to the army. All persons who do business are regarded as inferior by the others, who say they are not gentlemen, and they do not choose to live with them socially. These Virginians have all the aristocratic instincts, and when one sees them it is hard to understand how they came to enter a general confederation and to accept a government founded on perfect equality of condition. But the same spirit which has led them to shake off the English yoke may lead them to other action of the same kind, and I should not be surprised to see Virginia detach herself, after the peace, from the other States. Neither should I be surprised to see the American government become a complete aristocracy.

We have no political news here, you know already of the taking of Saint-Christopher, — a fine possession which the English have just lost. There is much talk about the evacuation of Charleston. Thirty transports have arrived in New York to fetch the troops. Forty or fifty were there already, armed for the same service. Our politicians differ much as to the object of this evacuation; some think it is to concentrate all their forces at New York, that seems to me little probable; others that it is to send succour to Jamaica in case of need. Since the capture and total dispersion of M. de

Guichen's convoy the English might feel easy in that direction, and I am more of the opinion of those who do not believe in the evacuation at all. What makes me doubt it is that General Clinton would never dare to take such a great step without orders from his Court, that such orders could only be the result of some plan of campaign, and that no plan, if made, has had time to get here.

The taking of part of M. de Guichen's convoy is a terrible loss for us. Besides the munitions of war and the commissariat stores with which the ships were laden, and which can be replaced, we lose time which cannot be recovered, and the expedition to Jamaica will fail. Admiral Rodney has arrived in the West Indies with ten sail of the line and troops. This makes him superior to M. de Grasse, and may change the whole face of things in that part of the world.

WILLIAMSBURG, May 27, 1782.

We are in great consternation on the subject of a battle between the fleets in the West Indies. The first news we received said that we had won the advantage, but yesterday we heard more through the English, that is to say, by a New York gazette, which reports that the "Ville de Paris," 110 guns, on which was the Comte de Grasse, was taken, with six other vessels, and that we were totally defeated. This news seems certain, because of the particulars that accompanied it. The ships taken are named, the number of killed and wounded on each ship is specified, and in short, it seems impossible that this should be news manufactured by a newspaper. We do not bear this reverse well; I see that we allow ourselves to be easily depressed. One would think we were not much accustomed to success from the excessive joy we show when we have any, and the gloom into which we are plunged by the slightest reverse. This reverse, how-

General Counte de Rochambeau

ever, is considerable, and will render the whole campaign
null; it gives the English the upper hand in the West
Indies, if they act well they can do us great damage there,
and reinforcements from Europe, if they get them, may cause
us to lose our conquests. This disaster will have a great
effect upon us here, and will force us to pass this whole campaign in total inactivity. This is dreadful, — especially if we
are unfortunate enough to stay in this place. The heat is already extreme; imagine what it will be in July and August.

We have no news as yet from M. de Lauzun; we expect
some with great impatience, — at least I do, and we are beginning to feel uneasy.

                                    PHILADELPHIA, August 8, 1782.

The last letter I had the honour to write to you, my dear
father, was dated July 6, also from Philadelphia. I came here
with M. de Rochambeau, who had a rendezvous here with
General Washington to confer together on the operation of the
campaign. The result of the conference was that I was sent
on the 19th to Yorktown, Virginia, with a commission then
secret, but not so at present: it was to ship as soon as possible our siege artillery, which we had left at West-Point,
eight leagues above Yorktown on the same river, and bring
it up the bay of the Chesapeake to Baltimore. This operation required great secrecy and much promptitude, for we had
but one forty-gun ship to escort the convoy, and the English
with two frigates could have kept us from leaving the York
River, or else have captured some of the convoy

I started ill with a very bad cold, which was considerably
increased by fatigue and the heat. As soon as I had at-
tended to the embarkation and seen that all was under way,
I returned to report to M. de Rochambeau, who was with
the army at Baltimore, and after remaining with him a
couple of days I started with the Chevalier de Chastellux for

Philadelphia, where the Chevalier de la Luzerne loaded me with care, attentions, kindness, civilities, and friendship. The army is to leave Baltimore on the 15th to come here, and go hence to the Hudson River.   I shall wait here till it arrives , I have need of rest, and I could not be in any house where I should be more agreeably and better situated.

Our campaign this year will not be as brilliant as that of last year   The defeat of the Comte de Grasse, the dispersion of M. de Guichen's convoy, the taking of that intended for the Indies — all these disasters united have deranged our plans and made all projects miscarry.   We have nothing now to do in this country but the siege of New York, and we are too weak for such an enterprise, the success of which depends entirely on superiority at sea, and that we have not got.   Admiral Rodney has taken good care of that; and besides, when we had it we did not know how to profit by it. We are daily expecting news from France.   We are told they are preparing to lay siege to Gibraltar ; for up to the present time it has been nothing but a fruitless blockade.   If the French are set on that difficult operation I fear that our campaign here will be very inactive, and will end in nothing but long and laborious marches.   I doubt if they can succeed in taking Gibraltar, though I fear the Spaniards will justify the witty saying of some one who replied to a friend who said it would be another siege of Troy, " Yes, but Spaniards are not Greeks."

The heat is very great here; I bear it very well.   The drouth has been extraordinary , all the brooks are dry, and our army has the greatest difficulty in finding water, which is very necessary in such hot weather.

PHILADELPHIA, August 17, 1782.

On the 8th of this month the army was at Baltimore, a little town at the upper end of the bay of the Chesapeake. Thence it was to march on the 15th of the same month to the North, or Hudson, River.   But the rumour and appearances of peace which we have received from England by way of New York have delayed our march, and we shall not put ourselves in motion till the 20th   This is the upshot of a deliberation that the generals had together. By this news from England (we have none as yet from France) it seems as though peace were near. England appears to be much inclined to it if France is modest in her demands. The Americans desire nothing else, now that the King of England has declared them independent, and I think that Holland does not find itself enough benefited to wish to continue the war.

The English seem to behave with less hostility in these regions; they have forbidden all their partisans, called "tories" or "refugees," to make incursions or expeditions into the country without a permit signed by the commandant of the station. They have sent back from England all prisoners, without demands for their exchange. General Carleton, who commands in New York, has informed General Washington in a very polite letter, that the king, his master, has granted the independence of America; that he has sent a man to Paris with full powers to negotiate; and he proposes to General Washington to agree to an exchange of prisoners All this seems to indicate peace; we all think that, if it is not already signed, it certainly will be in the course of the winter, and that we shall embark in the spring.[1]   This idea

[1] John Adams, Franklin, Jay, and Laurens signed a preliminary treaty of peace in Paris, November 30, 1782   The English evacuated Charleston, December 14 — TR

causes universal joy; it gives me a pleasure I cannot express; the hope of seeing you again, my dear father, is one that I can only feel.

CAMP AT CROMPOND [?], October 3, 1782

The last letter I had the honour to write to you, my dear father, was written in August. Since then we have been always on the march, and I have had no opportunity to send you a letter. The army has crossed the Delaware, also the North, or Hudson, River, and we are now encamped ten miles from the latter, and twenty-four miles from the island of New York. There is every appearance that we shall finish our campaign here, and start from here for our winter-quarters; no one yet knows where they will be, and I dare not tell you.

Charleston is evacuated, they say; consequently the English have nothing left in the South of this continent. Their possessions are reduced now to Long Island, Staten Island, and the island of New York. There is much talk of the evacuation of the latter; I do not believe it; while Lord Rockingham lived it seems to have been determined on; now all is changed. Our generals believe it, but I am not of their opinion. I think they are sending 2000 English troops to the West Indies, and are leaving the Germans with the rest, 10,000 in all, in New York If the evacuation takes place, we shall have nothing to do but return to France.

Though we have not seen the enemy, our campaign has been a very rough one. We suffered much from heat, and now the cold weather is making itself keenly felt. I bear these changes marvellously well, and I was never better in health This year I have a tent and a straw mattress, I am not very well off for covering, but a cloak supplements that.

BOSTON, November 30, 1782

The last letter I had the honour to write to you, my dear father, was dated November 3 from Hartford, where the army made a halt of eight days while the fleet of M de Vaudreuil was being made ready. We started on the 4th and reached Providence on the 10th, where our stay was prolonged until the fleet was able to take us on board I profited by this delay to go to Newport, which is only ten leagues from Providence, to see my friends there and bid them adieu.

We left Providence on the 4th and arrived here on the 6th; we embarked at once. I am on the "Brave," 74 guns, with the Comte de Deux-Ponts, and our three first companies. The Chevalier d'Amblimont commands the ship; he behaved very badly in the action of April 12; he ran away instead of obeying signals, and when M de Bougainville hailed him, asking the reason of such extraordinary conduct, he replied that, "the fleet being lost, it was best to save one vessel for the king." He is amiable, very polite, and has a good ship, I have good quarters and he keeps a good table. That is all I want; I let him off as to bravery

It seems certain that we are going to the Cape, under command of Don Galvez; it must surely be to attempt an enterprise on Jamaica, when that on Gibraltar, which has lasted five years, succeeds or fails; whether we make one on Jamaica will be decided before July, and it is probably on that decision that our return to France depends. A person worthy of confidence, who is in the way of knowing things, assures me that we shall not stay long in the West Indies, and that we shall surely be in France by next summer.

We do not yet know if the English have evacuated Charleston. This must seem to you very extraordinary; it is strange that having an army ten leagues distant from

there we should still be uncertain as to an event so interesting to us.   But the communications of this country are so
slow and uncertain that we get our news for the most part
from the " New York Gazette."   An express makes, bravely,
eight leagues a day, whereas it might make twelve or thirteen, but perhaps the fault is in the management.   There is
much talk of the evacuation of New York; they say the
English themselves are talking about it; I do not believe a
word of it   The rendition of that place will make a useful
balance in the treaty of peace

M de Rochambeau left us at Providence; the whole army
regrets him, and with reason.   He went to Philadelphia,
where he embarked on the frigate " La Gloire."   I gave him
a letter like this one, which you may receive at the same
time.   This one goes by the frigate " Iris."   Baron de
Viomesnil now commands the army, and will take us to the
West Indies, there he leaves us as soon as we arrive, and
returns to France.

I wrote you in my last letter that the Duc de Lauzun
remains in America with his legion   I thought we should
take away our siege train, but that is changed, it stays in
Baltimore, where it now is, with 400 men detached from the
different regiments, and about the same number of sick, who
will be in good health by the spring.   That makes in all
1400 men under command of M de Lauzun, who will probably have nothing to do but to wait here till peace is made.
The duke and his legion are in quarters at Wilmington, nine
leagues to the south of Philadelphia.

I cannot tell you, my dear father, how much attached I
am to the Duc de Lauzun, and how I like him; he has the
noblest and most honourable soul that I know.   Among the
personal belongings which he brought, and which were all
lost, there were several things for me that he knew I needed,

and a part of which I had asked him to bring me. He has never been willing to tell me what they were, always replying that it was only a trifle, not worth speaking of. I should never end if I told you all the delicate and kindly actions that I know of him.

The whole army is vexed at going to the West Indies; I myself am not much pleased We saw M. de Rochambeau leave us with pain, every one liked to be commanded by him. They will have to feel the same to the Baron de Viomesnil. As for me, personally, I ought to be much satisfied; the baron has always treated me with distinguished regard and courtesy. He is hasty and quick-tempered, he has not the precious *sang-froid* of M. de Rochambeau, who was the only man capable of commanding us here, and of maintaining that perfect harmony which has reigned between two nations so different in manners, morals, and language, and who, at heart, do not like each other. There have never been disputes between our two armies during the whole time we have been together; but there have often been just ground for complaints on our part Our allies have not always behaved well to us, and the time that we have spent among them has not taught us to like or to esteem them. M de Rochambeau himself has not always been well-treated; but in spite of that his conduct has been uniform. His example has compelled the same in his army, and the stern orders that he gave restrained every one, and enforced that rare discipline which was the admiration of all the Americans and English who witnessed it. The wise, prudent, and simple conduct of M de Rochambeau has done more to conciliate the Americans than the winning of four battles could ever have done

Our fleet at Boston consists of thirteen vessels, here is the list. . . . They will sail as soon as the wind permits. The

English fleet of twenty-three sail has left New York in two divisions, the first of twelve ships, under the orders of Admiral Pigott, departed October 27, the second of eleven ships, came out of the harbour on the 21st of this month, they say. Is it to await us and capture us, or is it to transport the garrison of Charleston to the West Indies? We do not know; but time will clear up the mystery.

BOSTON, December 21, 1782

It is not yet known whether Charleston is evacuated, a Philadelphia gazette, which has just arrived, says that the English are constructing two new redoubts there, and that the truce they had demanded, and which was supposed to be a certain sign of the evacuation, has come to an end, and the place is not evacuated.

We are all going on board to-night; the ships are ready, and if the wind is fair we shall sail to-morrow morning. As soon as we reach the West India Islands I will send you news of myself, my dear father, and I shall have the pleasure to assure you of my respectful attachment.

CHAPTER III.

1783–1791 — Return to France — Confidential mission of Count Fersen to
the French Court from King Gustavus III. — Letters to his father and
the King of Sweden on the political aspects of France at the opening
of the Revolution — The Emigration begins in July 1789

[COUNT FERSEN returned to France with the French troops
in June, 1783.   He was on the point of going to Sweden to
see his parents when he received an order to join his king,
Gustavus III, and accompany him during his journeys in
Germany, Italy, and France.   It was not until the close of
the year 1784 that Count Fersen returned to Sweden in the
suite of the king   As a well-deserved reward for his campaigns in America he was appointed titulary colonel in the
Swedish army, chevalier of the Order of the Sword, and
lieutenant-colonel on service of the light-horse cavalry of the
king.   The King of France appointed him second-colonel of
the regiment Deux-Ponts and chevalier of the Order of Military Merit.   In September, 1783, he was made proprietary
colonel of the Royal-Swedish [French] regiment, at the
request of King Gustavus III., who, during his stay in Paris,
protected Fersen and enabled him to obtain from France a
pension of twenty thousand francs, which was reduced to
thirteen thousand in 1788, and ceased altogether in 1791.

General Washington granted to Count Fersen in 1783 the
Order of Cincinnatus.   It was a flattering recognition of his
services in that memorable war which has had such immense
results   Though the King of Sweden would not allow him,
or any of the Swedish officers who had fought in that war, to
wear this decoration, it was still a great distinction to have

deserved a military Order of which the generals of the armies of France were proud to bear the insignia, with permission of their sovereign.

It was at this period — 1783 to 1786 — that young de Staël-Holstein began to be noted in the diplomatic corps and in the salons of the great world of Paris, and Count Fersen, who had been intimate with him from childhood, contributed much to make him so.   M. de Staël, born in 1759, saw service early in life, was an ensign when eighteen, a lieutenant, then a captain at twenty-three.   The court which he paid to Mlle. Necker established his fortunes.   Thanks to his known hopes of obtaining her hand, in which the queen and all the greatest ladies of her Court took an interest, M. de Staël was appointed in the same year (1783) *chargé d'affaires*, envoy, and finally, ambassador from Sweden to the Court of Versailles.   Count Fersen writes at this period to his father (August 19, 1784) —

" You will have seen already that the idea I had respecting Mlle. Necker cannot come to anything, even if you consented to it, on account of my friend Staël, to whom it is perfectly suited, — much more so than to me.   I really never thought of it, except to please you, my dear father; and I am not at all sorry that it cannot be realized."

We see from from this that Fersen had thought of Mlle. Necker for himself, and renounced his pretensions in favour of his friend, who saw in this match a first step to fortune. M. de Staël was, however, compelled to wait a long time for the consent of her parents, for he had many rivals, among them the famous minister Mr. Pitt.   Count Fersen writes to his father, October 15, 1785 : —

" M. Necker has at last decided to give him his daughter ; it is an excellent affair and I am enchanted for M. de Staël ; he had numerous and powerful rivals, among others Mr. Pitt,

the one who is at present at the head of English affairs; but
the young girl preferred M. de Stael.   I saw her a few days
ago.   She is not pretty,—on the contrary; but she has intellect, gaiety, amiability, has been very well brought-up, and is
full of talents.   The wedding will take place on the 10th or
15th of next month.

An illness of Mlle. Necker delayed the marriage until
January 1786.   It was concluded under very onerous conditions for Sweden.   King Gustavus III. agreed to give Stael an
annual pension of 20,000 francs, or an office in Sweden equiv-
alent to it in case he lost, through unforeseen circumstances
his embassy to Versailles during the first six months after his
marriage.   When the Revolution broke out in France this
agreement became very burdensome to the King of Sweden,
inasmuch as Stael sided, thanks to the influence of his wife,
with the enemies of the royal family, as we shall see
in the course of these Letters.   This obliged the King of
Sweden to conceal his real opinions in his despatches to his
ambassador to France, and it is important to know this, in
order to judge correctly of the epoch and also of its documents.   Baron Taube, first gentleman of the Bed-chamber
and confidential secretary of Gustavus III, wrote as follows,
to his intimate friend Count Fersen:—

"The king orders me to let you know that all Stael's
despatches are written in the spirit of the Revolution; his
Majesty is obliged to feign to pay attention to what he says
to him; but it is only that he may fathom their projects and
their views more completely.   The king orders you to
warn the King and the Queen [of France], so that they may
not be misled   Assure them that the king never varies in
his feelings and his attachment for them, as he will try on all
occasions to prove to them."

Count Fersen's service in the two armies of Sweden and

France obliged him to divide his time between the two
countries   During the summer of 1787 he was sent to
France with letters from the King of Sweden to Louis XVI.

"I passed a day in Paris," he writes, May 25, 1787, "to
deliver the letters with which I was laden and to see my
friends, and the next day I came to Versailles to pay my
court and give the letters to the king   It was the day of
the closing of the Assembly of the Notables, and I am very
glad to have seen that ceremony   It was very imposing,
and will probably never be seen again in our day. The
results of that Assembly are great reforms in the households
of the princes ; but most of them bear only on abuses and on
the old ostentatious splendour, which is scarcely noticed and
was of no use whatever except to absorb enormous sums.
The Comte d'Artois has already returned four hundred
thousand francs from his household to the king   The reform in the queen's stable amounts to two hundred and fifty
thousand francs , in short, it seems that they have taken a
firm resolution to correct abuses as much as possible   The
king has already reduced his packs of boar-hounds and wolf-
hounds, all the falcons, and the emoluments of the grand
falconer are to be suppressed, so they tell me.   There is
much else, but I cannot remember it.   They talk of a diminution of two-fifths of all pensions above ten thousand francs ;
but that is not certain "

In October, 1788, Gustavus III. sent Count Fersen again to
Paris to look after his interests and correspond with him confidentially.   From that time the Count remained in France,
sometimes in Paris, sometimes with his regiment, the Royal-
Swedish, which was in garrison at Valenciennes, Maubeuge,
and other towns.   The first rough shocks of the Revolution
were beginning to be felt, and Count Fersen bestowed much
attention on the study of them.   The loss of his Journal

from 1780 to June, 1791, was a great misfortune   Intrusted
to a friend at the time that he was obliged to leave Paris
when Louis XVI. and family started for Varennes, these
sheets were burned, from the fear that they might fall into
the hands of the revolutionaries.   They contained, as Fersen
himself said, precious information of the events of the time,
and the family of Louis XVI.   Nothing relating to that time
now remains but letters, written by the count to his father,
which contain some account of the political events in France
at the beginning of the Revolution.]

PARIS, December 10, 1788.

Affairs in this country are not in a more tranquil state
than they are in Sweden ; on the contrary, minds are furiously excited , but with what a difference !   Here we have a
patient with a good constitution and in all the vigour of his
age, for whom we need only a good physician , but the question is to find one.   There appears to be a great schism between the nobles and the *tiers état* ; the latter wants to be
represented in greater numbers and to have more influence
in the States-general than it has hitherto had.   The parliaments, which used to be united with the nobles, have been
abandoned by them in consequence of a late decree of the
parliament of Paris [abolishing feudal rights], which demands no less than the English constitution.   There were
two parties in the Chamber on that occasion ; all the old
members were against the resolution, but the young ones
carried it.   They say also that the provincial parliaments
are not all of one opinion, and that several are contrary to
the decree of that of Paris   So here is disunion among the
great bodies of the kingdom ; it remains to be seen what
will result for the king   But in any case, it seems to me
that things will go better than was thought at first, and that

France will recover in Europe the great influence that she ought to have there. The fermentation of minds is general, nothing is talked of but the Constitution, the women, especially, are mixed up in the matter, and you know, as I do, the influence they have in this country. It is all a delirium; every one is an administrator and talks of nothing but "progress;" in the antechambers the lacqueys are busy reading political pamphlets, ten or a dozen of which appear daily; I do not see how the printing-offices suffice for them all; they are the fashion of the moment, however, and you know, as I do, the empire that has here

We are having a very severe winter, freezing for three weeks, the cold has been up to 13° and at midday 2°, 3°, and 4°. For a week past there has been four inches of snow in the streets of Paris and the roofs are covered. The river is frozen, which hampers the provisioning of Paris, so that they fear a famine, it is also feared in the provinces. There is very little wheat, and what there is they cannot grind because of the lack of water, for there has been no rain since August.

PARIS, January 2, 1789

The country is still in a great ferment, but here great heats pass off in a short time and reflection comes. The grave question which divides all minds at the present moment is whether the deputies of the *tiers état* will equal in number those of the nobles and the clergy; opinions are much divided thereon, even among the nobles, the greater part of whom consent to this equality. The king has just decided that for one member of the nobles and one of the clergy there shall be two of the *tiers état*, which seems just. Meanwhile the public has been inundated with writings and pamphlets; there is not a day that five or six do not appear; most of them have no common-sense and contain

nothing but empty words or thoughts that are wholly sedi-
tious. Everybody is author and administrator, especially the
women, you know, as I do, how they give the tone here and
how they like to mingle in everything. They are occupied
now with nothing but "the Constitution," and the young
men, to please them and to have an air of good style, talk
only of States-general and systems of government, though
often enough their waistcoats, their cabriolets, and their
jackets make a diversion. I do not know whether the
kingdom will gain by all these changes, but society has lost
a great deal.

Valenciennes [in camp], June 26, 1789

The *tiers état* wants to be alone in the States-general.
The origin of the quarrel is that the *tiers état* claimed that
the powers of the deputies ought to be verified in common
in an assembly of the three orders; whereas the nobles
willed that, according to ancient custom each order should
verify its powers separately. This dispute heated all
brains; part of the clergy joined the *tiers état*, so did some
of the nobles; and they have constituted themselves a
National Assembly; whereupon the king held a royal session
at which he quashed the resolution of the *tiers état* The
National Assembly paid no attention to the king's action, but
continued its sessions. The nobles have joined the king.
The excitement is extreme. You know French heads, and
you can easily imagine to what lengths they may go; but
never could you have conceived the indecency of all that is
being done and written. The Archbishop of Paris, a man
respectable for his age and conduct, came near being stoned
at Versailles as he was entering his house, because he is not
on the side of the *tiers état*. Several of his servants were
wounded Three or four madmen lead the whole thing, and
God knows where it will end. The king seems decided to

hold to what he has said, and they have brought about 12,000 to 15,000 troops into the neighbourhood of Versailles, La Muette, Meudon, etc. What is most grievous is that they are not sure of the French soldier, and they are forced to employ foreigners as much as possible. They have also brought up forty pieces of artillery. It is impossible to foresee the end.

VALENCIENNES, July 22, 1789.

Heads are so heated that firmness is thought more injurious than useful The Baron de Breteuil is no longer minister. M. de Broglie and de La Vauguyon, who were appointed with him, the first as minister of War, the second to Foreign Affairs have gone too, the king has recalled M. Necker. The troops are sent back to their garrisons. The populace of Paris has seized the Bastille and has murdered the governor, M. de Launay, in a horrible manner. They have captured at the Invalides 36,000 muskets; they have hanged M. de Flesselle, provost of the merchants; all carriages are stopped; every one in Paris is made to go a-foot. The nobles are insulted. The Comte d'Artois and his children, the Princes de Condé, Conti, and Bourbon, with many other persons, among them the Baron de Breteuil, have fled, under assumed names to protect themselves from the people. No one is allowed to leave Paris; all is confusion, disorder, consternation. The assembly of the electors at the Hôtel-de-Ville has little power, as the execution of M. de Toulon and Berthier plainly shows.

At the present moment Paris is rather more tranquil, but not enough so to induce persons to remain in it. Every day great numbers of the inhabitants leave it, and by winter, unless quiet is restored, it will be deserted. The king has gone to Paris in the hope of producing calmness, but the effect has not been all that he expected

You will see in the " Journal de Paris " and other papers, the details of all this, which are fairly correct, nothing is exaggerated, for it is not possible to exaggerate what has happened, and is still happening. Riots are taking place in all the cities of the kingdom, but they seem to be only a parody of what is going on in Paris. So far all is confined to breaking into the tax offices and opening the prisons, for it is the lowest of the populace who make the disorder. The bourgeoisie was immediately armed and that did much to restore tranquillity. We have had our little riot here [Valenciennes], but it is all over Now, the idle scoundrels have spread themselves over the country districts; they are pillaging, or putting under contribution all the abbeys and châteaux, they are hunted everywhere, and yesterday, in one spot, we captured one hundred and nineteen, many more will probably be taken.

That, my dear father, is the sad news of this country; it is in a state of violent crisis; we must now see what the States-general will do, but at this moment all bonds are broken, obedience has disappeared in the army, and I doubt if it will be as easy to restore things as it has been to overthrow them.

VALENCIENNES, August 15, 1789

Disorder is increasing throughout the country, and God alone knows what will come of it. Paris is the focus of trouble, and nearly every one is in haste to leave it. Vagabonds and deserters are taking refuge there, and the number of the latter is very considerable. They are received into the new militia which is being raised under the command of the Marquis de Lafayette [the National Guard], they have better pay than in our regiments and there are no means not employed to entice them. It is said that according to the report of the regiments rendered to the war office, there

have been, since July 13, 12,750 deserters, without counting
the Gardes Françaises.   The king's authority is totally an-
nihilated, so is that of the parliaments and the magistrates;
the States-general themselves tremble before Paris, and this
fear greatly influences their deliberations.   There are no
longer in this kingdom either laws, order, justice, discipline,
or religion; all bonds are broken; and how can they be re-
established? that is what I do not know, but these are the
effects of the progress of the ideas of anglomania and philoso-
phy, France is ruined for a long time to come.

VALENCIENNES, September 3, 1789

All bonds are broken; the king's authority is null; the
National Assembly itself trembles before Paris, and Paris
trembles before forty to fifty thousand bandits or vagrants
established at Montmartre or in the Palais-Royal, from which
they cannot be driven   In the provinces the people are
intoxicated with the idea, long spread by philosophers in
their writings, that all men are equal; and the abolition of
feudal rights and others (voted so glibly by the Assembly in
three hours time, after a supper) has persuaded them that
they have nothing more to pay.   Everywhere they are rush-
ing into frightful excesses against the châteaux of the nobles,
which they pillage and burn, with all their deeds and papers;
they even maltreat the owners if they find them there.   You
will see the details in the newspapers and there is nothing
exaggerated in them.   In all the towns the people have
broken into the offices and driven away the clerks of the
farms,[1] in nearly all the provinces they refuse to pay.   The
taxes cannot be collected; the troops are won over, or seduced by the hope of liberty, or money.   The king will soon

[1] The farms, *fermes*, it will be remembered, meant under the old monarchy the farming out of the public revenues to "farmers-general," who
levied them for the royal treasury at a profit to themselves — TR.

be unable to meet his engagements, and bankruptcy is imminent The nobles are in despair, the clergy are, as it were,
struck demented, and the *tiers état* is wholly dissatisfied:
it is the *canaille* who reign, and are satisfied because, having
nothing to lose, they can only gain. No one dares to command, and no one is willing to obey.

Such is the liberty of France, and the state in which she
is at this moment. One shudders at seeing what is going on,
and it is impossible to foresee how these things will end. All
this makes me very unhappy. I share with you, my dear
father, the attachment you feel for France, and I cannot see
its ruin without the keenest sorrow. Many regiments have
mutinied, some have even laid hands on their chief officers
In our regiment things have not gone so far as yet, but for
three days the soldiers forced the gates of the quarters and
of the town, and went to drink in the country, where they
committed very horrible excesses. On the third day they
would certainly have pillaged and fired the town if the
générale had not been beaten [call to all citizens to assemble].
Aided by the bourgeois militia, we have now re-established
order and quiet

The extraordinary part is that the same thing has happened in nearly all the garrisons, and that throughout the
kingdom the mutinies have all been alike. Secret agents
distribute money; these men are known nearly everywhere;
the leaders of the seditions, tried and hanged, have de-
nounced them; but whether it be weakness, or fear, or
complicity, or the absence of laws or the lack of means to
enforce those that still exist, — certain it is that the magistrates dare not take steps, nothing is done against these men,
and they are left in peace to stir up anarchy, mutiny, license,
and to work for the ruin of the State. The Duc d'Orléans
[great-grandson of the Regent, who presently took the name of

Philippe Égalité] is strongly suspected of being the leader and motive-power of all this.

If I were writing from Paris I should not dare to tell you these things, the epistolary inquisition has been very close; the letters of the king and queen have not escaped it. I think it has ceased at present, but it is more prudent not to trust to this When you write to me, my dear father, you can freely say what you please; coming from you it can only do good; but you must be kind enough not to refer to what I have written to you on this subject.

PARIS, October 9, 1789

All the public papers have told you, my dear father, of what happened at Versailles on Monday, 5th, and Tuesday, 6th, and of the coming of the king to Paris with his family. I was witness of it all and I returned to Paris in one of the carriages of the king's suite; we were six hours and a half on the way. God keep me from ever again seeing so afflicting a sight as that of those two days.

The people seem enchanted to see the king and his family; the queen is much applauded, and she cannot fail to be when they know her, and do justice to her desire for the right, and to the kindness of her heart The States-general are to come to Paris and begin their sessions, I do not yet know on what day.

[Towards the close of the year 1789 Count Fersen rejoined his regiment, still at Valenciennes. He pacified a sedition which had just broken out, and punished the leaders of it. He then received orders from King Gustavus III. to return to Paris and remain there near the King of France, to convey to him letters, to explain to him the sentiments of the king, his own master, and to facilitate to the utmost of his power communication between the two sovereigns, as will be seen by the following letter · —]

To His Majesty, the King of Sweden

Aix-la-Chapelle, January 7, 1790

Sire, — I received last night at eleven o'clock the letter which Y. M., deigned to do me the honour to write to me by Baron d'Ugglas. Nothing could flatter me more than the expressions and assurance it contained, they will always be precious to me and I have been deeply touched by them. . . .

To fulfil the intention of Y. M., I think it would be better not to hasten my return to Paris; it might give rise to conjectures at a time when all actions, even the simplest, are watched and interpreted Baron Taube is of my opinion, it will be, after all, a delay of only ten days; I shall be in Paris on the 17th or 18th.

The details into which Y. M. has entered as to the affairs of Sweden and France are a new proof of kindness by which I am deeply touched. The affairs of France are distressing, and Y. M. has seized them from the right point of view. I believe, as you do, that M. Necker is very guilty, and that nothing but a civil or a foreign war can restore France and the royal authority, but how is that to be brought about, with the king a prisoner in Paris? It was a false step to allow himself to be brought there. Now it becomes necessary to try to get him out of it, and the declaration made by the king in October that he was free and, to prove it, would visit the provinces in the spring, is a good pretext to leave the city, meantime the Assembly must be allowed to commit its follies.

Once out of Paris, the king ought to be able to give birth to a new order of things. If he is prevented from leaving

Paris, his captivity will be shown to the provinces, and in that case a great change may be looked for. His party is already much increased in the Assembly and in the provinces, the courage, firmness, and good conduct of the queen have brought many back to her. All the nobles, except a few, not worthy of being such, are devoted to her, the clergy the same, so is nearly the whole of the good bourgeoisie, and the number increases daily. There are none now but the *canaille* who are still stirred up by the famous words "despotism" and "aristocracy;" but a winter of experience and poverty — for everybody is saving and reforming, and nobody spends or gives — such a winter may calm and change a great many.

The noble, feeling, and generous manner in which Y. M. expresses yourself on the situation of the king and queen of France is worthy of Y M All the world shares that sentiment of indignation; but none of them dare to undertake anything for fear of compromising themselves; they all seem awaiting the moment when the king shall be out of Paris before declaring their intentions openly. The letters that Y. M. sends to the king and queen, can only touch them, one is always more sensitive to kindness when unhappy. The commission which Y. M gives me is too agreeable to let me fail in endeavouring to fulfil it myself. Besides which, I know no one to trust. . . .

I came here from Valenciennes two days ago to see Baron Taube. I am not satisfied about his state of health . .

I am, Sire, with the most profound respect, Your Majesty's very humble and obedient servant and faithful subject,

AXEL FERSEN.

[In consequence of these orders Count Fersen went to Paris at the end of January 1790 and remained there until

Louis XVI.'s abortive attempt to escape in June, 1791.   His letters to his father continue as follows : —]

PARIS, February 1, 1790

I profit eagerly by the return of M. d'Ugglas to write you freely and without restraint, for the post is not safe ; there is such great inquisition, so many committees of search, and so much conspiracy, that no one dares to either speak or write. What a frightful situation this fine kingdom is in ! no force within, and no respect without ! It is null in the political system of Europe ; within, it is in complete anarchy.   All bonds are dissolved ; there is no obedience to laws, no respect for religion, which does not exist except in name   They have taught the people to feel their strength, and they are using it with ferocity.   The nobles, clergy, and parliament, who set the first examples of disobedience and resistance, are the first victims they are ruined and their châteaux burned.   The upper bourgeoisie, who were also seduced, repent now, but too late.   The workmen, manufacturers, and artisans, all are ruined and dissatisfied, for purses are closed.   Every one is desiring another order of things; but — the populace is armed, and having nothing to lose, it has everything to gain. A mass of persons, whom hatreds, jealousies, and private revenge have led to conduct themselves ill to the king and to forget their obligations to him, hoping for no oblivion of what they have done except in a total subversion, are inciting the *canaille* with the great words " Liberty," " despotism " and " aristocracy."

The Assembly [the Constituent Assembly] is divided into three parties the aristocrats, the impartials, and the fanatics.   The first are at present for the king, because that is also for their selfish interests.   The impartials are the most reasonable, but, from that cause alone, the weakest.

The fanatics are the strongest, and are all against the king ; and M Necker, as ignorant in administration as he was said to be learned in finance, imbued with philosophic ideas, has never reflected that he ought to win opinions for the king. He looks on means of seduction as not honest ; he has wanted to remain an honest man in the midst of rascals, and he has been their dupe. His immoderate conceit made him believe he could persuade them, but England's money has stronger and more irresistible arguments. M Necker is not only guilty through ignorance, he is also guilty of treachery. He wished to be the minister of the people, to reign through them, and to force the king to be unable to do without him. He sacrificed the king and the State to his ambition. It is true that he is punished for it , his influence is completely null to-day, punishment, however, repairs nothing ; and the king was wrong not to reign by him, inasmuch as he saw that he could not reign without him.

Among the ministers there are none but MM. de la Luzerne and Saint-Priest who are well-intentioned towards the king , the others are all imbeciles or knaves, in whom no confidence whatever can be placed. M. de Saint-Priest joins to intellect both character and firmness, and if occasion should present itself he is the only man on whom the king can rely. I am on very good terms with him , his house is mine ; he loads me with kindness, civilities, and confidence. I know from him all that happens, and sometimes he even consults me. In spite of that, I only tell him what I choose ; I am prudent, for reserve is more than ever necessary.

The National Assembly continues its folly. The provinces are more in a ferment than ever, and the king is a prisoner in Paris. His position — but above all, that of the queen, who feels it much more keenly than he does — is dreadful.

The queen has shown and still shows a courage, character, and conduct which have won her many adherents.

At this moment a party of the fanatics, with M de Lafayette at their head, want to let themselves be won over to the king. The opportunity ought not to be lost; because a change for the better might then be hoped. You will certainly hear of the step the king has taken towards the Assembly [agreeing to its abolishment of the rights of primogeniture] ; this step is blamed and approved ; one party of the fanatics desired it ; at that price they promised to put back into the king's hands all executive power and the army. A fraction of the aristocrats is displeased with it, the others have decided to remain faithful to the king and to contribute all in their power to the good of the cause. It is impossible to see the result of the king's action ; but, at least, if it does no good it cannot do harm.

PARIS, April 2, 1790.

Little change. The States-general do what they choose, without the slightest opposition, they reform and destroy everything with the utmost levity ; but they do not create so readily, and what they establish takes root with difficulty Poverty and discontent are increasing, they are beginning to touch the people, especially the populace of Paris, which now finds itself without resource, owing to the diminution or annihilation of fortunes occasioned by the degrees of the Assembly. There are persons who have lost 40,000 to 50,000 francs a year, and others their whole revenue, by the abolition of feudal rights. Most of the workmen and artisans have come to beggary The shopkeepers are earning nothing. for nobody buys. The best workmen are leaving the kingdom, and the streets are full of paupers One and all they blame the Assembly, they reproach it for the absence

6

of the great world, who were their subsistence, and for
the diminution of fortunes which forces every one to econo-
mize.   The royal treasury is exhausted; the taxes are very
ill-paid or not paid at all, there is neither credit nor confidence, money has disappeared, every one hoards it; nothing
is seen but bills on the *caisse d'escompte,* which lose six per
cent in realizing them.

There, my dear father, is the present state of things.   God
knows how it will end   M. Necker is worse than ever; his
health is quite destroyed, and I do not believe he can live.
He will be regretted by very few.

PARIS, June 28, 1790.

You will see by the public papers about the state of the
army, there is no longer any order or discipline.   All heads
are turned, the soldiers form committees; they dismiss,
break, judge, and sometimes execute their officers.   Every
day we hear new horrors, and there is no longer any pleasure
in serving.   My regiment [the Royal-Swedish] has behaved
marvellously well up to the present time, though everything
has been done to seduce it   There has not been the slightest
insubordination, and I hope that this may continue.

PARIS, July 16, 1790

The famous Federation, which had inspired such fears and
was made such a bugbear, driving so many persons out of
Paris, passed off very quietly   The ceremony, which might
have been very august, very fine, and very imposing, from
the enormous mass of assistants and the beauty of the scene,
was made ridiculous by the disorder and indecency which
reigned there.   You will see a description of it in the public
papers, and you know the situation of the Champ de Mars.
But what the papers will not tell you is that there was no
order, no one was in his right place, the soldiers, who ought

to have lined the arena as guard, obeyed no one; they ran
about hither and thither, dancing and singing, and before
the arrival of the king and the Federal troops, they took a
priest and two monks from the altar and, putting grenadier's
caps on their heads and muskets on their shoulders, they
marched them round the amphitheatre, singing and dancing,
like so many savages before they eat Christians At the
moment of the mass people sang and danced, and no one
knelt at the elevation of the Host, which made many
persons who were present declare that the mass was not
said at all.

Those, my dear father, are little anecdotes which will give
you an idea of what happened, and which I am sure you will
not find in any newspaper.   I ought to add that the populace
and the National Guard, even those who were armed and on
duty, forced the sentinels and entered, with their acquaintances, into the box of the ambassadors to shelter themselves
from a shower; and we should have been forced, if they had
been more numerous, to vacate the place   They were not
turned out.

PARIS, November 5, 1790

The disorders increase daily, and, to crown all evils, we
cannot foresee the end.   Poverty is felt everywhere, coin has
disappeared, *assignats*, which were substituted for it, have
little or no credit; a thousand objections to receiving them
in payment are made, in many of the provinces the people
will not take them at all.   The merchants sell nothing;
manufactories are at a standstill; provisions grow dearer,
the quantity of paupers has increased so much that their
number is terrifying.   Paris, which is tranquil and safe
enough for individuals, is full of thieves; one hears of nothing but robberies committed, and as there is little law and
order they are not prevented and remain unpunished.   This

state of things cannot last, and the discontent, which is becoming general, will lead slowly to a change in affairs When once the discontent rises to its height the new order of things will be as quickly overthrown as the old order was; this is the effect of the vivacity and volatility of French heads.

PARIS, January 3, 1791

The affair of the clergy is making a great noise here at this moment, and the consequences cannot be foreseen. The Bishop of Clermont, who tried to propose a modification of the required oath and a form of adhesion to the decrees of the Assembly in all that concerns temporal matters, was not listened to, they forced him to answer "yes" or "no", he answered "no," and was followed by the majority of the clergy. Ninety-five refused the oath, against sixty who took it, among the latter two bishops. — the Bishop of Autun and the Archbishop of Bordeaux All the other bishops of France, except the Archbishop of Sens and the Bishop of Lidda refused likewise, and from that moment schism was established. Many persons think that this will make a great turmoil in the provinces; I do not believe it. The people do not understand this article of faith,— it is not within their range; and they will be delighted to choose their own bishop and their own rector. But I shall not be surprised if there are massacres, and if evil-minded persons profit by the refusal of the rectors of Paris to excite the *canaille* against them and so create an uproar. Those men have all to gain and nothing to lose by tumult Unhappy country!

February 15, 1791

My position here is different from that of every one else I have always been treated with kindness and distinction in this country by the ministers and by the king and queen Your reputation and your services, my dear father, have been my passport and my recommendation; perhaps a judicious, circumspect, and discreet conduct have won me approbation and esteem and some success.   I am attached to the king and queen, and I ought to be for the manner, so full of kindness, with which they always treated me when they were able to do so, and I should be vile and ungrateful if I abandoned them now when they can do nothing more for me and while I have still the hope of being useful to them.   To all the many kindnesses with which they loaded me they have now added a flattering distinction — that of *confidence;* and it is all the more flattering because it is limited to four persons, of whom I am the youngest.[1]

If we can save them, what pleasure I shall have in returning a part of the many obligations I am under to them; what sweet enjoyment to my heart if I am able to contribute to their welfare!   Yours feels it, my dear father, and you cannot but approve of me.   This conduct is the only one that is worthy of your son, and, though it may cost you something, you would be the first to order me to follow it, if I were capable of taking any other.   In the course of this summer all these events must surely develop and decide themselves: if they are unfortunate and all hope is lost, nothing shall then prevent my going to you.

[In the month of March, 1791, the king and queen asked the advice of Count Fersen as to their situation, and he gave them his opinion in the following paper —]

[1] These four persons were (1) the Baron de Breteuil, lately minister of state, who had emigrated in July, 1789, and was now the confidential agent of the King of France to the European Powers; (2) the Marquis de Bouillé, commanding certain troops in Metz, (3) the Comte de Mercy, minister and friend of the late Empress Maria Theresa, at one time Austrian ambassador at the French Court, now minister of the Low Countries under the Archduchess Maria Christina; (4) Count Fersen himself — TR.

Memorial of Count Fersen to the King and Queen of France

March 27, 1791

There seems no doubt that it is necessary to act, and to act vigorously, if order and prosperity are to be restored, the kingdom saved from total ruin, its dismemberment prevented, the king replaced upon the throne, and his authority returned to him. The steady, uniform advance of the Jacobins in their wickedness, the disunion of the democrats in the Assembly, the discontent of the provinces, which visibly increases but has no vent for want of a centre and point of union, the determination of the princes, particularly the Prince de Condé, to act if the king does not act — all this indicates that the moment has come to take a course; it seems a favourable moment, and the more delay there is, the more difficult it will be.

But how act — after the news received from the emperor [Leopold II., the queen's brother], the slowness and indecision of Spain, and the difficulty of finding money? Two courses present themselves · one is to undertake nothing before having formed alliances and obtained from the different Powers all necessary help, in men as well as money; the other is to leave Paris, waiting only to be assured of the good-will of the foreign Powers and to obtain the necessary money to pay the troops for two or three months, by which time a loan can be made in Switzerland.

The first of these courses is, without contradiction, the safest; it presents less dangers for Their Majesties, and the advantage of a less doubtful, or at any rate, a less disputable success. But as it is not possible to see the period of it, must we not fear that the ills of the State, increasing during that time, may become more difficult to repair? Will not habit and discouragement become so fixed that it will then be impossible to conquer them? Will not the now excited brains calm down and then unite to create an order of things still more disadvantageous to the king, but which private persons will prefer, for the tranquillity it will give them, to the convulsions of civil war? Moreover, will not the princes, before the period first mentioned can arrive, themselves make efforts which, if successful, will give them the honour and the fruits, rallying to their side the nobles and all those discontented with the present régime, and will they not then be masters of the kingdom and of Their Majesties?

The second course is the most hazardous. The Comte de Mercy and Baron de Breteuil seem to indicate it Their hope of success is founded on great probabilities. The emperor and Spain are well disposed, but Spain will do nothing without the emperor; and the latter, from mistaken policy and timid forethought, wants to delay the period of manifesting his good-will (The Northern powers are well-intentioned, but their distance and the war with the Turks hinders them from seconding the views of Their Majesties in a more active manner.) We are almost sure of Sardinia and Switzerland, and it is probable that a very marked advance of Their Majesties to those two Powers would decide them, for they are perhaps undecided only by a doubt of the firmness of Their Majesties' resolution, and by a fear of committing themselves uselessly should that resolution change; M. de Mercy seems to indicate as much in his letter.

Such a course would have something grand, noble, imposing, and audacious, the effect of which, both on the kingdom and in Europe would be incalculable; it might bring back the army and prevent its total decomposition, it would fix the Constitution, and prevent the factions from making such changes in it as would consolidate the revolu-

tion, and, if done at this moment, would make the movement of the princes useful to the king, whereas, if they act
alone and meet with reverses they could not, at the later
period, be of service to his cause.

Whatever may be the course which Their Majesties adopt,
it seems necessary to await the answers of Vienna and Spain
on the plan communicated to them, in order to fully understand their disposition and what can be expected of them.
If the first course is adopted, Bouillé's preparations must be
stopped and negotiations continued. If the second is preferred, preparations must go on and all be made ready for
execution, the necessary money must be found; a well-
intentioned and capable person chosen to go at once to
England and sound, skilfully and without compromising
himself, the intentions of that Power. This person should
not receive his instructions till the moment of departure; they
should be to negotiate with that Court for its absolute
neutrality, either by reasonable sacrifices or by forcing it
with the help of the Northern Powers, whose disposition is
not equivocal, but who, in consequence of their great distance, cannot assist the king in a more direct manner.

From the certainty which Their Majesties have of the
intentions of the King of Sweden and his desire to be useful to them, would they feel any impropriety in authorizing
me to communicate to him the plan they may adopt, and
their intention to profit by the good disposition he manifests,
and claim his good offices to restrain England in case that
Power refuses to listen to any proposal for accommodation and
tries to put obstacles to the execution of Their Majesties' project ? This mark of confidence would flatter the King of
Sweden and could only interest him the more in the ultimate
results. As this overture would pass through Baron Taube,
whose attachment to his master and to Their Majesties is

known to me, I would tell him to make no use of it but that which he believes necessary and most advantageous for Their Majesties.

I have the honour to send to the queen a few reflections on the present state of affairs, also the translation of a letter I have just received; it will prove still further to H. M. how earnestly the King of Sweden is interested in the [word omitted] of Their Majesties and the means of being useful to them.

To his father.

Paris, April 10, 1791.

It seems as if the Assembly has taken upon itself the task of ruining this unhappy kingdom, it is succeeding. The revolutionaries have destroyed everything and put nothing in its place. Coin has disappeared, — there are nothing but bank bills at six per cent discount, they wish to substitute others, called *assignats*, which will be forced and bring in four and a half per cent, these are to be hypothecated on the sale of the property of the clergy. But there is no confidence, and this property will barely suffice to pay the debts of the clergy and public worship. Credit is gone, for everybody is ruined; the suppression of feudal rights upset all fortunes and diminished them by more than half; sometimes it destroyed them utterly. Up to that point the state of France resembled that of Sweden; but add to it that the châteaux are pillaged or burned, the owners massacred or fugitive; that there is neither authority nor order, that the Assembly is led by the most perverted and infamous men, who have no interest except in general disorder and misfortune, that the kingdom groans under the despotism of the multitude, which is the most dreadful of all — and you will have a true idea of the state of France. God knows how the country will come out of it; we must hope that the misery of which each individual will soon feel the weight may change opinions, and from that change alone can we look for a change in the state of affairs

The situation of the king, especially that of the queen, is pitiful, her conduct and her courage have brought minds back to her. The army is lost ; the regiments have mutinied ; they no longer obey their leaders, and are taking part in the popular cause.

NOTE. — The second plan referred to in Count Fersen's "Memorial to the King and Queen of France" is the one that Louis XVI. adopted. It is nowhere fully explained in all its details, but in general it was as follows . To escape from Paris to Montmédy and there raise a rallying standard, gathering the loyal of the army and the *émigrés* about him, and issuing a proclamation to France, dealing more especially with the pressing financial situation, the question of bankruptcy, and the redemption of the *assignats*. This was the plan that was frustrated at Varennes. Louis XVI. was not attempting to escape from France at that time. — TR.

CHAPTER IV.

1791   Preparations for the Escape of the King and Royal Family — The King has a settled Plan, not fully revealed — Safe Departure from Paris, driven by Count Fersen — The Arrest at Varennes.

Count Fersen to Baron Taube

PARIS, April 18, 1791

MY DEAR FRIEND, — I hope you have received all mine, I am awaiting your answer with the greatest impatience   I wish my letter of April 1 may have reached you soon.   They are making the design for my carriage, and I hope to send it to you very soon.

[*In cipher.*]   An answer has come from the emperor, still in the same style; he fears England, and will not bind himself to anything until the King of France is at liberty and in a place of safety.   They have written to him to know whether, in that case, they can count upon him, his answer is now expected.

The Marquis de Bouillé has proposed to the King of France to cede some possessions in India, or even all of them, to England, reserving the right of commerce there. The king is repugnant to such a sacrifice, and is now awaiting the advice of Baron de Breteuil upon it; but all this cannot be negotiated until he is safely out of Paris   The King of France seems to wish to make this escape the latter part of May.   To find the money is the difficulty,

The chaplain of our ambassador [M de Staël] is a decided democrat.   For a long time he would not pray in church for the King of France, but for " the King of the French " as decreed by the National Assembly.   Many persons, shocked by the change, induced the ambassador to stop it, but the chaplain, to avoid saying "King of France" now says "Louis XVI.," to the great scandal of part of the congregation.

Entreat the king [of Sweden] to be cautious if he comes to Aix-la-Chapelle, even with the best-intentioned persons, for they will put meanings on the slightest words that escape him, and their indiscretions might be as hurtful at this moment as the savage espionage which will certainly seek to discover the sentiments of the king. He may rest assured that these madmen, who fear him, will surround him with spies; his reputation makes them tremble, for he is much admired here.

From several conversations I have had with the Russian minister I think I see that the empress [Catherine II] dares not trust too much to the king's dispositions relatively to herself and England.

The King and Queen of France will not perform their Easter duties, for they have heard that the *canaille* are to be excited to make a disturbance because they have both determined not to employ the priests who have taken the oath, they have changed their confessor for the same reason

[*In plain writing*]   Yesterday there was a sort of mutiny at the king's service. The grenadiers of the guard refused to go into the king's chapel during mass, because it was said by a priest who did not take the oath. They wanted to prevent any one from entering, and the priest from officiating. M. de Lafayette appeared for the first time to prevent an indecency, he spoke to them and succeeded in pacifying their minds by saying they were there as a matter of military duty and not for worship   Since the evening before, this guard had been worked upon, they had been kept drinking all night and during the morning. . . .

The king and his family leave this morning for Saint-Cloud, they will return on Wednesday or Thursday week.

[*Added to the preceding letter.*]   At half-past eleven the king went to mass, — M. Bailly [mayor] having previously come to warn him that his departure for Saint-Cloud would occasion a disturbance, and that the people seemed inclined to oppose it.   The king replied that liberty having been decreed to every man to go and come as he pleased, it would be very extraordinary if he were the only man who could not go two leagues to get fresh air , and that he was quite determined to go.

He came down with the queen, Madame Élisabeth, the children, and Mme. de Tourzel, and as the carriages had not been able to enter the Cour des Princes, he turned to go and meet them in the Carrousel.   On being told that the crowd was enormous, he stopped in the middle of the Cour des Princes, and the queen proposed to him to get into a carriage which was in the court, although it was only a *berline*   They all six got into it, but when the carriage reached the gate the National Guard refused to open it and let the king pass.   In vain M. de Lafayette [their commander] talked to them, declaring that none but enemies of the constitution would behave in that way; that by thwarting the king's will they gave him the air of being a prisoner and defeated the decrees which he had sanctioned.   They answered only by invectives and assurances that they would not let the king pass out. They used the most insulting terms, calling the king a ⸺ aristocrat, a fat pig, incapable of reigning ; that he ought to be deposed and the Duc d'Orléans put in his place ; that he was only a public functionary to whom they paid 25,000,000, which was a great deal too much, and he would have to do as they chose.

The same talk went on among the people.   M de Lafayette called upon the mayor to proclaim martial law and display the red flag, he refused. . . . Detachments of grenadiers as they arrived swore that the king should not leave Paris, several showed balls, saying that they would put them into their muskets and fire upon the king if he made the slightest motion to go   All the people of the household who approached the carriage were insulted : . . . M. de Gougenot, the steward, having gone to the queen's side to take her orders about the dinner, was dragged away and came near being hanged. The queen leaned forward to tell them to let him be because he was in the king's service, on which they told her they had no orders to receive from her; others said : "There's a pretty b—— who thinks she can give us orders!" . . . M. de Lafayette asked the king if he wished him to force a passage and make the law respected.   The soldiers cried out that he had no power to do it for they had all taken out their bayonets and would never serve against brave citizens.   The king refused to employ force, and said: "I will have no blood shed for me, when I am gone you will be master to employ all means you please to make the laws respected."

Some of the grenadiers who were near the carriage wept; a few advanced and said to the king: "Sire, you are loved, you are adored by your people; but do not go; your life would be in danger; you are ill-advised; you are misled; the people want you to send away the priests, they are afraid of losing you"   The king silenced them, saying it was they who were misled, and that no one ought to doubt his intentions or his love for his people.

At last, after two hours and a quarter of vain attempts, and useless efforts on the part of M de Lafayette, the king ordered the carriage to be turned round   On getting out of it the soldiers pressed in crowds around them.   Some said "We will defend you."   The queen answered, looking proudly at them : " Yes, we count on that , but you must allow that at present we are not free."   As they pressed closely and entered the vestibule in crowds, the queen took the dauphin in her arms, Madame Élisabeth took Madame Royale, and they hurried them in as best they could   The king then slackened his pace and when the queen and Madame Élisabeth had reached the queen's room and entered, he turned round and said, " Halt, grenadiers ! "   They all stopped as if their legs were cut off . . .

In the Cour des Princes there was no one but the National Guard ; the people were in the Carrousel and the gates between were closed   Nothing was said there against the queen, but horrors against the king.   They both spoke with much firmness and coolness , their bearing was perfect.   All was quiet within the palace.   At eight o'clock the king was notified that the National Guard had decided to enter all the rooms that night, even those of the king, under pretext of seeing that no priests were there   This resolution was, however, changed at ten o'clock.   In the Carrousel a man read aloud, by the light of a torch, a paper full of horrors about the king, exhorting the people to force the palace, fling everything out of the windows, and above all not to miss the opportunity they had lost at Versailles on the 5th of October.

PARIS, April 22, 1791

It is thought to be the faction of the Duc d'Orléans that caused what happened on the 18th, for the leaders of the Jacobins are, with good reason, much disturbed by it   This affair gives proof of the imprisonment of the King of France, and consequently nullifies all the sanctions, and even the Constitution. After this event, which I do not regard as unfortunate for the King of France, his conduct ought to change ; he ought not to oppose anything , on the contrary,

he should yield in every way, and do all they ask of him, in
order to show that he is not free, and also to put them to
sleep about his real projects, to which he ought to hold more
firmly, and to the execution of which he ought to sacrifice
everything, however painful it may be to do so.

Their Majesties are running great dangers at this moment, the things that are said about them are dreadful,
they are no longer respected, and their life is threatened
openly and with impunity   But to make sure of their personal safety and tranquillity the *means must be good* . . .

Last night M. de Lafayette sent in his resignation, the
majority of the National Guard and all the sections of Paris,
except three, desire him to remain, and have asked him to
do so.   It is not known what course he will take.   I think
he will remain if he can.

[Louis XVI. having determined to leave Paris, Count
Fersen took charge of all the arrangements and carried them
out successfully, although in the end his efforts were fatally
defeated at Varennes.   The following letters relate to the
affair.]

Count Fersen to the Marquis de Bouillé

PARIS, April 28, 1791.

The king [of France] will be ready to start the last two
weeks in May, and he is very determined not to put it off
any longer; but he must have until the fifteenth to receive
the answer from Spain.   He feels how urgent the circumstances are, and all that happened on Monday of last week
makes him more resolved than ever.   He recommends you to
make on your side no more open preparations than are absolutely necessary.   He fears, and with reason, that by drawing
attention in your direction it may increase the watchfulness
here and that his departure will be more difficult, and suc-

cess less certain. They are negotiating for the money, but nothing is yet settled as to that. M. de Mercy intimates in all his letters that as soon as the king is safely out of Paris the Powers will declare themselves and favourably for him.

From the Baron de Breteuil to Count Fersen.

April 30, 1791 [1]

I have received your letter of the 22d of this month. I needed the approaching execution of the plan to calm my distress about that cruel day of the 18th

I will be as quickly as I can at the place indicated ; but I warn you that the order to leave here should not be sent to me at the time the king leaves Paris, and not until he has joined M. de Bouillé; because, having, before I leave, to take certain steps towards the Cantons, in order to put them in motion, it would be equally imprudent, dangerous, and useless to let those steps become public before His Majesty's project is entirely carried out. I hope that this reflection will seem as right as it is necessary.

As it is impossible, no matter what diligence I may make, that the king will not be some days before me at the place where he is to go, I request that (excepting military operations, as to which it is important not to embarrass or delay the views of the general [de Bouillé]), His Majesty will be so good as to take no resolutions as to persons or things before I have received his orders   Nothing is more essential

---

[1] In the French, no date of place is given to the letters of the three men who, with Fersen, made arrangements for the king's escape. From the context it appears that the Marquis de Bouillé was in a position of command at Metz; M. de Mercy was Austrian minister at Brussels ; and the Baron de Breteuil was in Switzerland. Baron Taube was in Stockholm , he was first gentleman of the Bedchamber to the King of Sweden, and had his entire confidence — Tr

for the service of the king than to avoid all precipitate steps, which one might be compelled to retrace.   I venture to add that it is not less essential that His Majesty should make known, even in the slightest details, the extent of the confidence with which he honours me for the conduct of affairs.

The king may regard this request of my purest zeal in the light of ambition; I should be from that moment incapable of becoming of any utility in the difficult position in which the kingdom is now placed   You will judge of this truth as I do.

Count Fersen to Baron Taube.

May 2, 1791.

MY DEAR FRIEND, — I received three days ago your letter of April 8. As for the Prince de Condé, I have already given to the king [of Sweden] very precise information in my letter of April 1, sent by a Russian courier, also in one of the 11th of that month.   In those two letters you will see [*the rest in cipher*] that the Prince de Condé is intrusted with nothing and is ignorant of all the projects of the King of France.   His ambitious nature, his indiscretion towards the men of his own party, would compromise the secrecy so essential to this great object.   The conduct of the princes, who have always chosen to act without consulting the king, and even in spite of him, without considering the dangers to which they expose him, but above all, the dependence in which the king would be if he charged them with so great an undertaking, — all these things have led His Majesty to confide nothing to them and not to make use of any of their resources until he is at liberty.

Nevertheless, the Prince de Condé continues to work, but it is on his own account; and in spite of the weakness or nullity of his means and the impossibility of success, he seems decided to attempt something. The king takes all possible means to delay this enterprise until he is at liberty, without, however, confiding anything to him, for if he did the secret would be betrayed and all would fail.   The king may be forced by the Assembly to issue a proclamation against the Prince de Condé, this will be another proof of his want of freedom, and His Majesty may give it, as he has decided to yield everything in order to lull to sleep the factions as to his real project, and inspire them with the confidence so necessary to enable him to leave Paris.   He still seems determined to attempt it during the last fifteen days of this month.   There is much ferment in Paris, but it is chiefly against M. de Lafayette, who has resumed command of the National Guard, which is very lucky, otherwise we might have had some one more capable and worse.

The Danish minister tells me there is much political excitement in Sweden, which is waiting for the departure of the king [Gustavus III.] to break out . . . When H M. arrives at the place where he intends to stop, I shall at once go to him; but if he gets there before the King of France leaves Paris, it will be impossible, for it is quite impossible that the escape can be made without me; I am the sole person here in his confidence, and he has no one on whose discretion he can rely to take my place

Count Fersen to the Marquis de Bouillé.

PARIS, May 3, 1791

M. de Giliers has just proposed a strong plan, namely, to carry off the king by force of arms either from here or from Fontainebleau. He says that M. Heimann, who is here, is in concert with him, and that the general, who is very well disposed, will pledge himself. They would send six hundred thousand francs to win over the troops and induce them, as well as the departments, to demand the king's liberty and

L cf C

to march at once to obtain it. He says there are sixty squadrons and eight thousand men sure. M. de Klingin will also be with them, and M. de Gihers wishes to go and speak with you. He says that the Jacobius have given Heimann three millions with which to go to Prussia and bribe the favourites, and that Heimann wants to take that money and use it for the king. As he has always been the creature of the Duc d'Orléans it is feared that the whole thing is a trap into which M. de Gihers has fallen. Here is the answer signed by the king and queen   They have also sent word verbally that if M. Heimann wishes to give a proof of attachment he will transfer the three millions to the king.

Copy of letter from the King and Queen of France annexed to the foregoing.

The king, being decided at the present time to follow the impulsions of the Assembly and to work in concert with that body, for the restoration of order and tranquillity, cannot and will not admit of any measure which is contrary to its projects; that which is now proposed to him, while giving him fresh proof of M. de Gihers' attachment, nevertheless seems to him more than doubtful as to success, and might only expose uselessly the good and faithful servants who undertook it. From the prudence and disposition that M. de Bouillé has manifested down to the present time, the king has reason to think that he would not enter into any project of that nature.

Baron Taube to Count Fersen.

STOCKHOLM, May 6, 1791

MY DEAR FRIEND, — The king orders me to tell you that he charges you to say to the King and Queen of France that he will employ all possible means to try to succour them. His opinion is, if Their Majesties can escape from Paris, that they should at once convoke all the parliaments of France and have the National Assembly declared illegal, the usurper of the rights of the throne and royalty, the individual members declared rebels and traitors and the whole country ordered to attack them, all the great officers, and the chiefs of the army who were obliged to escape from the country, also all the priests, should be recalled; everything should be re-established as it was before the revolution, the clergy should be replaced in their old régime and worship, the three orders of the State, which have been abolished by usurpation of the Assembly, should be re-established, but declared at the same time to be without difference as to the payment of taxes; the Duc d'Orléans should be arrested, and tried and condemned by one of the parliaments, and no mercy shown to him; above all, the army should be brought back to discipline and the most absolute subordination, and rigorous examples should not be spared to compel this; and, finally, no compromises should be made with no matter who, no mixed government permitted, royalty should be replaced in its omnipotence, the king ought to leave Paris forever, and cause that haunt of assassins to perish through the total oblivion of its existence for as long as there is a Paris in France there will never be kings; history proves this.

The king also thinks that it is very prudent not to confide any secret negotiations to the Prince de Condé, but he also thinks it would not be prudent to show him distrust, and that it would be best to make use of his military talents without admitting him into the administration

The king is convinced that none of the sovereigns will act with hostility against the King of France as soon as he is out of his prison, — not even England, which at the present time sustains the animosity and anarchy by money and underhand proceedings.

I have not tried to prevent the king's journey, for it would be in vain, besides, his health needs to be restored after the extreme fatigue of body and mind which he has borne during the last three years of war. I took another way to increase his hatred to the National Assembly, which he already detests from the bottom of his heart. I told him that you had begged me to warn him that he would be surrounded by spies of the Assembly, who would explain to suit themselves every word he said; that he ought to distrust even those whom he thinks well-intentioned, but who, by their indiscretions do almost as much harm as the madmen who surround the King of France. He charged me to thank you for that advice, which he would confide to no one, and to say that his talk in future would be more republican than monarchical; and he requests you to warn Their Majesties of this.

The king disapproves of the emperor's conduct.

Count Fersen to the Marquis de Bouillé.

PARIS, May 6, 1791.

Here is a copy of the letter of M. de Mercy. It is possible to place troops along the frontier of Luxembourg, but any movement beyond the frontier would be impossible at the present moment. The most essential thing is the safety of the flight. The escort should be scattered along the route; one shudders in thinking of the horrors that might happen if they were betrayed and arrested.

The route agreed upon is by Meaux, Chalons, Reims, Île-Réthel, Pauvre. Write me if you wish it changed, and what the precautions are that you mean to take. There are

none of the body-guard at Chalons ; the town requested that
it might have no more of them

Count Fersen to Baron Taube

PARIS, May 9, 1791.

MY DEAR FRIEND — I received two days ago yours of the
19th.   The cipher of yours of the 8th was so incorrect, and you
had forgotten so many things in it that I had the greatest
difficulty in the world to make out its meaning   Towards
the end the cipher was plainer; I managed to guess that the
king [of Sweden] had ordered M. de Staël to say to Montmorin that H. M would not receive the new envoy, but
preferred to keep the present secretary of the embassy.   The
squabbles which increase daily between our neighbour [the
Empress of Russia] and the other Powers are very injurious
to [*changes to cipher*] the projects of the King of France, but
his position is such (and it is becoming day by day more
dreadful) that it is impossible he can bear it much longer;
he has therefore decided to risk all for all rather than live
in the daily humiliation into which a mass of factious men
have cast him   It is towards the end of this month that
he means to act.

[*In plain writing.*]   Nothing is changed here.   The Jacobins still have the upper hand.   M de Clermont-Tonnerre
just missed being hanged the other day, on leaving the Assembly, for having spoken against the union of the *comitat* of
Avignon with France, and without the assistance of the
National Guard he indubitably would have been.

The domestic household of the king is about to be sent
away in a body, and a new one is to be formed; it is not
known yet how it will be composed, but they think that all
the old appointments will be changed and the places filled
indiscriminately by nobles and *roturiers.*   Since April 18

the emigration is enormous; every one is departing for foreign countries, Paris is almost deserted. The matter of religion is one which drives a great many persons to other countries where they can practise it freely. Besides, as everything goes for fashion in this country, it is good style to go away. People are awaiting with much impatience to know what course the pope will take relatively to his nuncio. Since the letter of M. de Montmorin and the insults offered to the effigy of His Holiness, which was publicly burned together with his brief at the Palais-Royal, it is said that they mean to do the same with all the sovereigns, beginning with the emperor and the King of Spain. Our master will surely not be forgotten, especially as they are now saying, and the rumour is spreading among the people, that he is coming to Aix-la-Chapelle to put himself at the head of the counter-revolution; even sensible people believe this!

The Marquis de Bouillé to Count Fersen, in cipher.

May 9, 1791

Send me M. Goguelat; he must be with you now. He will be very useful to me in making the necessary reconnoitring of the route in the Reims division, hereafter named; he could bring the money I asked of you, which is needed. From M. de Mercy's letter it is to be feared that the Austrians will not join the king, but we must absolutely obtain that the king may have seven or eight thousand men in his pay, even if they are not auxiliaries. This reinforcement is necessary to restrain the troops we assemble, for though they are nearly all German, they are liable to be bribed; whereas with this reinforcement they will think all is possible, and their fidelity will be secured. Concern yourself above all in obtaining the money.

All reflection given, the shortest, safest, and simplest route is by Meaux, Montmirail (whence they must not forget to take the road by Ferté-sous-Jouarre), Chalons, Sainte-Mene-hould, Varennes, Dun, and Stenay. From Sainte-Menehould to Stenay there will be good detachments placed for escort; the distance is twelve leagues. Could we not admit M. d'Agoult into the secret a few days before the start, and get him to go to Chalons, with some thirty of the most resolute of the body-guard on pretext of looking after the horses which are there, and removing them as the town requests? Those thirty guards could be on horseback at the gate of the town at a fixed hour and escort as far as Sainte-Menehould Tell M. Goguelat to take that route in coming here, and to make a report to the general

Write me what they think. You see how essential it is to be notified in time of the day fixed; and that it be irrevo-cable It must not be later than June 1. Here is the route in detail. Paris to Meaux, 25 miles; Meaux to Ferté-la-Jouarre, 12 miles; Ferté to Montmirail, 21 miles; Montmi-rail, to Chalons-sur-Marne, 35 miles; Chalons to Sainte-Menehould, 25 miles, Sainte-Menehould to Varennes, 12 miles; Varennes to Dun, 12, Dun to Stenay, 7; Stenay to M . . . , 5 miles. You can see this route on the map of the departments. It makes in all about one hundred and fifty-three miles. By leaving at night and travelling through the next night they would arrive on the second day.

Count Fersen to the Baron de Breteuil.

PARIS, May 16, 1791.

I have received your two despatches of April 30 and May 3. The king approves of all you say touching your de-parture. His Majesty feels as you do the necessity of your making some overtures to the cantons, but he thinks you ought first to prepare the way with the *advoyers* [supreme judges in certain cantons of Switzerland] in those cantons of which you are sure, in order that you may get to him as soon as possible, you might also charge the Bishop of Pamiers (or any other you may indicate) to continue the negotiation, which is for a loan of several millions and twenty or thirty thousand men to be employed at will. The cantons would have to pay them, at least during the first three months.

As it is important to take no hasty resolution from which we might have to retreat, and as circumstances may arise in which decision must be made before your arrival, the king wishes you to put in writing your general ideas and views, which might guide him in taking a steady and uniform course This paper should be sent by a safe man to Luxembourg early enough to reach the king on his arrival at Montmédy. This man is not to be in the secret, and must be told to remain in Luxembourg till further orders. You must send me his name.

We have four millions for the first wants. It would be, I think, good policy to take a decided course at once about the bankruptcy, whether to be made, or not made, and about the *assignats*. The property of the clergy, when returned to them, could pay off the latter. This would make fewer enemies, and would interest all who hold them and also all bankers in the success of the king's enterprise. What do you think of this ?

The king is very uneasy about the junction of the Comte d'Artois with the Prince de Condé. He charges you to write to him and try to prevent it; without, however, telling him anything in detail of the king's projects, but reminding him that H. M. has always promised to do nothing without him, but that the moment and the means can be decided by no one but the king

You will add from him that H. M. desires that the Comte d'Artois shall not join the Prince de Condé, of whose proceedings he disapproves, inasmuch as they only render the king's projects more difficult of execution; but, on the contrary, he wishes him to keep near to the King of Sardinia, in order to maintain that prince in the good inclinations he has always shown, and to guide the Southern provinces, so that all may work together, in concert with the king, for the approaching execution of the ideas he has adopted. You will make the Comte d'Artois feel the necessity of the greatest secrecy, as much towards Worms as towards the provinces and his whole party. All would be lost if the slightest project were suspected And you will add that the king, having no means of corresponding directly with him, makes his communications pass through you. You will send him your courier wherever you may be, whether *en route* or at Worms

The Marquis de Bouillé to Count Fersen, in cipher.

No date.

The movement of Austrian troops on the frontier is necessary It is absolutely necessary that a body of troops shall be at Luxembourg, and that squadrons be stationed at Arlon and Verton, and that other points be guarded; without that, I may not be able to leave Metz and take out the four German and Swiss regiments which at the present moment compose the whole garrison, and I could not bring to the frontier the cavalry who are now scattered over the flat country. Thus, if it is desired that the king should maintain himself with his own troops in his kingdom, he absolutely must wait until the Austrians arrive and I can make the movement on the frontier with that pretext. But if, on the contrary, the king merely wishes to leave the kingdom I can escort him at once wherever he pleases. But I believe, if there are no imperative reasons at this moment, such as the safety of the king, that it would be better to do as I propose and wait till the 15th or 20th, at which date the Austrians will surely have arrived at the line indicated. If the emperor sincerely desires to help the king, he will lend himself to this step and hasten the march of the troops to Luxembourg, inasmuch as the success of the plan depends upon it so entirely, and the delay increases the difficulties and the risks daily.

The route is fully agreed upon, except that they will have to go as far as Clermont. We are now reconnoitring the road from Clermont to Dun; they can take the cross-road easily, horses are all ready for that purpose, so that there may be no delay at the post-house. We shall manage to send a detachment of hussars who will meet the king at Chalons and escort him to Sainte-Menehould or Clermont, where there will be other detachments. You must see to the safety of the route as far as Chalons.

Count Fersen to the Marquis de Bouillé, in cipher.

May 26, 1791.

I have written to Goguelat to go to you, and do all that you order. He is a safe man; he needs only to be moderated The king approves the route; it will be fixed such as you have sent it. They are now occupied about the body-guard. I shall send you by diligence to-morrow or Tuesday, in a roll of white taffeta addressed to M. de Contades, one million in *assignats;* we have four millions, of which one is out of the country. We have received a very good letter from the emperor, and they have written to him to reinforce the line towards Luxembourg with eight or ten thousand men, disposable at will.

The king intends to start during the first eight days of June, for at that time he receives two millions from the civil list. If you want more money they will send it. Between the lines of this writing are written in white ink the numbers of the notes that I send you   Make the white ink show out before you decipher the last two lines of this letter;[1] the word for the two is *battre*. There are no precautions to take between here and Chalons; the best precaution of all is to take none. All will depend on celerity and secrecy, and if you are not perfectly sure of your detachments it would be better to place none; or at least, place none this side of Varennes, so as not to excite attention in the country. The king will then pass simply

Count Fersen to the Marquis de Bouillé, in cipher.

May 29, 1791.

The departure is fixed for the 12th of next month. All was ready, and they could have gone on the 6th or 7th, but they do not receive the two millions till the 7th or 8th , besides which, the dauphin has a maid who is very democratic, and she does not leave till the 11th. They will take the last route agreed upon. I shall not accompany the king, he does not wish it   I shall go through Quesnoy and come out by Bavay to Mons   I will notify M. de Vauban, who is at Quesnoy, and I shall write you more positively on Wednesday. Let me know at once of the arrival of my letters; this is very important now, and I will do the same by you.

[1] Throughout the correspondence from this point, especially in the letters of Queen Marie-Antoinette, "white ink" is used and mentioned , it was made visible by heating the paper or by washing it with some chemical preparation   In many places gaps in the letters occur, where the words were illegible at the time, or later when Count Fersen himself copied them. — TR.

Count Fersen to Baron Taube, in cipher.

May 31, 1791

MY DEAR FRIEND, — The king and queen charge me to tell
the king [of Sweden] that they cannot sufficiently express
their feelings for the marks of interest and friendship which
he never ceases to give them, they will always feel it a
pleasure and a duty to be grateful for them. Their departure was fixed for June 12th, but M. de Bouillé wanted it
delayed till the 15th or 20th, to give the Austrians time
to reinforce the cordon of troops about Luxembourg and
thus give him a pretext for assembling those of the
king.

The Comte d'Artois and the Prince de Condé seem determined to act in spite of the weakness, or nothingness, of
their means. Such a course will be of the greatest danger,
and as the Comte d'Artois will doubtless see the king [of
Sweden, then at Aix-la-Chapelle], Their Majesties desire
that His Majesty should dissuade him, by proving to him
that he neither can nor should act against the will of the
king, that he can only expose Their Majesties and himself
uselessly. The king [of Sweden] may add that he has reason to think the king desires to act, but it is necessary, for
the success of his projects, to leave the sole direction of them
to him, and to second him in the manner that he desires, — he
being more in the way of judging of means and the proper
moment of execution than others.

But H. M. must not tell Comte d'Artois the king's plan, because the Prince de Condé, who rules him, might induce him
to anticipate the king's action so as to gain the whole credit of
it for himself. Persuade the king not to give ear to all the
exaggerations of the aristocrats at Aix-la-Chapelle; above all,
not to let them know anything of the king's projects, for all

would be ruined. I will write you again two days before I start.

I send this to Aix-la-Chapelle, believing you to be there already. Take care of yourself for the sake of all Frenchmen. Count Esterhazy knows nothing.

Count Fersen to Baron Taube, in cipher.

PARIS, June 2, 1791.

The king has just received news from the Comte d'Artois, who tells him of the result of his interview with the emperor at Mantua The disposition the emperor showed in that interview does not accord in any way with what he has previously written. He manifested the most decided will to serve the king with all his forces; he said he was fully assured of Spain and Prussia, and thinks that there is nothing to fear from England , but as to that he agreed that more assurances were needed. As for the King of Sardinia, the Swiss, and the German princes, there was no doubt whatever as to their intentions, and he hoped that peace with the Turks would soon be made, which would enable him to employ all his forces in this direction; he also said that the Powers nearest to France would furnish troops amounting in all to 100,000 to 150,000 men.

In consequence of this, Comte d'Artois urges the king to wait in Paris until, towards July 15, all these troops can be set in motion and enter France at the same moment, and then, by a manifesto which would make the city of Paris responsible for all events, the life of Their Majesties would be safe, and they could then deliver them.

The Comte d'Artois assures the king that the Prince de Condé knows nothing of this plan , he asks to be alone charged with the execution of it; and that the king will disavow the Baron de Breteuil and all that he has done. It is

M. de Calonne who is leading the Comte d'Artois at the present moment. The king, feeling that the passive rôle they want to make him play in this affair is contrary to his inclination, and would put him later into too much dependence on those who would have the credit of having done all, and being decided not to abandon the men who serve him, has resolved to follow his first project, and to profit, as soon as he gains his liberty, by the good intentions of the Powers, whose aid he will himself invoke. Moreover, as this news is brought only verbally by a man sent by Comte d'Artois, and the king has several times received missions which have been contradicted by subsequent letters, he has just sent a courier to the emperor to make sure that this news is true, asking him as a first proof of his good-will to give him 8000 or 10,000 troops from the Low Countries on the frontier, and to wait till the king is out of Paris to make the rest of his good intentions effective.

The king is still fixed to his plan and expects to start from here on the 15th, 16th, or 17th   If Comte d'Artois speaks to the king [of Sweden] of his plan, Their Majesties desire he should answer that he cannot enter upon any negotiation of that nature except at the request of the King of France himself   All this has been arranged by M. de Calonne that he may have the merit of it, enter the ministry, and exclude the Baron de Breteuil. The King of France is extremely surprised at the certainty the emperor appears to have as to the good intentions of Prussia and England, which does not agree at all with what M de Mercy and even Prince Kaunitz have always written to Baron de Breteuil. Write me if you have any notions thereon.

Count Fersen to the Marquis de Bouillé, in cipher.

No date.

Try, if possible, not to send the Duc de Choiseul here [he had already started]. No one, certainly, is more attached; but he is a young man, a blunderer, and I fear some indiscretion, he has too many friends, relatives, and possibly a mistress to save Send back Goguelat instead, on any pretext, to M. Duportail. I have had much difficulty in finding your horses, I hope to send them to-morrow.

Make sure of your detachments, and do not send them beyond Varennes.

Count Fersen to the Marquis de Bouillé, in cipher.

June 13, 1791.

The departure is fixed, without delay, for the 20th at midnight. A dangerous maid of the dauphin, whom they could not get rid of, and who does not leave till Monday morning has forced them to put off this departure till Monday night; but you may count upon it. No relays will be sent to Chaintrix; it is simpler to go on with post-horses. The king will wear a red coat, and will make himself known according to what the Duc de Choiseul may tell him as to the good intentions of the troops. To avoid all suspicion, and all excitement at Chalons the detachment for the bridge of Sommevesle should not get there till Tuesday at midday, the king can be there by half-past two.

I will write you again by the courier of to-morrow. The departure is fixed, unchangeably, for midnight on the 20th, it is now too late to change it. Trust to me. I am much pleased with the Duc de Choiseul. If all should fail he will be at Metz Friday morning; if he is not there, you can start Sunday morning, and rely that they will start from

8

here Monday at midnight. I will take measures to have you warned if the king should be stopped. There has been no way of getting rid of the maid without compromising secrecy.

Count Fersen to the Marquis de Bouillé, in cipher

June 14, 1791.

Nothing is changed ; they start without fail Monday, 20th at midnight ; they will be at the bridge of Sommevesle, Tuesday, half-past two, at latest ; you may count upon this. Have you reflected that *Monsieur* [the Comte de Provence] will arrive at the same time ? Can you lodge him at Montmédy, or else send him to Longwy ? If you could get me a room at Montmédy you would do me a kindness. We have no answer as yet from the Comte de Mercy ; they have written him again to start the troops.

Be certain that the start will be Monday, 20th, at midnight. *Monsieur* will take another route than the king. The gray horse is for you ; the little stallion for your brother, unless he prefers the bay ; the two others are for Goguelat.

Count Fersen to his father, Field-Marshal Fersen

Mons, June 22, 1791. 6 A M

I have this instant arrived, my dear father. The king and the whole family left Paris safely on the 20th at midnight. I drove them to the first relay. God grant that the rest of their journey may have been as fortunate. I am expecting *Monsieur* here at every moment. I shall continue my way along the frontier to join the king at Montmédy, if he is so fortunate as to get there.

AXEL FERSEN.

Count Fersen to Baron Taube.

MONS, June 22, 1791. 11 A M.

MY DEAR FRIEND, — The king, queen, Madame Élisabeth, the dauphin, and Madame Royale left Paris Monday at midnight. I accompanied them to Bondy without any accident. I am this moment starting to meet them.

AXEL FERSEN.

Count Fersen to the King of Sweden.

June 23, 1791. Midnight.

SIRE, — All has failed. The king was stopped at sixteen leagues from the frontier and taken back to Paris. I am going to see M. de Mercy and take him a letter from the king, asking the emperor to take steps for him. From Brussels I shall go to see Y. M.

I am, with the most profound respect, Your Majesty's very humble and very obedient servant,

AXEL FERSEN.

Count Fersen to his father.

ARLON, June 23, 1791.

All is lost, my dear father, and I am in despair. The king was stopped at Varennes, sixteen leagues from the frontier. Judge of my grief and pity me. It was M. de Bouillé, who is here, who told me of it. I am just starting for Brussels to take to M. de Mercy the letter and orders with which the king intrusted me. I have only time to assure you of my respect and love.

AXEL FERSEN.

From the Diary of Count Fersen.

June 11, 1791. *Saturday.* Lafayette wanted to double the sentinels and look over all the carriages of the palace.

Montmorin said, "That will be a bolt the more. I will not take upon myself to speak of it."

12th, *Sunday*. Journey put off till 20th, cause a chambermaid. Lafayette s case sent to court-martial.

13th, *Monday*. Oath for officers. They say the guard is to be doubled and all the king's carriages watched.

16th, *Thursday*. Went to the queen at 9.30 ; carried all the luggage myself; nothing suspected; nor in the city. Oath for officers , that will make many depart.

17th, *Friday*. Went to Bondy and Bourget. Dined at home.

18th, *Saturday*. With the queen from half-past two till six. Good letter from the emperor; they say the English fleet has sailed.

19th, *Sunday*. With the king. Took charge of eight hundred francs and the Seals. Remained at the palace till midnight

20th, *Monday*. [The Diary for 20th is written in pencil, on detached pieces of paper, of which half are missing.] . . . remark, and asked what he wished to do. Both answered me that there was no hesitation; they must go on. We agreed as to hours, etc, etc.; if they were stopped I must go to Brussels and act for them, etc., etc. On leaving me the king said · "Monsieur de Fersen, whatever may happen to me, I shall never forget what you have done for me." The queen wept much. At six o'clock I left her , she went with the children to the gardens. No unusual precautions. I went home to finish my affairs. At seven to Sullivan's to see if the carriage had come. Went home. At eight wrote to the queen to change the rendezvous of the maids and instruct them carefully to let me know the exact hour by the body-guard. Carried the letter; no excitement. At eight and three quarters the guards joined me and gave me the letter for Mercy.   Instructed them, went home; sent on my own carriage; gave them my coachman and horses to start with.   Went to fetch the carriage.   Thought I had dropped the letter for Mercy.   At ten and a quarter in the Cour des Princes   At eleven and a quarter the children came out, brought without difficulty, Lafayette passed twice; at eleven and three quarters Madame Élisabeth, then the king, then the queen.   At midnight started, joined the carriage at the Barrière Saint-Martin   At half-past one reached Bondy; there they took the post-road, I the cross-roads to Bourget.

21st.   Fine.   All went well; delay on the cross-road.   The commandant of militia asked my name; I was alarmed, crossed the Quesnoy and came out by Saint-Vast.

22d.   Fine   Very cold last night   Reached Mons at six. Sullivan, Balbi, *Monsieur*, many Frenchmen very glad.   A monk in the street asked me if the king was saved.   Left at eleven, plain as far as Namur, then mountains.   Everybody glad the king had escaped.

23d.   Fine weather, cold.   Reached Arlon eleven at night. Found Bouillé, learned the king was taken; the details not well known.   The detachments did not do their duty, the king lacked firmness and head.   Rested there.

24th. Started half-past four in the morning; fine.   Everybody grieved that the king was taken.   The French wanted to burn two villages near Longwy.   Felt awful sadness.   The whole country about Luxembourg in despair that the king was taken.   What a change ! . .   Reached Namur at midnight. Found *Monsieur* there.

25th.   Fine and warm.   Started in the morning; reached Brussels two hours after midday.   Many Frenchmen lodged at the Hôtel de Bellevue.   Went to Comte de Mercy's house, did not find him; left the king's letter for him.   Many persons came to question me.   Talked with Mercy in the evening.

Resolved to make an attempt to write.   He sees black; says, "Say nothing to the princes, *Monsieur* ought to take charge of all   All must be done over again"   No order given here, notwithstanding the two letters of the emperor to the queen, he is a thorough Italian, that Leopold.

26th. Fine and warm   At one o'clock went to the arch-duchess [Maria Christina, sister of Marie-Antoinette, Regent of the Low Countries]; very kind to me and much touched. Mercy spoke to *Monsieur*; he is beneath the work he ought to do.

27th. Fine and warm   Paid my court to the Comte d'Artois; nothing said.   Spoke to *Monsieur*; he is very reserved and embarrassed.   All that gives me a bad opinion of the state of things.   People talk to me of the departure from Paris; they know it was my doing, and they consider me much at Court.

CHAPTER V.

1791. Vain efforts to induce the European Powers to take steps in behalf of the King and Queen of France — Gallant Proposal of Gustavus III., King of Sweden.

[In July the King of Sweden sent Count Fersen to Vienna to negotiate with the emperor certain measures to facilitate a descent on Normandy which Gustavus III desired to undertake with Swedish and Russian troops, simultaneously with the efforts of the other Powers, for the purpose of res- cuing the royal family of France, and restoring the monarchy According to the king's instructions Count Fersen was to request the emperor: (1) that the King of Sweden be per- mitted to disembark his troops in the port of Ostend; (2) that facilities be given to obtain supplies and recruits; (3) that an artillery siege train be lent to him   If Count Fersen found the emperor favourably inclined he was to try to make him recognize the King of Sweden as the leader of the league, and the one who was called upon to put the said project (of the descent on Normandy) into execution personally.

Count Fersen reached Vienna August 2, 1771. The nego- tiation advanced very slowly, owing to the indecision of the Emperor Leopold, the ill-will of his ministers who were little inclined to lend any active succour to the King of France, and the intrigues of the princes, the Comte d'Artois and the Prince de Condé; the former of whom went to Vienna with M de Calonne to work in their own interests, and not in those of the King of France   Count Fersen, obliged to ac- company the imperial Court to Prague, where it went for the

coronation of the emperor, returned to Brussels in October
without having succeeded in his mission.]

Diary. June 28th. Fine and warm. News from Paris
of the king's return there. Barnave and Pétion in their carriage — what a horror! No applause. Letter from Bouillé, —
bad, Crawford offers to go to England. The archduchess
proposed to me to go to Vienna; accepted. The National
Assembly usurps the executive power. The king in the condition of a prisoner. Talked with Comte d'Artois, much won
over, but light-headed and too hasty; talked to me of wrongs
done him in relation to the Baron de Breteuil, etc.; said he
was sure of England and Prussia; complained of Mercy because he will not march at once and compromise himself.
Boasted of Calonne, who came in just as I was leaving

30th. Reached Aix-la-Chapelle at 3.30. Saw the king
[Gustavus III], very well inclined Wished me to go to
England. Proposed Crawford for that, and myself for Vienna.
Accepted. Warm feelings of all the Frenchmen to me; I
was touched by them.

July 4. Brussels. Went to Mercy at five P. M. Letter
from the queen. The emperor did send orders to march twelve
thousand men to protect the king's escape. Very good
memorial of Kaunitz to the emperor on the affairs of France.
Dined with Sullivan. Conversation with Mme. de Lamballe;
gossip and nonsense.

13th. The king and queen [of France] are not lost sight
of a moment: all doors are kept open; guards in the room
adjoining the bedchamber. The doors are only closed for one
moment while they put on their chemises, as soon as they
are in bed they are looked at, and several times during the
night. Never alone. Cannot speak to each other unless in
whispers. No one allowed to enter the palace except by

tickets from Lafayette or the mayor. Grieved by the letter; still, it may be well.

17th. Started at midday; reached Aix-la-chapelle 18th at nine A. M , and Spa 19th at nine A M. Alexandre Lameth, Barnave, Lafayette, Duport, Merreville have coalesced and separated from the Jacobins, they have made overtures to Mercy through Père Laborde to get him to induce the king [of France] to come to an understanding with them; Mercy told them strong truths.

Found Crawford at home. Agreed together about what he should say in England; we must know if that Power regards the continuation of anarchy in France as more advantageous than order, representations should be made of the danger that will come to England itself through the disaffected.

Orders positive and urgent from the emperor to succour the king. Writes very well of me; says Kaunitz has an abstracted air in affairs, but is not so really. Agrees that we must absolutely exclude the princes, and that the whole affair must be negotiated between the foreign Powers, because of the intrigues among the persons who surround the princes; says a congress should be formed to settle all. They talk openly at Coblentz of two parties · that of the queen, and that of d'Artois.

21st. Presented Crawford to the king. Agreed upon everything Dined with the king. Wrote the whole evening for him — a note in reply to questions. Talked with him. Bouillé enters the Swedish service; he talks, like all Frenchmen, with much levity.

22d. Sent Crawford off to England this morning. He hopes much. Gave him a letter for the king [of England] and one for Pitt, and a note from myself for the archduchess. Details from Paris from my man · dreadful.

24th. I was despatched Letter for the emperor, for

Kaunitz, instructions, copy of letters to Berlin; etc., etc.; started at 2 o'clock.

25th. Reached Coblentz at 4.30. At 7 went to the princes. They breakfast at midday and dine at 7. *Monsieur* better than d'Artois. Read the papers of the king to him.

Comte d'Artois wants no negotiation, only force without regard to dangers. Dissatisfied with the papers; wants them suppressed, full powers not necessary. Showed him Breteuil's letter announcing 20,000 Spaniards, and 6 millions in Holland for the king at liberty. D'Artois said he knew all that. *Monsieur* showed signs of feeling, d'Artois talks always, and never listens, — being sure of everything, wants only force, no negotiations. *Monsieur* would do better alone, but is entirely subjugated by the other. Calonne is coming from Aix-la-Chapelle; they asked me to wait for him. . . . Condé here, and a number of others. The princes want to dispose of all foreign forces, divide them, and appoint the general officers They have sent for Broglie and Castries; the former will come; doubtful if the other does, on account of Calonne.

26th. Wrote all the morning to Mercy, Taube, Crawford At 4.30 to the princes to talk. Vaudreuil told them that Lafayette wished that the king and queen should be killed. *Monsieur* said. "I have no ambition for his esteem, but he must despise me very much to have such an idea." D'Artois proposed to stir up Paris with money. I opposed the idea from the danger of defection and a single bad agent. Proposed also, at the moment of the manifesto, safety and forgetfulness of the past to Lafayette, with permission to leave by any port in safety Replied: that alone he was nothing; the same thing must be offered to his companions, whoever they were; and besides, the means were not safe. They agreed. . . . I dined there; much company; the Elector of Trèves, with his sister, Princess Cunégonde; very good to the French. The elector defrays the expenses of the princes for their table, lodging, and horses; he gives pensions to the priests and lodges the body-guard.

At 8 o'clock news came that Calonne was overturned into the Rhine, his carriage lost, he saved by swimming, why did he not stay there! Arrived all wet at 9 o'clock. Comte d'Artois begged me to see him. He told me that he was sure of England and of her perfect neutrality, that he had nothing in writing, but verbal promises from the king and his ministers, that the Prince of Wales and members of the Opposition had told him that action should be taken at once because Pitt had refused to do anything. . . . In short, he was sure that England would respond well if the other Powers took steps.

27th. Started at 4 30 and reached Vienna August 2

August 2d. Looked for lodgings. Quantities of strangers, especially Poles dissatisfied with the new government and with their throne being made hereditary. At 6 to the Prater to see Blanchard go up in a balloon very good. Fine place, much company, superb drive along the Danube; full of tea-gardens, very lively.

3d. Dined with Bildt and Asp at Augarten, a pavilion belonging to the emperor, where he only breakfasts and dines; the garden always open to the public; fine establishment for dinners, — species of Vauxhall. Dined very well for two florins and a half.

Vienna grand, especially the faubourgs; much movement and magnificence, but that does not strike one as much.

The emperor has forbidden the French ambassador, M. de Noailles, to appear at Court, his master being a prisoner; a half-measure which is worth nothing.

4th. At 11 o'clock went to the emperor; much company,

it was audience. I had written on the day of my arrival to
Prince Rosenberg, the grand-master. No one was there to
announce, two valets at the door, whom they called *Kam-*
mer herren   At the end of half an hour they ushered me
in. The emperor talked much and listened little. He
asked: " Where is the king [of Sweden] ? Has he come
away for important affairs ? what is his project ? what are
his views ? "

Fersen. The king's project is to furnish troops and
vessels conjointly with the Empress of Russia, with whom
he has negotiated on this subject, but as he cannot disembark in France he asks Your Majesty for the port of Ostend
in which to disembark and leave his vessels.

Emperor. Yes, but I am waiting for answers from the
empress, to whom I have sent a courier; and so I have to
England, I must be fully assured of the latter's neutrality
— though she can't do anything else.

Fersen. The princes charged me to tell Your Majesty
that M. de Calonne assured them that England would be
neutral, he has just come from there.

Emperor. Did you see him ?

Fersen. Yes.

Emperor. What did he say ?

Fersen. That — etc., etc., etc.

Emperor. But he is rather light-headed; I know him,
I don't trust him much; he believes so easily.

Fersen   I think as you do; and for that reason M.
Crawford has now been sent.

Emperor. Ah! I know him and his pretended Mme. Crawford. (*Details about her*)   He is a man of intelligence.

Fersen.   He is authorized to — etc, etc., etc.

Emperor. Ah! that is very good; but we must first
know what the King of England means to do as Elector of

Hanover. I have urged the Diet to explain itself as to the project of the Elector of Mayence, which is very reasonable. Naples is all right and will give vessels. The King of Sardinia gives all his troops, but there is excitement in his country about the flight and arrest of the king; I have sent into Italy on his frontier 10 battalions and a regiment of cavalry to ensure tranquillity. Prussia, and the King of Prussia personally, are all right; he has sent the men on furlough [*semestricis*] to their homes, but he has kept the corps of Prince Hohenlohe to act on this side. I know that the King of Sweden has appealed to Hesse.

Fersen. Yes, and to Bavaria.

Emperor That help will not be much — but it is always something.

Fersen. Little as it is it will be increased, and besides, it has an effect.

Emperor. There is a very bad man there; I believe he has the spirit of the Assembly; he commands the troops; he is very bad. He is M. Johnson, an American, but he can't do much. Spain is the one from whom we must expect least help, not that she is ill-disposed, but she is in a bad state. Since the arrest of the king I have had no news from there.

Fersen. I must inform Your Majesty of the answer made by Spain to the Baron de Breteuil, etc, etc; but this was in case the king was at liberty; perhaps it is changed now.

Emperor. I do not think so; I know that Spain continues to send troops to the Pyrenees, but of eight regiments of cavalry she could only get together three thousand men; she is raising ten thousand men in Switzerland, but on ridiculous conditions There is not to be a single one that is not Catholic! The Dutch consent to lend her money, but

on ridiculous terms. They want her to put Corunna and
Manila into their hands. She is trying to make a loan in
Portugal, which holds out hopes to her. The declaration of
Spain is as unmeaning as it can be; one can't tell what it is;
it would have been better to say nothing. Naples gives
vessels to go to the coasts of Provence, but the king
cannot supply troops I await the answers of Spain, England and Russia before deciding, England is the most
important.

Fersen. I think, as Your Majesty does, that before undertaking anything we must, to ensure success, have a great
concurrence of means, which shall impose respect and insure
the individual safety of the king, the queen, and their family.
Your Majesty must feel more than any one how very necessary that precaution is.

Emperor. Yes, no doubt; I feel it and I believe that
nothing but an imposing force can save them; all half-measures are worth nothing; we must not act before all is ready;
when that is so, a first proclamation must be made, then a
second, in short, all that is necessary, and after that we must
act, for threats without anything to carry them out only do
harm.

Fersen. I desire to render account to Your Majesty of
the projects of the Comte d'Artois He has one of sending
persons to Paris with money to form a party. I have opposed it with such and such reasons

Emperor All that is of no use, they are half-measures,
petty schemes which can only do harm

After talking a little about the state of France I said: —

" The archduchess is very much embarrassed in Brussels by
this great influx of Frenchmen, especially officers. She
fears that their presence will have an influence on the soldiers, and may make them discontented."

Emperor. Oh, our men are of a different kind, it would be very difficult to do that. Besides, if we ever saw the slightest sign of it we should immediately make a terrible example, when it is a question of discipline there is no venial fault.

He did not ask me for details of the king and queen leaving Paris, in fact he talked much and listened little

I left him and went to dine with Asp and Bildt at Schönbrunn, a château about half a league from the town, where the empress often goes. It is a very large and long building, but in bad taste, backing on a hill which is made into a garden. At the top is a pavilion, where the chateau ought to have been placed.

Went to see Kaunitz; a very extraordinary man, who affects to be more extraordinary still; his wig was two inches from his eyebrows on all sides; red coat, black breeches, top-boots, for his sole mania is to ride daily in the riding-school. As he entered he distributed nods to all present, who seemed very eager to receive them. He is very deaf, but he assumes that no one perceives it. He dislikes perfumes, never takes the fresh air, when he crosses the courtyard at five or six o'clock, he holds his handkerchief before his mouth, and in spite of the great heat he keeps all the windows closed He said very flattering things to me about my recommendations. I gave him the king [of Sweden]'s letter, which he put in his pocket without reading it. At the end of half an hour he began to ask me details about the king and queen [of France]. As there were many persons present, among them Baron d'Escars, I was very laconic and he did not press me.

6th. At six o'clock went to dine with Prince Kaunitz I arrived too late to see him in the riding-school which is his sole passion, he is vain of his riding, and it is a means

of paying court to him.   In summer he lives at his country-
house, which is in the suburbs of Vienna.   Madame de Clary,
a little widow and his relation, does the honours.   She is the
echo of the prince, when he speaks she repeats all he says
We sat down to table at half-past seven   Casanova, the
painter, was there; he is the sycophant of the prince, who is
never in good humour unless he is with him.   As the prince
is very vain the painter flings flattery at his head in a dis-
gusting manner, but the other swallows it with delight.
The latter talked very well at dessert on the affairs of
France.   He enunciates with clearness and precision, but
slowly and methodically, he listens to himself.   One of his
manias being that he cannot bear fresh air, all the windows
were closed, notwithstanding the extreme heat   We did not
leave the table till nine o'clock   He ate a great deal.   He
spoke insultingly of the French, whom, as a general thing, he
does not like.

9th. At 5 30 went to the riding-school to see Kaunitz.
He kept strictly to the answer of the emperor, which he
repeated at length and methodically.   He seemed to doubt
the sincerity of England, and dwelt on the necessity of being
sure of her.   He asked me what had been the project of the
King of France, and what proposition he would have made to
the Assembly had he escaped   I told him he would have
based it on his declaration of June 23, which the prince could
not remember.   He made a note of this.   He made a great
eulogy on the King of Sweden, whom he called " Gustavus,"
and told me that the object of my mission seemed to him to
present no difficulty, but that it was a secondary measure to
take, *after* all the Powers had agreed.   On the whole, it seems
to me that the thing will be long delayed, and that no great
warmth will be put into it.   For that reason I should be
glad to shorten my stay here, but I am afraid I shall be

obliged to go to Prague   Prince Kaunitz was extremely polite and obliging to me

14th. Saw the emperor.   He has received a long letter from the queen [his sister Marie-Antoinette] through M de Noailles, in which she said that the Assembly was acting well and that they had nothing to fear except from those without.   She ended by saying that he had only to " compare what she now wrote to him with what she had always written to him, and draw the necessary conclusions by which to act."   The emperor concluded from that sentence that the letter was forced, and that she still wished for help.   He seems decided to give it, — but with precautions to assure their safety from the *canaille*   He is awaiting the answer from Spain; he has no doubt of that country's goodwill, but much of her ability to act   The answer of England is good; he seems satisfied with it, although it says nothing positive; but it could not be otherwise.   He does not doubt the Empress of Russia   He said to me: —

" They all say that they must see, that the means must be agreed upon, they want to be assured of payment, and how is it possible to assure them?   I see that they want some pledge; but if they had it, would they return it?   For you know what is good to take is good to keep; and I fear lest that should be their principle.   They say, moreover, that they must have an answer from England.   But I shall see the King of Prussia at Dresden, and learn his private sentiments, and then we may be able to take a course.   Meanwhile I shall take advantage of this letter of the queen to reply to her through the same channel; I shall pretend to think it safe and confidential and shall tell her certain truths, but the letter will be ostensible, it will be opened and read, the opportunity is too good to lose   What do you think about it?"

Fersen. I think as you do, sire, that you had better profit by it, and appear to be the dupe of those fellows; it is the system the king and queen have followed for some time, and it is the only one to adopt.

The emperor then spoke of Comte d'Artois' scheme of offering a pardon to M. de Lafayette and Company. He did not seem to approve of that course. He seems to me to wish to act. I have made up my mind to go to Prague, and return to Brussels from there.

Dined with Rasumoffski. Count Bergen came after dinner to tell us that Madame de Polignac had arrived . . . Went to Madame de Polignac. She wept on seeing me. I felt pleasure and pain at seeing her.

24th. Went to see the Duchesse de Polignac. She talks much of public affairs, and little of her friend.

Prague, 29th. Prague is a very lively town; many carriages; customary to go about the streets with four or six horses.

31st. Declaration of the emperor and King of Prussia pretty good, but time is passing. Entry of the emperor into Prague at three o'clock. Eighty carriages with six horses; those of the Court not very fine. Equipage of Prince Swartzenburg fine; the others hideous, those of the Court very shabby. Bourgoisie on horseback very good; German guards in extraordinary red uniforms much befrogged, a long *soubreveste* [sleeveless outer coat] of black velvet braided; they are not mounted, and on occasions like this the first regiment of carbineers lends them its horses. The prettiest was the Hungarian guard and the detachment of the carbineers and cuirassiers was superb; so were the grenadier battalions formed from the different regiments.

The Duc and Duchesse de Polignac arrived at three o'clock.

Prague, September 2d. Saw the emperor this morning.

Mme Vigée Le Brun

The Duchesse de Polignac

Met Polignac on my way.   He showed me a manifesto of the princes in which they say' that if the king is not set at liberty by the 15th of October in some frontier place in Hainaut, Alsace, or Franche-Comté (where he must be guarded by foreign troops, not being able to rely on the French army until order be restored in France), *Monsieur* will then declare himself *Regent*, until the moment when the king is at liberty.   Polignac told me he had just given a copy to the emperor, begging him to sign it, but the emperor asked him to let him keep it, and said he would reply to-morrow.

I asked the emperor for an answer respecting the port of Ostend, — saying that the King of Sweden was fully prepared to act, and was only awaiting the emperor's answer to start at once.

Emperor.   But they tell me the king wants to disembark at the Hogue.

Fersen   I can assure Y. M. it is not so; it would be impossible without revictualling after so long a voyage.

Emperor.   Yes, yes, I understand: but the Empress of Russia will ask the same thing, I am expecting every day to hear from her.   I must know whether her vessels are to come in separately from those of the King of Sweden; after that we can arrange the whole thing together.

Fersen.   Will Y. M. permit me to see the answer of the King of Spain to Y. M. and to the King of Sweden?

Emperor.   Yes, you can ask Count Coblentz for them.   I will have a copy given to you.

Fersen   I should like to send it to Sweden in case the courier from Spain should have been delayed.   Besides, for all the arrangements with the King of Sweden I am provided with full powers from the king and even with blank agreements in case Your Majesty desires to sign yourself.

Emperor. As for the item about Ostend there is no need of it; those are orders which must be given in the Low Countries.

Fersen. The king [of Sweden] desires as to that a written agreement.

Emperor Yes, but we must wait for the answer from Russia.

Fersen Has the Duc de Polignac shown Your Majesty the draft of a manifesto?

Emperor. Yes, I do not approve of it.

Fersen. I think Y. M is right. Any step whatever taken before the troops are ready is harmful. The idea of the regency is also harmful; and will furnish a pretext to turn against the princes by making it believed that they wish to seize the government and put the king under guardianship. None but imbeciles will think they act for the king in act-ing for the princes. The project of having him guarded by foreigners will never succeed

5th. Wrote to the queen. Saw Coblentz in the morning. He gave me copies of the letters of Spain, the demands of the Comte d'Artois and the answers, the declaration of Spain to Paris, and that of the emperor with the changes made by Spain; all this confirms them more and more in the idea of a congress, to shorten the affair and settle everything He liked my idea of insisting on the liberty of the king and fixing the place to which he should then go, without entering upon any detail of the Constitution or any negotiation with the Assembly. He told me that in the declaration sent to the Courts it was proposed to recall all the ambassadors from France and assemble them in congress at Aix-la-Chapelle. I asked if that proposition had been sent to Sweden. He answered, after a moment, that he was not sure, but would ask and let me know; whereby I saw that it had not been sent. There is great slowness. He told me that the King of Prussia had been against a congress, and wanted everything negotiated in Vienna by the ambassadors now there. Also that the King of Prussia advised no immediate action, but previous consultation as to the declarations that ought to be made.

6th. Coronation of the emperor in the chapel of Saint-Wenceslas in the castle; small, not fine, no preparations to make the fête beautiful. Ceremony lasted from 8 A. M. to 11 o'clock The Archbishops of Prague and Olmütz officiated; he of Prague put on the crown, every one applauded and cried, "Viva!" — little order. They dined in the Salle du Serment — the emperor under a dais. After he had drunk, the company sat down to the other tables of which there were twelve, of twelve covers each. I was not at the dinner, but I went to see it from the gallery with Prince Hohenlohe, the Prussian general. I was rather displeased at not being at the dinner. As a general thing, foreigners receive little attention here.

General Hohenlohe comes on the part of the King of Prussia [Frederick-William] to concert a plan of operations and urge the emperor to act; the king is all ready. They want to go too fast and do not really know the situation in France, but this may hasten the emperor a little. Hohenlohe is a great man, solely military; from his talk I see that the animosity between the two countries still exists. He spoke to me with disdain of the Austrian troops, nevertheless, they are fine He told me he was empowered to make proposals for marching the Prussian troops; that his master was ready; that he would do nothing that the emperor did not do at the same moment; that he had given half a million of florins to Comte d'Artois, that Bischoffswerder was charged in Italy to make proposals to the emperor to cede to the

Elector Palatine certain districts in Alsace; to Prussia, Bergue and Juliers and something in Hainaut, that the emperor had refused; but the matter ought now to be re-vived, as it would be a means to make the emperor bestir himself in behalf of the king and queen, if he meant to act. I saw in all this Prussian intrigues and the distrust which exists between the two Courts. They want to make a mere intrigue of this matter

7th   Went to see Hohenlohe. He wants the King of Sweden, on the reply of Spain, to start for Ostend without awaiting any answer from the emperor. Dined with Polignac; he has nothing with him but his silver service and his cook. Hohenlohe came there, he had dragged nothing out of the emperor, whom he saw at midday, he told him all the tales and intrigues that I had told him of Calonne, Condé, and the hatred of the princes for Breteuil and the rest of us, he said the queen was against them and disapproved of them. All this he repeated before Polignac. Fortunately he did not quote me; he is amazingly indiscreet, nothing should be told to him.

9th. Went to the emperor at midday : I was ushered in at once before every one. The emperor spoke to me like a man decided to act at once; but results do not follow speech   I cannot understand it. He seems to feel the advantage it would be to the tranquillity of the Low Countries, Normandy, and the Mouth of the Seine to have the Swedish and Rus-sian troops land at Ostend, in fact, it was he who said so to me.

10th. Dined at Court; one hundred and four persons at table, not very magnificent. The emperor told me he had received a letter from the queen through Mercy, asking that the Powers should act, but cautiously, and without the princes, she said she feared — as we supposed — that the

Assembly was alarmed and had decided to do something and employ force, and was about to issue orders. I said: " Your Majesty, it would be well to frighten it." " No, no," he replied, " we must act."

Went to a ball and concert at Czernin's; superb, house magnificent, a perfect palace, eight hundred persons at supper at little tables. The empress spoke to me very well. The Archduchess Marianne, who is abbess here, told the ambassadress of Spain that her father talked well, but she feared he would do nothing.

13th. Went to the ball at Kolowrath's at half-past eight. Talked with the emperor.

Emperor. I received your paper, and I think it very good.

Fersen. I thought that it expressed the result of the views of Y. M. and all that you did me the honour to say to me.

Emperor Yes, yes ; perfectly right.

Fersen I believe that a congress unsupported by troops will have no effect, the object is to awe them.

Emperor. Yes, yes, no doubt, and I have already given orders for two regiments of cavalry and several battalions to march to the Brisgau; the requisitions will be sent at once; that will have an effect; and the recall of the ambassadors will have more.

Fersen. I am told that Y. M. has received the answer of the Empress of Russia.

Emperor. Yes, but not the one by my courier. The letter of the empress is good, she proposes a congress, the recall of the ambassadors, and a declaration of the stoppage of all communications and commerce with France

Fersen Yes, but that concerns only the maritime Powers. England might do it, and that is another reason why she should be pledged to neutrality.

Emperor. Yes, yes, I understand, it would be very advantageous to her, and have a great effect on the commerce of France and on the financiers

Fersen. What would really have a great effect in the king's favour would be the ability to reassure the country as to bankruptcy; at any rate as to that of the annuities [*rentes viagères*] and the redemption of *assignats.* He would then have on his side all the capitalists and bankers, it is they who made the revolution or helped to consolidate it; they are very much dissatisfied; they fear bankruptcy; and I am certain that if they are reassured as to that they will be for the king.

Emperor. Yes, but that is very difficult; and if the bankruptcy occurs it will be general.

Fersen. I do not think the operation so difficult. At the time the king left Paris, his project was to begin by reassuring the country as to the payment of the annuities in full by reducing the *agiotage* [traffic with the public funds] and the onerous loans to a reasonable rate, also, when returning to the clergy their property to saddle it with paying off the *assignats;* this was possible, and their property would still have been sufficient to furnish several millions; but the Assembly can never derive as much from it.

Emperor. Oh! I know that; for this very day I have a parallel affair in a convent reformed by the late emperor: in order to give eight or nine old women pensions amounting to six thousand florins there is a cost of eleven thousand florins in administrating the property; it is bad economy. That idea of the king was very good, and would have had great effect.

Fersen. Would Your Majesty, in consequence of the empress's letter, decide about the king's troops and the port of Ostend?

Emperor. I must wait for another courier, which the

empress informs me will arrive in two or three days, giving
me in detail what she intends to send. I imagine that she
wants to concert about that with the King of Sweden, and
let me know the result.

Fersen. It is important that the matter be decided as
quickly as possible, for the season is advancing, and if the
troops do not start this autumn, they cannot arrive before
June or July of next year.

Emperor Yes, yes, I understand ; it would be better if
they were there, no harm will come of that, and if they are
there, there will be no waiting for them.

He seemed to agree with me about it, and to desire to act.
Were he alone it might be done ; but he has not the force
to resist his council, Baron Spielmann and the others are
against it. Nevertheless, the conversation gave me some
hope.

16th Count Coblentz tells me that the answer of the Empress of Russia is very favourable, she encourages the emperor
to act. As to Ostend, he told me that vessels of war cannot
enter that port ; the merchantmen are obliged to wait for the
tide, and when it is low they lie on their sides, that the season was far too advanced to send troops this year, moreover,
we must know what England and Holland would say to
the arrival of a fleet in that port. — I see clearly that they
are dragging things along purposely to prevent the King of
Sweden from sending troops this year, they fear his activity,
and also that he may command in person ; they want to
avoid acting, or else to act alone if it becomes necessary.
Nothing is being done ; the requisitions have not been sent,
although they assure me the troops are to march at once.

They are all agreed that the congress must be an armed
one ; but they are losing time awaiting replies and doing
nothing positive. The emperor is inclined to act, and wishes

it, but his ministry hold him back. He is afraid; he feels
about him; he does not venture to act, and the work will be
harder in the end. — He hopes to gain all by getting over the
winter — My conversation with Count Coblentz has made me
lose heart. I see a well-formed plan to do only trifling
things during the winter; to try to patch up matters for the
time being, and not to act until spring, and not then unless
it is absolutely necessary. This is very shameful and dreadful towards the queen.

17th Received a despatch from Sweden. It seems that
the empress will act only indirectly; this will delay operations very much, and all hopes of acting this year is lost
for the king [of Sweden]. The assembling of the congress
and the preliminary declarations will take all winter, we
shall be lucky if we obtain the right to support it with
troops.

18th. Prince Hohenlohe came to see me this evening.
He had talked a long time with Baron Spielmann, who told
him that the emperor would raise the number of his troops
in the Low Countries to fifty-eight or sixty thousand men,
that he could then act with thirty, or thirty-two thousand of
them; but first, he must await the reply of England. He
added that an army would be raised from the German States;
that the intention was not to form *têtes-d'armées* to support
the congress; that the first thing necessary was to know what
reply the King of France would make about sanctioning the
Constitution; if he accepts it, there will be difficulty in acting; there will then be new inquiries to make of all the
Courts, to know if they recognize the sanction of the king as
free or compulsory; that it would be only after all this that
any action could be taken, that the season was already too
late, and nothing could be undertaken till the spring.

21st. Saw the emperor Communicated the reply of Eng-

land. He thought it good Was of my opinion on everything, and sent me away as soon as possible The whole
matter embarrasses and annoys him. He told me that the
King of Prussia writes to him to place no confidence in
Prince Hohenlohe, who is not charged with any mission
Never have I seen an affair conducted as this has been ! I
am not surprised that it goes so badly

25th. News that the king [of France] has sanctioned the
Constitution — There are terrible intrigues at the Court here,
as everywhere. The Archduchesses Theresa and Marianne are
strongly for France, the empress and all the sub-orders
against it; the emperor is weak and indiscreet. All sorts
of tales are told of the French, many invented The archduchess in Brussels writes against them. The emperor tells
all this. They say that the queen is letting Barnave lead
her, that she holds back the emperor, that she is against
the princes. All goes ill.

26th. Took leave of the emperor; he agreed that the
King of France was not free; that it was necessary to insist
on his liberty; that it was fortunate he had sanctioned the
Constitution without restrictions, as that showed it was under
compulsion. In the evening he said to another person that,
now that the king had sanctioned the Constitution, there was
nothing more to be done ! This is just what I feared.

28th. Started at five o'clock in the evening, enchanted to
get away.

Coblentz, October 3d. Reached Coblentz at five o'clock.
Went to the princes. They said they had excellent news;
march of Austrians and Prussians to the number of twelve
thousand men, etc., etc. I denied it all, and they would
hardly believe me. The crowd of French officers at Coblentz
is enormous and alarming; they arrive more than ever, by
hundreds, even bourgeois are among them. The princes are

forming corps, restoring red companies, etc. Maréchal de
Broglie is living here   The princes have a numerous Court ;
the intrigues diabolical.   The princes dined at nine o'clock ;
there was much company   Everybody came to ask me for
news ; which I did not give them, to their astonishment.   I
started after dinner and slept at Andernach ; I gave the
difficulty of finding lodgings as an excuse for getting away.
The follies that this assemblage may commit are incalculable.   When they have spent all their money they had
much better be in France.   The Prince of Nassau keeps
them in great state, the empress gave them two millions.

Brussels, 6th.   Reached Brussels at six in the morning.
Saw Mercy ; the queen writes to him that the king must go
a little by the Constitution ; the princes must be checked ;
she asks for the calling of a congress, the pretext to be
Avignon.   Mercy thinks a congress useless at this moment,
for he does not see what it would find to do, it cannot give
the lie to the king as to the Constitution.   I proved to him
its utility, and the necessity of some ostensible step being
taken in order to check the princes.   He agreed to suggest
to the emperor to ask for its announcement at once ; and
also for the selection of place and members,— the object
to be Avignon.   He spoke very well, but thought that
nothing could be done (the king having accepted the
Constitution) except to wait until the new legislature
committed follies which would give the Powers a pretext
for interfering

7th   The princes sent Cazalès and Burke's son to persuade Baron de Breteuil to go to Coblentz, he refused.
Quantities of Frenchmen here ; they pass the frontier by the
fifties daily.   The Duc d'Uzès is their leader in Brussels.
They are all mad.

15th.   Du Moustier passed through and saw the Baron de

Breteuil   He said that the King of Prussia in a conversation he had with him (in which he asked H. M. what he was to say to the king [of France] as to his intentions) answered, laying his hand on his sword, that he would help him with all his forces, that he was ready, but the emperor stopped him; that he would march 50,000 men if the emperor would march as many, that he was keeping 12,000 men on a war footing ready to march at once, and the rest should follow. Du Moustier having told him that he had a plan of finance by which to bring coin back to France and save the king all embarrassments as to money, but in order to do this he needed a credit of one hundred millions in *écus,* and hoped to obtain it from him, the king replied that if the money were wanted for that object he would lend it to the king on sufficient security and fixed dates for repayment.

Baron de Breteuil represented to him that he ought not to speak of that project until the king recovered full power. He agreed, and seemed decided to serve him; but he, du Moustier, is a rascal on whom no great dependence should be placed.

18th   La Marck arrived; I went there; he made me an apology for his conduct, saying that he had done nothing except with a view to serve the king; that was the motive of his intimacy with Mirabeau; he said that in the month of October, 1789, he had made Mirabeau make the plan for the counter-revolution; that he had seen *Monsieur* clandestinely, and had read and given the plan to him; that the basis of this plan was the king's departure for Beauvais   He said shocking things of the French nation. He has bought a house here, he will not be looked upon favourably, but if he gives good dinners every one will go to them.

23d. Mercy gave me a letter from the queen; he deciphered to me four or five lines.

29th. Saw the Princesse de Lamballe, who started to return to Paris.

November 13th. M de Mercy now says that he thinks the emperor will accept the congress, and that this is the result of the conduct of Sweden and Russia. On the other hand, they sent me word from Vienna that the emperor will do nothing, and I believe it. The Duke of York says that the King of Prussia is sincerely for us, but that he cannot act without the emperor; and the duke thinks the latter means to do nothing

15th. The King of France has not sanctioned the decree against the *émigrés*, he used his veto. This has caused agitation; evil minds are exciting the populace. The king will lose in this way the little popularity that he has, and will be again where he was in April; they may prevent him from riding on horseback, great commotions are expected in Paris, and a crisis. Lafayette will be mayor through the ascendency of the Guard, which, being unable to have him as general, is determined to have it thus. He will then have great and very dangerous power. Letters from Paris are terrifying; the newspapers are as incendiary as ever, and point to the probable flight of the king in order to inspire distrust. The "Journal Général," published by the Abbé Fontenay, an aristocrat, says frightful things against Breteuil, Mercy, and Thugut, and warns them not to attempt the flight of the king. This article was certainly written in Coblentz. It is abominable!

18th. Finished my great letter to the queen.

20th. Went to Mercy. He gave me a letter from the queen, they are very unhappy, but wish to act.

December 6th. M. Luisey has arrived from Berlin. Says the emperor has written to Prussia and Russia to prevent them from doing anything; that he wants to ally himself with Prussia and Holland and invite England to join them —which she will not do; that Prussia is very right towards France, but will not act without the emperor.

10th.   Baron de Viomesnil, a poor negotiator, is going to Cologne and Coblentz to commission the Marquis de Castries to be the king's man in the council of the princes. A false step. The queen is now very sorry to have sent him; my letter arrived too late to prevent it.   He came to see me this morning, I was tempted to prevent his going on, but I dared not, because they would have thought it was by agreement with Baron de Breteuil, whom they would then have accused of getting rid of every one in order to have sole control himself of affairs   In the conference I had with Viomesnil at Breteuil's house I proposed changes in what the former was to say, which weakened his commission and made it as little important as possible.   It is to be hoped that Castries will not agree to go.   Viomesnil wished, not being able to agree, that Calonne should go away. I opposed it, ostensibly under pretext that it would be dangerous in view of the nobles, but really because the king would then be obliged to correspond directly with the princes, which he cannot do without compromising himself, because of their indiscretion There is no danger, they cannot act without the Northern Powers; and it is better to let them be guided by them.

CHAPTER VI.

1791   Correspondence of Queen Marie-Antoinette with Count Fersen —
Official Letters of the same Period, showing the vain Efforts employed to
induce the Powers to act in behalf of the King of France and his Family.

[DURING the time already noted in the Diary, letters were
passing between Queen Marie-Antoinette and Count Fersen,
in his capacity of intermediary between the King and Queen
of France, the King of Sweden, and the Courts of Europe.
The chief object of their hopes and efforts was to convoke
an armed congress, to meet either at Frankfort on the Main
or at Aix-la-Chapelle, and awe by that means the National
Assembly.   Eleven letters from the queen and ten from
Count Fersen in 1791 (also seventeen from the queen and
twenty-two from Fersen in 1792) still exist as a testimony
to the count's last efforts for the expiring monarchy   Nearly
all these letters were written in cipher or with "white ink"
— invisible ink ; sometimes in both.   They were deciphered
and copied by Count Fersen himself, and are now at Stockholm in possession of his family.   Among these papers is a
memorial, dated November 26, 1791 (called by the count in
the foregoing diary " my great letter to the queen"), in which
he explains to her the political situation of Europe as regarded the affairs of France, suggests a plan of conduct for
the king and queen, and advises the writing by them of certain personal letters to friendly Courts asking them to guard
Their Majesties' interests.   This plan was adopted.

Other letters of the same period, explanatory of current
events, are here interpersed with those of the queen]

Count Fersen to Queen Marie-Antoinette.

BRUSSELS, June 27, 1791.

The dreadful event which has just happened [king and family stopped at Varennes and virtually imprisoned] will change entirely the course of affairs, and if the resolution is persisted in to let others act (no longer being able to act personally), it is necessary to begin the negotiations over again and to give full powers for that purpose. The mass of Powers who may be brought to act must be sufficiently strong to awe, and thus preserve the precious lives. Here are questions to which answers should be made : —

1. Is it desired that they should act in spite of all prohibitions that may be received ?

2. Is it desired to give the full powers to *Monsieur*, or to the Comte d'Artois ?

3 Is it desired that they shall employ under them the Baron de Breteuil, or do they consent to M de Calonne, or do they leave the choice to them ?

Here is the form for the full powers : —

" Being detained a prisoner in Paris, and not being able to give the necessary orders to re-establish order in my kingdom, restore to my subjects happiness and tranquillity, and recover my legitimate authority, I charge *Monsieur*, or, in default of him, the Comte d'Artois, to watch for me over my interests and those of my crown, giving him for this purpose unlimited powers , I pledge my royal word to keep religiously and without restrictions all the stipulated engagements which may be made with the said Powers ; and I bind myself to ratify. as soon as I am at liberty, all treaties, conventions, and other compacts made by him with the different Powers who may be willing to come to my defence, also all commissions, brevets, and posts which *Monsieur* may have

10

thought necessary to give; and to this I pledge myself on the word of a king.   Done in Paris, this twentieth day of June, 1791 "

This form should be written in white ink and given as soon as possible to the person bearing this letter.   As the number of the above questions has been kept, the answers can be very brief.

I am very well treated here.   Your sister [Archduchess Marie-Christine] *ebstien* [?] for you and for me.

Queen Marie-Antoinette to Count Fersen.

June 28, 1791.

Be reassured about us, we live   The leaders of the Assembly seem to wish to be gentle in their conduct.   Speak to my relatives of steps to be taken outside.   If they are frightened, we must compound with them [*il faut composer avec eux*]

Queen Marie-Antoinette to Count Fersen

June 29, 1791.

I exist . . . How uneasy I have been about you, and how I pity you for having no news of us!   Heaven grant that this letter may reach you.   Do not write to me; that would only expose us, above all, do not come here under any pretext. It is known that it was you who took us out of here; all would be lost if you appeared here   We are kept in sight night and day; I do not care . .   Be easy, nothing will happen to me.   The Assembly means to treat us gently. Adieu. . . . I cannot write to you again. . . .

The King of Sweden to Louis XVI.

AIX-LA-CHAPELLE, June 30, 1791

I beg Y. M. not to doubt the feelings with which we all share your misfortune.   Your friends will never abandon you. Sustain your present position with firmness, as you have already sustained the dangers that surround you ; above all, do not allow them to degrade the royal dignity in your person, and the kings will come to your support. This is the advice of your oldest ally and your most faithful friend.

Powers given by Louis XVI. to Monsieur *and the Comte d'Artois.*

PARIS, July 7, 1791.

I rely absolutely on the tenderness of my brothers for me, on their love and attachment to their country, on the friendship of the sovereign princes my relations and allies, and on the honour and generosity of the other sovereigns, to agree together as to the manner of, and the means to be used for, negotiating, the object of which should tend to the re-establishment of order and tranquillity in the kingdom ; but I think that all employment of force . . . [1] that, placed behind negotiations, I give all power to my brothers to negotiate in that sense with whom they will, and to choose the persons to employ for these political purposes.

LOUIS.

Queen Marie-Antoinette to Count Fersen.

July 8, 1791

The king thinks that the close imprisonment in which he is held and the state of total degradation to which the National Assembly has reduced royalty, allowing it to exercise no action whatever, is sufficiently known to Foreign powers to need no mention here.

The king thinks that it is by negotiations alone that their help can be useful to him and to his kingdom ; that all show of force should be secondary, and only in case all means of negotiation be refused here.

---

[1] Wherever these omissions occur in the letters it means that the parts omitted were either lost or undecipherable — TR

The king thinks that open force, even after a first declaration, would be of incalculable danger, not only to him and to his family, but even to all Frenchmen in the interior of the kingdom who do not think in agreement with the revolution. There is no doubt that a foreign force could enter France, but the people, armed as they are, leaving the frontiers and the foreign troops, would instantly turn their arms against those of their co-citizens whom they have been incessantly taught during the last two years to regard as their enemies, and above all . . .

The king thinks that unlimited full powers such as proposed, even if dated on the 20th of June, would be dangerous for him in the position he is now in. It is impossible that they should not be communicated ; and all cabinets are not equally discreet.

It is announced that during the next fifteen days the articles called constitutional will be presented to the king ; that he will then be set at liberty, and be left master of going where he pleases, in order that he may decide whether to accept them, yes or no ; but by keeping his son in Paris they make this illusory. All that has been done during the last two years must be considered null as regards the king's will, but impossible to change so long as the majority of the nation desire these novelties. It is to change this spirit that all our attention must be turned.

Summary. He desires that the captivity of the king be fully stated and known to the foreign Powers ; he desires that the good-will of his relatives, friends, and allies, and that of other sovereigns who may wish to concur, be manifested by a species of congress, at which the method of negotiation shall be adopted, understanding always that an imposing force be there to support it, but always sufficiently in the background not to provoke to crime and massacre.

It is important that the Baron de Breteuil be united with the king's brothers and with those they may select for these important negotiations.

The king does not think he ought to give unlimited powers; but he sends the enclosed paper, written in white ink, to be given to his brothers. [See foregoing]

We dare not answer the King of Sweden. Be our interpreter to him of our gratitude and attachment.

The King of Spain to the King of Sweden.

MADRID, August 3, 1791

MONSIEUR, my brother and cousin:

If things were still in the state in which they were six months ago, I should not delay a moment in accepting the plan which Y. M has sent me in your letter of July 16, and in concurring therewith by every means in my power. But to-day circumstances have changed so much that there is far more need for reflection, prudence, and sagacity than for active force in favour of Louis XVI. That sovereign might be sacrificed to popular fury on the point of being placed by those who have torn his liberty from him in a safe and free place, where he may accept and sanction the reformed code of constitutional laws which will be presented to him, or else reject it wholly or in part If that were to take place it would then be the proper time to sustain him in order that his subjects may submit to the modifications their king will make in it [the Constitution]; and Y. M. may count on my assistance, pecuniary especially, as far as my possibilities can go.

Meantime it would be useless to undertake a war against a nation enthusiastic for its apparent liberty and seduced against its monarch, and the life of that prince would be exposed to the greatest dangers. Armed conquerors, whoever they be, can only possess the territory they occupy, the people and the misled multitude being their enemies, they must exterminate them and ruin the country.[1] Time must be given to clear understanding, after all that has been lost without my yet obtaining a clear answer from the Powers to whom I disclosed my intentions. I formed a plan according to the circumstances of the month of April when there was, even then, few resources; I communicated it, but I have been unable to learn any result. At present, the plan of escape of the Very Christian King having failed, and the general aversion of the French for monarchy being still more heated than in the beginning, it is absolutely necessary to await calmness and the effects of negotiation for his liberty, and the re-establishment of his power.

It is thus that I understand the matter, and say it plainly to Y. M., whose ideas in themselves, even if they be not realized, will obtain for you an immortal glory and make you worthy of eternal gratitude, not only from the Bourbons, but from all the sovereigns and even from humanity itself ever interested in the maintenance of society and legitimate authority. I forestall them to thank Y. M. in their name, and to assure you of the constant and cordial friendship with which I have the honour to be, Monsieur, my brother and cousin,

Your Majesty's good brother, cousin, and friend,

CHARLES (IV).

After writing this letter, I have received one from the emperor, in which he expresses ideas that agree with ours. I beg Y. M. to come to an understanding and concert with H. I. M., to whom I will propose and request the same.

---

[1] This autograph letter is translated literally as it stands in the French; the wording is obscure, though the meaning is tolerably plain. Royal personages were very deficient in the art of writing — and spelling — TR

The King of Sweden to Count Fersen.

DROTTNINGHOLM, August 5, 1791.

M. de Calonne arrived the day after your departure [for Vienna]. I had a conversation of four hours with him, the details of which would be too long and useless to send to you. The news from England alone seems to me important. He brings a letter from the King of England to the princes, in answer to one which Comte d'Artois wrote to him. The King of England expresses himself with the utmost feeling about the affairs of France. As to succour, M. de Calonne announces none. Nevertheless, he let it be seen that the king and even the Prince of Wales (who on this point agrees with his father) give some hopes of Hanoverian troops. But M. de Calonne positively assured me that the King of England, and even Mr. Pitt promise the strictest neutrality, and the latter added that if he took part in the cause of the princes, it would do harm, because the Opposition would take the contrary view, and it was therefore more useful to the good of the thing that the King of England should be neutral. This language seems to me that of truth, and if the English disposition is really such our emissary will have no trouble in passing.

Postscript : Since writing the above I have received letters from Petersburg in which they tell me that the first news of the disaster of the King of France made the greatest impression on the empress. She received the news in the midst of the fête which was given on the anniversary of her succession. The Prince of Nassau is working with all his strength to obtain succour; but neither my despatch to Baron Stedingk [Swedish ambassador to Russia] nor my memorial, sent July 6 from Aix, had arrived before the departure of the letters. You know already that the empress has surmounted all obstacles, and the allies have yielded everything to her. This, joined to the victories won by the Russians in the Caucasus over the grand-vizier, make peace almost certain That will give Russia more ability to aid France. Nevertheless, it seems to me essential that you should engage the emperor to warmly promote the success of my negotiation with Russia. . . . *that the orders given to the ambassador from Sweden in Paris.* . . . she tells me she will write to Vienna to induce the emperor to give the same to his minister in Paris. I think it necessary that you should know all these circumstances, so as to compare them with the notions which you yourself obtain in Vienna, and regulate your proceedings accordingly.

Your very affectionate

GUSTAVUS.

Count Fersen to the King of Sweden.

VIENNA, August 17, 1791.

The emperor is still awaiting the answer from Spain. H. I M seems to be less doubtful of the good inclinations of the King of Spain and his willingness to act than of his means and the possibility of making them effective. The answer of England, though not positive, seems to him good. He does not doubt the sentiments of Y. M. and the Empress of Russia; but he does not seem well assured of the sincerity of those of the King of Prussia; he thinks there is more demonstration of eagerness than of will to act. He told me that the king seemed to wish to be reimbursed for his outlays, and to know how and by whom it would be done; and the emperor fears he will ask to be put in possession of some lien on lands [*hypothèque*], which later he could not be made to give up. This does not agree with what M. Bischoffswerder [envoy of the King of Prussia to settle

terms of treaty with the emperor] told me on the evening
before his departure. He repeated to me how much his
master desired the emperor to act, and for that purpose he
was keeping on a war footing the corps of Prince Hohenlohe,
the garrison of Magdebourg, and the troops in Westphalia
As for the reimbursement of the outlay such an expedition
would occasion, the object, he said, was in itself too important for such considerations to stop it or delay it, and the
treaty which had just been signed ought to reassure the
emperor as to the intentions of his master.

It seems it has not, for the emperor has again told me
that when he has seen the King of Prussia and heard from
himself what he thinks, he will take a definite course.
This reply induces me to go to Prague, so that I may the
sooner get a positive answer and know definitively what the
emperor means to do. He seems to me in opposition to his
ministry, which makes delays and wants to wait before
doing anything for the action of the National Assembly
about the Constitution, and the reply that the King of France
may make to it. I have endeavoured to show them how
illusory all that is, how necessary it is for the success of the
operation not to lose time, and how useful, even from their
point of view, a demonstration of force would be in making
the Assembly more tractable. As soon as the emperor has
had his interview with the King of Prussia I hope to send
Y. M. his definitive answer.

The King of Sweden to Count Fersen.

DROTTNINGHOLM, August, 23, 1791.

I send you inclosed several extracts from despatches relating to the affairs of France. You will see the necessity
of urging the Empress of Russia through the emperor. I
add nothing more at this time, because I hope to have let-

ters from you by the next post making plain the intentions
of the emperor. By the news from France, I see that the
Constitution will soon be ready to be presented to the king.
It would be very fortunate if the king could be induced to
refuse all answer, on the ground of his captivity. He would
risk nothing, because it is notorious that they dare not attack
his person from fear of the foreign powers; and he would
thereby greatly strengthen the efforts of his friends.
If you still have communication with him, give him that
necessary advice.

Baron Taube has arrived and gives me the best assurance
of the firmness of the princes in not entering upon any
negotiations. They have written to the empress by M.
de . . . that the Prince of Nassau had amused them with
words of consolation from Her Majesty. I think it is very
necessary to warm up the empress in their favour, and you
would do well to talk with the Russian ambassador in
Vienna about the affairs of France, in order that he may
write about them to the empress. That princess is a
woman who will never have a moment's peace until she
obtains what she wants.

On which, I pray God to have you, Count Fersen, in his
holy keeping, being

Your very affectionate

GUSTAVUS

The King of Sweden to Count Fersen

The little castle of HAGA,
September 8, 1791.

I have received to-day an answer to my letter to the King
of England, of which I send you a copy; as a mark of the confidence I like to show to the emperor, I request you to show
it to him. You will see that the King of England expresses

himself in a positive manner about the neutrality he is resolved to hold as to the affairs of France, and when one
considers the peculiar position of that king in view of the
spirit of his people and the British constitution, the resent-
ment he has a right to retain concerning the war in America,
and the jealous feelings of the English against their former
rival in greatness, it seems to me that we can hardly look
for anything more favourable or more positive than this
letter of H. Britannic M. announces. And if to that one
adds (with regard to Sweden) that the King of England, by
declaring himself neutral, puts himself in the position of not
being able to refuse entrance to his ports of Swedish vessels,
if forced by accidents to take refuge there (the old treaties,
especially that of 1662, always recognized as subsisting
between the two nations, give us positive rights as to this),
you will see that the words of the King of England's letter
express more than appears at first sight.

I think that the emperor will judge the matter in the same
light, and being thus assured of the intentions of the King of
Prussia and those of the King of England, he will feel the
necessity of hastening operations   The position of the
King and Queen of France is too cruel for them to be able to
bear it much longer, the season is advancing, prompt measures are absolutely necessary, especially for the Northern
Powers. The Empress of Russia, being now delivered from
all the embarrassments of the Turkish war, will be able to
second efficaciously the efforts of the other crowns, and her
grandeur of soul joined to the high regard she feels for the
emperor, will no doubt bring her to adopt the measures
necessary for concurrence, still, I think it is essential that
the emperor should urge her vigorously, and I charge you to
speak of this to H. I. M. when you communicate to him the
letter of the King of England.

I flatter myself that the emperor will recognize in all this
the zeal and friendship which inspire me for him and for the
safety of the queen his sister, and his brother-in-law the
king.

Your very affectionate

GUSTAVUS.

The King of England to the King of Sweden.

St. James, August 13, 1791

MONSIEUR, my brother and cousin:

In consequence of the friendly letter that I have just
received from Y. M., I profit by this opportunity to testify
how sensible I am to the assurances you give me of your
esteem and personal friendship. It will always give me true
pleasure to cultivate those feelings as well as to preserve and
increase the good understanding which has so long and so
happily existed between our States.

My conduct in relation to the troubles which agitate the
kingdom of France has been guided by the principles of a
strict and perfect neutrality, and never, in any of the
occasions which have arisen, have I departed from that system.
I am far from wishing to involve myself in the internal
affairs of that kingdom in order to profit by this crucial
moment, or obtain advantages which circumstances might
offer to me. As a result of the same principles I intend to
take no part in the measures which the other Powers of
Europe may see fit to adopt in this matter, neither to second
them, nor to oppose them. The wishes I form in this affair
tend solely to the welfare of Their Very Christian Majesties
and their subjects, and to the restoration of public order and
tranquillity in a kingdom so adjacent to my own States
and with which my subjects have relations of friendship
and commerce.

I shall see with pleasure all events that may contribute to

such important results, and if the new order of things appears to present consequences which might affect the interests of my subjects, I shall feel no difficulty in expressing myself ultimately on the subject in the frankest manner to the different Powers of Europe with whom I have the happiness to live in peace and a good understanding. I beg Y. M. to be convinced of the friendship and high consideration with which I am, Monsieur, my brother and cousin,

Your Majesty's

good brother, cousin, friend, and neighbour,

GEORGE R.

Baron Taube to Comte Fersen.[1]

DROTTNINGHOLM, September 9, 1791

I received your letter of August 20 this morning, my dear friend; it is very curious that the reflections which you make in the cipher part of your letter as to the reasons of the emperor's slowness I had already said to the king some days ago. I do not doubt that the former is jealous of the king's success and of the reputation he has won; he will be still more so when he learns that the empress refers herself to him and to his decision relatively to the affairs of France, and relies on him for the execution of their joint operations. There may be still a second reason why the emperor should not wish the Northern Powers to take an active part in the restoration of the King of France. we know that Prussia has never made a treaty in favour of any one without turning it to good account and getting leg or wing from her closest allies (for as yet none of them, except England, have failed to be her dupes). It may be that in the treaty just con-

---

[1] Baron Taube was, it must be remembered, the first gentleman of the Bedchamber to the King of Sweden and in his closest confidence, for this reason his letters are of great importance as expressing the views, intentions, and real policy of the king in French affairs — TR.

cluded between the emperor and the King of Prussia they have mutually guaranteed to each other some portions or possessions of France as indemnity for the cost of succouring the king; but that cannot be done *now* without the co-operation of the Northern Powers.   The emperor's slowness looks very suspicious to me since the signing of the treaty with Prussia; it is certain that if they can delay action for another five or six weeks it will be a physical impossibility for us and our neighbours to get out of the Baltic.   The answer of England reached us yesterday, and I think it is perfect and just what we wanted; it seems to me that all we could ask of the King of England is not to take part for or against the operations that other Powers may attempt for the restoration of the French monarchy

There is one thing, however, that we must ask of England (and the King of Sweden has rights by which to do so)   it is that our fleets may winter in English ports; England exacted this of us at the beginning of this year (when she thought there would be a rupture between herself and Russia), by reason of an old treaty existing between Sweden and England.   The king refused it only for the Baltic ports, not for the ports of the North Sea, such as Gothenburg, Marstrand, Uddevalla, etc.; but the Russians have not the same claims. We must obtain this, and money, for what the empress gives is not sufficient, now that Spain will pay nothing at the present moment, the latter promises to send it when things reach the point of being able to act — but that point never comes for Spain.   Everything is going with abominable slowness, we are all ready to leave our ports by the end of this month, the Russians the same; but they don't want us to do so, my friend; I am more and more convinced of that. The princes were to send Baron d'Escars here, but he has not arrived.

I annex to this letter a project for the descent on Normandy, which the king desires me to send you. It is certain that if we could get there and operate, that would soon settle the existence of the National Assembly, for we should then find ourselves in the heart of France. I am now getting further information on this memorial; the descent, if made at a spot called the Fosse de Colleville, is very practicable; but it remains to be seen where our fleet can then stay, for the roadstead of La Hogue is not tenable during the winter months; for this reason we must obtain permission for the joint fleets of Sweden and Russia to winter in English ports, because it would be impossible to get them back to Sweden. All our sailors say that the entrance to the port of Ostend is impracticable in the autumn, and, to judge by the charts they show us, it must be so on account of the many sandbanks which form at the entrance of the harbour.

Return to me this memorial by the courier; the king is much bent on the execution of this plan. I think it very feasible as to the descent at Colleville, but we must have safe ports for fleets of some thirty or more ships of the line and frigates. By this plan we should be rid of the embarrassment of acting with the combined troops of several Powers, which always retards all operations, there would be none but ourselves and the Russians, and such of the French as would rally to us It would be best in every way, even for us, if this project could be carried out, it would cause us fewer embarrassments and less expense; for we should take with us on the ships what we needed in the first instance, and once on shore we could find means of subsistence, and even ports, later.

Count Fersen to the King of Sweden.

PRAGUE, September 14, 1791

I have Y. M.'s despatch of August 19. Yesterday the
emperor received an answer from Russia, which he communicated to me himself. The empress proposes to him a congress, the recall of ambassadors, a declaration in common to
the Assembly, and the cessation of all communication and
commerce with France. She informs him that a second
courier will bring him information as to the troops she
means to send and the steps she proposes to take   The emperor supposes from this that she is waiting to concert with
Y. M, and he will determine nothing until the arrival of that
courier. He is more decided than ever on the congress, and
all we can obtain from him is to have it supported by troops.
He seemed to me to feel the necessity of that. He told me
yesterday that orders were about to be given to march two
regiments of cavalry and some battalions of infantry into
the Brisgau, and that the requisitions were ready to be
sent.

M de Mercy has been to England and brought back the
assurance of the perfect neutrality of that Court.

If, after all this, the emperor takes no steps, I shall feel
sure that he is only seeking to gain time and so prevent the
Northern Powers from sending troops this year, in that
case I shall send him, before his departure from here which
is fixed for the 20th of this month, a note demanding a positive answer.   It will be useless for me to prolong my stay
any longer, the emperor not intending to return to Vienna
till October 23   From what he *says to me* I ought to believe that he is determined to act, and feels how important
it is, even for his Low Countries, that the Swedish and Russian troops should arrive ; but there is a wide difference be-

tween words and actions I gave him on the 9th a rather
detailed memorial on what I thought necessary to be done
at this moment. I insisted on the utility and necessity of
the immediate arrival of the Swedish troops. We shall see
what that will produce. . . . It will be useless to negotiate
with the other princes of Germany; they will consent to
nothing without the advice of the emperor, and he, having
declared himself head of the league, will lend himself to no
foreign negotiation with them. The subordinates here all
assure me that he will do nothing, and I know that that is
their advice to him ; I fear their influence much.

Count Fersen to Baron Taube.

PRAGUE, September 21, 1791

The king's courier arrived last night, and I received your
letter, my dear friend. I do not think it is solely from aversion or jealousy that the emperor delays and drags along the
operations ; I think him personally inclined to act; but his
ministry holds him back and he has not force enough to
resist it. I think their plan is all made : they want to await
an answer from England which they have asked for through
the King of Prussia; they want to form an army of the
Cercles [German States]; they want to wait and see what
answer the King of France gives touching the Constitution, and then consult anew all the Courts to learn what
they think; *then*, if the king is at liberty after that, they
will propose a congress at Aix-la-Chapelle; but I doubt if
they will permit columns of troops to support it, or that
they mean to do anything before the spring.

The king will show you the memorial which I have given
to the emperor. It was written solely to induce him to agree
to this step [the arrival of Swedish and Russian troops];
but what I say in it about the proper method of interference

11

in the affairs of France is, I think, the only way, namely: not to enter into any question of government, but to demand, solely, that the king be set at liberty either at the Hermitage or at Montmédy.   By this method we should avoid all the delays into which discussion of governmental details would lead the congress, and it would destroy the argument which the Vienna ministry has already used to me, namely: that *if the King of France sanctions the Constitution freely, he will be shown to be master in his own kingdom and the Powers can interfere no further.*   That is incontestable; but the king must be really free, not apparently so.   That is the one thing to insist upon, and it simplifies matters very much. . . .

I am seeking a means of correspondence with the King of France to inform him of all that is going on, and induce him to make requests to the emperor and our master, which would be very useful.   Perhaps the position of the king and queen (of which I have no knowledge at this moment) may make them desire the project of our master and the empress. I will get information as to this, and if it be so, my God, what happiness!   I will send you a courier at once, and the landing could be made effectually.   It seems to me a good scheme, but the important, indeed the absolutely necessary point is that the ships may have a safe roadstead in order to have a sure retreat in case of disaster, and that this roadstead should be susceptible of defence to prevent the vessels from being insulted, or burned.   For this reason I should prefer the roadstead of La Hogue, in spite of its distance from Caen; it can be defended; whereas that of the Fosse de Colleville is open and the fleet would be exposed   The idea of disembarking the troops there and then sending the ships to La Hogue seems to me hazardous, the fleet might have contrary winds, and part of the troops must be left on board to seize the forts which defend the entrance to La Hogue.

However, the navy can best judge of these operations; I do not know the coast.

But, in any case, an enterprise of this kind can only be part of a general plan concerted with the emperor. All partial advance would involve great danger to whoever undertook it, and would only expose the king and queen so long as they are in Paris. By all that I have told you, my friend, you will see that I could be more useful in Brussels than in Vienna for it seems to me clear from all that I am told that the strongest impulsion comes from the Comte de Mercy and the archduchess [Marie Antoinette's sister, governor of the Low Countries]. I know that to them is communicated all that happens, every thing is passed upon by them, it is therefore on them that we should act, and if there I should be better able to keep the king informed as to what is happening and what are the intentions of the King of France. . . .

You are very right in all you say of the Comte d'Artois, . . his visit to Vienna has done more harm than good; all vehement action checks the emperor and his ministry still more, and the consequence is that the former has decided to act without the princes, he fears the intrigues of those who surround them, and he is confirmed in this idea by letters from M. de Mercy, and letters from the queen written before the attempt to leave Paris, and one which he received through M. de Mercy since the arrest, in which she asks that the Powers will act without the princes; she fears their reckless behaviour; she fears to find herself dependent upon them, if it is through them that matters change, she fears, and with reason, that their proceedings will only irritate the factious without alarming them, whereas those of the foreign Powers will terrify them. The emperor has therefore decided to act without the princes in concert with the other Powers; we must, however, induce the king to keep on good terms with the princes, for that may be useful to him, but not to bring them forward in any negotiations with the other Courts, especially that of the emperor.   Make any use of this that you think proper, without compromising any one.   We must also induce the king to make no partial advance without the consent of the King of France, or else in concert with the other Powers; the danger would be too great for him, and even for the King of France. . . .

I leave on the 28th for Brussels, where I hope to open a correspondence with the King of France to find out what he wants and if we can concert something with him in which our master and Russia can take the leading part, but, as I could from there give ideas to the king's ministers at the different Courts, I must have the cipher, for with the one I have I cannot communicate with Vienna   If the king desires this, send me the cipher at the earliest moment.

Adieu, my dear friend; God preserve you; love always the most tender and most sincere of your friends.

Queen Marie-Antoinette to Count Fersen.

September 26, 1791

Your letter of the 28th has reached me.   For two months I have had no news of you; no one could tell me where you were.   I was on the point, if I had known her address, of writing to Sophie [his sister, mistress of the robes to the Queen of Sweden] . . . [*seven lines missing*[1]] we are here in a new position since the king's acceptance [of the Constitution], to refuse it would have been nobler, but that was impossible under the circumstances in which we are.   I could have wished that the acceptance were simple and

---

[1] The queen's letters are nearly all in cipher, or in "white ink" mingled with plain writing, and various undecipherable or missing passages occur. — TR.

shorter, but that is the misfortune of being surrounded by villains ; indeed, I assure you it was the least bad project they presented.   You can judge of this some day, for I have kept for you all that ex . . . [*two lines missing*] there, which I had the good fortune to find, as there are papers in it belonging to you.   The follies of the princes and the *émigrés* have forced us to this step.   It was essential, in accepting, to remove all doubt of its being sincere.   I believe that the best way to sicken every one of all this is to seem to be in it wholly ; that will soon show that nothing can go on.

In spite of the letter that my brothers have written to the king (and which, by the way, did not at all have the effect here which they expected) I do not see, especially in the declaration of Pillnitz, that foreign help is very prompt. That may, perhaps, be fortunate, for the farther we advance the more these wretches will feel their misfortunes, perhaps they will even come to desire the help of foreigners themselves.   I fear that rash heads may lead your king to do something which may compromise him, and us with him. Much wisdom is needed   I shall write to M. de Mercy.

As soon as you are in Brussels, let me know ; I will write to you simply ; for I have a sure means always at my orders. You could never imagine how much all that I do in these days costs me ; and yet, this vile race of men, who say they are attached to us and to whom we have never done harm, are furious at this moment ; it seems as though one must have a base soul to do with satisfaction that to which one is forced, and it is their . . . and their conduct which has dragged us into the position in which we now are.   I have had but one happiness, that of seeing once more the gentlemen who were imprisoned for us, — especially M. Goguelat ; he is perfectly reasonable and his head has become balanced during his imprisonment.

Count Fersen to Queen Marie-Antoinette

BRUSSELS, October 10, 1791.

I am here again.

[*Four lines missing.*]

I pity you for having been forced to sanction [the Constitution]; but I feel your position, it is dreadful, and you could take no other course   I have at least the consolation of knowing that other reasonable persons are of the same opinion.   But what are you going to do?   Is all hope lost?   If any remains, do not allow yourself to be disheartened, if you desire to be aided, I hope that you can be, but for that we must know your desires and your plans, in order to moderate or excite the good-will and efforts of the King of Sweden and the other Powers; for, in any case, the princes must be only auxiliaries.

The Empress of Russia and the kings of Prussia, Naples, Sardinia, and Spain are very satisfactory, especially the first three, Sweden will sacrifice herself for you   England assures us of her neutrality.   The emperor is the least willing· he is weak and indiscreet, he promises all, but his ministry, which fears to compromise itself and wants to avoid interference, holds him back.   Hence the contradiction which you notice between his letters and his acts.   I was sent to him by the king with full and unlimited powers, to propose and consent to whatever might serve you.   I have been unable to do anything except prevent a few foolish acts of the princes and persuade him to have nothing to do with them. I made him a detailed memorial in which I proposed to him to recall the ambassadors and have them meet in congress, to insist on nothing except your liberty in the terms of the Pillnitz declaration; to exact, as a proof of your liberty, that you shall go to the Hermitage or to Montmédy, and call the body-guard and whatever troops you wish around you; to advance columns of troops on all sides toward the frontiers; to demand them from Sweden and Russia and allow their troops to land at Ostend. I asked the emperor to make this demand at once, inasmuch as the other Powers have all said that they would do what he did. He was of my opinion about everything; but nothing has been done, all has been allowed to go on until now you have been forced to sanction the Constitution. But if you have any project, we can push it by the other Powers, and as I am charged by the king [of Sweden] to correspond with all his ministers, I will guide myself in doing so by what you will write to me.

Here are certain questions to which it is necessary to reply, but to save length I keep the numbers and you can mark your answers 1, 2, 3 : —

1. Do you intend to put yourselves sincerely into the revolution, and do you think that there is no other means?

2. Do you wish to be aided, or do you wish us to cease all negotiations with the Courts?

3 Have you a plan, and what is it?

Pardon these questions; I flatter myself that you will see in them only the desire to serve you with boundless devotion.

October 12.

M. de Mercy has just communicated to me your letter and I write in consequence He was against the congress until now, but I have decided him to support it in Vienna by proving to him that some ostensible step must be taken to check the princes and the assemblage whom they have collected about them; it is alarming. The affair of Avignon is a good pretext for a congress, and I intend to write to the ministry of the King of Spain asking them to induce the pope to call for an intervention of the Powers. You must

urge the emperor to form the congress, or, at least, to announce it at once, indicating the place and naming the members.   Exaggerate your fears about the princes and say that
this announcement will calm them.   Insist that the congress
be supported by a demonstration of armed force.

Comte Fersen to Queen Marie-Antoinette.

October 13, 1791

I have nothing to add to my letter of yesterday.   Continue to insist with the emperor and urge him; ask him to
tell you frankly whether he intends to do what you request
of him; I will try to have him urged by the other Courts.
Do not let your heart go out to those madmen; they are
scoundrels, who will never do anything for you; you must
distrust them, and use them.

I have confided to the Chevalier de Coigny a part of my
negotiations; I know no other fault in him than that of liking Calonne.   I have had no time to decipher more than the
beginning of your letter.   It is the fear of compromising us
which has kept me from writing to you.   I am just now
overwhelmed with writing.   I cannot return to Sweden because I am charged with the king's correspondence   The
rest of this cipher means nothing, it is only to fill up the
paper.

Queen Marie-Antoinette to Count Fersen

October 19, 1791.

It is impossible to bring out M. de Breteuil's writing on
the papers with the liquid that the Chevalier de Coigny has
brought us.   Send me word at once, by post, the right way
to use the liquid and of what it is made, because if this is
bad we must get some more made.

I have written to M. de Mercy to urge the congress, I
told him to communicate my letter to you, therefore I will

enter into no details about that matter here. I have seen M. de Moustier, who also desires the congress. He has even given me some ideas for the basis of it which I think reasonable He refuses the ministry, and I advised him to do so. He is a man to preserve for better times; and he might be lost.

Reassure yourself, I shall not let myself go to these madmen, and if I see them, or have any relations with some of them, it is only to make use of them; they inspire me with too great a horror ever to let myself go to them They intend, I believe, to put the Comte de Ségur in M. de Moustier's place. I wish he would take it; he knows how to speak, and that is all we need at this moment when we cannot have ministers who are good for us, and it may ruin him; there would be no harm in that.

The body-guards make us very anxious, it is certain that they will be entirely lost for us by forming them into a corps, as is now being done; I am assured by these madmen themselves that nothing will be more easy than to bring them back later; but there certainly is an air of intending to do something down there [là-bas], and then it would be impossible. I have written of this, and so has the king, to his brothers by the *senaubr* [?], to see if there is no way of doing something to prevent it The point is not to unite them into a corps, and, if nothing is done this winter, to send some of them back here We must not, however, urge their return, because we have a project very much like that of the month of June, it is not yet fully determined, I will let you know about it in eight or ten days, if it takes place it will be from the 15th to the 20th of November. If we cannot go then we shall do nothing more this winter, but go on waiting for the congress, which I shall urge strongly.

I cannot tell you how touched I am, the king also, by

what that good M. Crawford is doing for us. I will write you in a few days what you must say to him from us. We should be very glad to be able to do anything for him. There are so few persons who show us true attachment! It is known here that he is concerned in our affairs, and I have had many fears about his house.

All is tranquil enough for the time being, apparently, but this tranquillity hangs by a thread, and the people are always as they were — ready to commit horrors. We are told they are for us, I do not believe it, certainly they are not for me. I know the value to set on all that; most of the time the people are paid, and they only like us as long as we do what they choose. It is impossible to go on much longer in this way; there is no more safety in Paris now than there was before [the acceptance of the Constitution], perhaps less, for they are now accustomed to see us degraded

You tell me nothing of your health   Mine is good . . [*two lines missing*]. Frenchmen are atrocious in every way, if those here get the advantage and we have to live on among them, we must take great care that they shall have nothing to reproach us with; but we must also remember that if those now without [the *émigrés*] should ever again become masters we must do nothing to displease them . . . [*five lines missing*]

Baron Taube to Count Fersen.

STOCKHOLM, Oct. 21, 1791

The treaty of alliance [between Sweden and Russia] was signed yesterday   The empress gives the king 12,000 infantry and 4000 Cossacks and hussars, and 12 ships of the line. What I am to tell you now, my friend, is of the greatest secrecy, and you will see how necessary it is that I shall not be compromised. The king has just received an extremely friendly letter from the empress, with copies of one she has written to the emperor and of one she has received from the princes. In her letter to the king she says she perseveres in her idea of contributing with all her power to the overthrow of the new Constitution in France, in spite of its acceptance by the king of France, which should be regarded as forced and null; if, however, the King and Queen of France accepted it in good faith, so much the worse for them, and in that case the King of France must be regarded as *non ens* You can judge what advantage can be drawn from the opposition of a person who thinks as strongly as she does.

To the emperor she says : " We must assist the princes efficaciously and begin operations without delay." You see from that how necessary it is that the King of France should himself write to the empress and tell her of his affairs and his designs, — to her directly, or to her through the king [of Sweden], to whom she seems to give herself up with the utmost confidence

As for the affairs of France, here is what the princes say in their letter to the empress . " The spirit of delay which is conducting the cabinets of Vienna and Madrid, the bad faith of the latter, which we have good reason to believe is sold to our enemies, the intrigues of the Baron de Breteuil (for it is time to name him to Your Majesty), who prefers to upset everything rather than see any projects succeed but those he conceives himself," etc., etc. You can tell all this to M. de Breteuil, without naming me , I rely, my dear friend, on your regard and discretion. Advise the baron to keep up a steady correspondence with the king [of Sweden] . the king has a great esteem for him and has loved him from childhood. Try, in God's name, that the king may have money so that he may be in a position to rule all the others , for if he does not begin this affair, the other Powers will never do anything.

Count Fersen to Queen Marie-Antoinette.

October 25, 1791.

Continue to urge the emperor for this congress; without a very decided and prompt step in that direction, I fear all from the folly of the princes and the *émigrés;* they are much excited, and if they think themselves abandoned I will not answer for what they may do. I have written to the ministers of my king at all the Courts, telling them to urge the emperor on this point, he needs to be pushed, or he will do nothing. Do not fear any rash advance on the part of my king; I can stop that. His conduct in your affairs deserves your gratitude, if all had behaved like him you would not now be in your present state.

Stael says horrors of me; he has even bribed my coachman and taken him into his service, which pains me. He has prejudiced against me many persons who now blame my conduct and say that I act from ambition only, and that I have ruined you and the king. The Spanish ambassador and others are of that opinion. They are right: I have had ambition — to serve you, and all my life I shall regret that I did not succeed; I wanted to return to you a part of the obligations it has been so sweet to me to owe you, and I wanted to show others that one can be attached to persons like you without any selfish interests The rest of my conduct might have proved to them that *there* was my sole ambition, and that the glory of having served you was my dearest reward

My horses have arrived [those with which he drove the royal family to Bondy]. I know that you have seen the wife of my valet. How kind! but I ought to be accustomed to that. They say here that you prefer to remain as you are, and to make use of the princes, that is very proper, but take care; it must not be said openly, or it will be dangerous for you.

My father wants me to return to Sweden, but I hope to bring him round to my ideas; it is chiefly the matter of money which alarms him. Tell me what you wish me to do with that I sent for you to Holland. Am I to invest it, or leave it on deposit where it is? M de Bouillé, though I told him to remit to me what remained of the million, had the weakness to give it to the princes; it was seven hundred thousand francs, which would have been very useful to you to have. If the princes can be restrained the present vast emigration may not be an evil for you; it may serve to enlighten the people and bring them back through want and poverty.

Count Fersen to Queen Marie-Antoinette.

October 29, 1791.

I have received perfect letters from Sweden. The king urges the empress strongly, and she is very well inclined. She desires an interview with him, which is to take place as soon as the frontiers are settled. It is important that your letter should reach her before this interview; it would have a good effect. I have already told the king what you desire should be done, and I will repeat it to him again. Baron Taube has come round to my idea for the congress, and I am sure that the king will urge it. The departure of the ministers and ambassadors should be on leave of absence, and this should take place as soon as possible; but it is necessary to insist to the emperor that a demonstration of armed force be made to support the congress; or, at least, that preparations be made to march the troops, without which the congress will not have the power or the consideration it ought to have. The emperor, Spain, and the King of Sardinia could give orders to hold their troops ready to march. The King of Prussia could order his in Wesel to prepare their war equipment and hold themselves ready : Sweden and Russia the same. Insist on this to the emperor. I shall write the same everywhere   Disunion is in the councils at Coblentz [among the princes and *émigrés*]; the Bishop of Arras has departed.   They are weary of Maréchal de Broglie Calonne and Jaucourt have quarrelled, the first will not remain if the other does; they even say that he is going back to England   M. de Castries is here; he inclines to go to Coblentz, but he is very reasonable and wants to induce M. de Breteuil to go with him, which he will not do; but I hope Castries will put him into relation with the princes sufficiently to prevent their follies.   Even the two princes [d'Artois and Condé] have quarrelled, and I hope there will be nothing to fear from them   We must, nevertheless, make use of that scarecrow to urge the emperor, who needs it, or he will do nothing.   If the *émigrés* return just now it will be a great misfortune, but they had far better never have come out; as they are here, however, their return would be a great triumph for the madmen, and you would lose much of your power to control the latter   I therefore think it best to have an air of wishing the return of the *émigrés* but do nothing to promote it; it is only necessary to restrain them; and the congress will do that

Whenever you receive blank paper or a book with blank leaves or engravings it will be written upon in white ink; when the date is at the bottom of the letters, the same.

CHAPTER VII.

1791. The same continued. — Efforts to obtain a Congress — Memorial of
Count Fersen to the Queen, explaining the political Situation of the
Powers and advising a Course of Action for the King and Queen of
France

Queen Marie-Antoinette to Count Fersen

October 31, 1791.

I received your papers by M. de Brige yesterday; the
writing came out perfectly with the liquid which I obtained
from the apothecary. The kind sent to us from down there
[*là-bas*] must have evaporated, but that is no matter now.
I shall try to answer all in brief, and I will do so as often as
I have time up to Thursday, when the man who takes charge
of this letter will start.

I was so hurried the last time I wrote to you that I could
not speak of M. Crawford. Tell him that we know the perfect way in which he has acted for us ; that I have always
taken pleasure in thinking of his attachment, but that now,
in the dreadful position in which we are, every new proof of
interest is a claim the more, and very sweet, upon our gratitude. — *Monsieur's* letter to the baron [de Breteuil] surprised
and shocked us ; but we must have patience and not show
too much anger at this moment ; I shall, however, copy it
and show it to my sister. I am curious to know how she will
justify it in the midst of all that is happening. Our interior
is a hell ; with the best intentions in the world there is no saying anything. My sister is so indiscreet, and so surrounded by
intriguers, and above all so ruled by her brothers from without, that there is no way for us to talk to one another, or we
should quarrel all the time. I see that the ambition of the

persons who surround *Monsieur* will ruin him entirely, he believed, at the first moment, that he was everything, but do what he will, he never can play a rôle; his brother [the king] will always have the confidence of others and the advantage over him in all cases, from the constancy and invariability of his conduct.

It is very unfortunate that *Monsieur* did not return at once when we were arrested, he would then have followed the course he had always announced, — that of never quitting us; and he would then have spared us much pain and trouble which may perhaps result in a formal summons [*sommation*] which we shall be forced to issue for his return, to which we feel, especially if made in that manner, he could not consent.

We groan at the number of *émigrés;* we feel the injury, as much for the interior of the kingdom as for the princes themselves. What is dreadful is the manner in which these worthy persons are deceived and have been deceived, so that soon nothing will remain to them but anger and despair. Those who have had enough confidence in us to consult us have remained, or, at least, if they thought it for their honour to go, they have heard the truth from us. But what good was that? the tone and mania are not to do our will; to say that we are not free (which is very true); that consequently we cannot speak our real thoughts, and that the reverse of what we say should be done. This has been the fate of the memorial sent by us to my brothers, which you saw and approved. The answer came that we were forced to write that memorial, that such could not be our sentiments, and that consequently they would take no account of it; and then they beg us to have confidence and speak to them frankly; which is really saying · "Do our will and then we will serve you, but not otherwise."

As it is possible, however, that they may at this moment

be committing follies which would ruin all, I think we ought to stop them at any cost; and as I hope — from what your documents say and from the letter of M. de Mercy — that the congress will really take place, I think we ought to send them from here some safe person who would show them [the princes] the danger and the extravagance of their scheme, and also show them our true position and our desires, and make them see that the only course for us to follow at this moment is to gain the confidence of the people here, that that is useful, necessary even, to any project whatever; for all should go on together, and the Powers not being able to come to the help of France with great forces during the winter, nothing but a congress can rally and unite the means that may be possible in the spring. But, in making this confidence [to the princes] we must beware of their extreme indiscretion; for that reason, we can say to the person who goes from here only that which we want to make openly known *là-bas.*

M Grimm has arrived here. He wished to see me, but I answered that it was impossible for me to receive him, and that is true in a certain way; I am too closely watched. But I have had him told my reasons by a person who, at the same time, will tell him in suitable terms of our feelings for the empress [of Russia] It is very important that we should succeed in making her adopt the idea of a congress; by her character she can bring all the Powers to decide upon it, and she can also restrain the princes I fear only the levity of M. de Calonne and the petulance of M. de Nassau

There is nothing to be gained from this Assembly; it is a crowd of scoundrels, madmen, and fools; the few who want order and less evil than the rest are not listened to, or dare not speak. It is in the mud, among the populace even, that the Assembly tries in every way to create excitement, but that succeeds no longer. Nothing but the dearness of bread occupies their minds, and the decrees The journals do not even speak of it [excitement]; in this there is a great change, very visible in Paris, where the great majority, not knowing whether they want this régime or another, is weary of troubles and does want tranquillity I speak of Paris only; for I think the provincial cities are worse at this moment; and yet from Coblentz they never cease to tell us that they have great good understandings throughout the kingdom, but the affair at Lyon makes us cautious and little credulous on such assurances. The King of Sweden, in sending back to the king his letter notifying his acceptance [of the Constitution] without reading it, did a thing which I wish had been done by all the other Powers, but done alone, I fear there was imprudence in the step. Nevertheless, it is impossible to be more touched than we are by the frankness, the loyalty, the nobleness of his conduct to us, and I hope that some day we may at last benefit by all that he is good enough to do for us.

I have just read two despatches from Spain, one of October 13th, the other of the 20th. They are very well, and I think that Spain will make no difficulty about the congress The idea of it is even a part of her own plan; but she wants that the king be free and able to go where he pleases *beforehand* That idea is impossible; for they will always say here that he is now the master of going where he pleases; but in point of fact he cannot do so, for besides the danger of getting out of Paris (where he might be obliged to leave his wife and son), his personal safety would be no greater in other places. for there is not a town, and no troops, on which he can rely. It seems to me, on the contrary, that it is only in seeking to win daily more confidence and popularity here that we can

succeed, after the congress is opened, in joining it, or at least
in going to the frontier, to be in some sort charged with the
interests of this country. If we could gain that point, it
would be all, and that is the object for which we ought to
aim, for that, all our daily actions should combine to inspire
confidence. The misfortune is that we are not seconded
here by any one, and, no matter what efforts I make, I cannot
alone do all I wish and feel so necessary for the general good.

Spain has still another idea, but I think that detestable:
it is to have the princes return, accompanied by all the
French, supported only by the King of Sweden as our ally,
and announce by manifesto that they do not come to make
war, but to rally all good Frenchmen to their side and declare
themselves protectors of true French liberty. The great
powers to furnish the necessary money for this operation,
and remain themselves outside with a sufficient number
of troops to awe, but do nothing; so that no pretext of
invasion or dismemberment could be made.

But all that is not practicable, and I think that if the
emperor would hasten to call the congress, *that* is the only
useful and suitable manner to make an end of it all I do
not understand why you wish the Powers to withdraw their
ministers and ambassadors at once. It seems to me that,
this congress being supposed, at least at first, to be called as
much for affairs that concern all the Powers of Europe as
for those of France, there is no reason for this sudden
recall. And besides, is it sure that all the Powers would act
alike? and do you not think that England, Holland led by
England, and Prussia, in order to outwit the others, will
leave their ministers? Then there would be disunion in the
opinions of Europe, which could only injure our affairs I
may be mistaken, but I think that nothing but great harmony,
at least in appearance, can impose respect here. Distrust

Denmark; from the despatches she seems detestable, especially towards Russia and Sweden

I must have expressed myself ill about the body-guard, our intention was not to recall them, but to prevent their being formed into a corps, and, if nothing were done this winter, that the officers, or the richest among them, should return here to show themselves. The same thing exists for the *émigrés;* I know perfectly well that, once out of the country, and in such a manner, their return is impossible; but this is a great misfortune, greater even for the rest of France than for Paris, for the provinces are now delivered over entirely to themselves, or to a horde of scoundrels and factious persons. In the position in which we are, with the horrible mistrust they are always trying to excite against us, it is impossible that we should not do publicly all that is necessary to bring back every one. The decree of the parliament proposed at the council of the princes was crazy; I am not astonished that it was rejected. It seems to me that the best heads in that of Paris would reject such extravagance, and not desire to leave their place here.

I understand very well all that concerns the cipher, but you must always put two full stops when two words end at the same time and leave the *j* and *v ;* that will facilitate things for us. We have read very easily all that was in white; but in future the king will dispense with ceremony, it will be easier to say "you" only I also desire that the bishop, or some one with legible writing, shall write these letters, and not you, who are already worn out with writing You must, by the next safe opportunity, send us word how much money we have outside, at Brussels and in Holland, and the name of the bankers. Send me word also what we owe to Mme. de Korff, and how and when we can pay it.

As Maréchal de Castries is right-minded, the baron [de

Breteuil] might agree with him as to our interests and our ideas, so that he could go to Coblentz and speak in our name to our brothers. We will try to find some one to send to him from us with the authorization. I should like it to be the Baron de Viomesnil, but I do not know if he would be willing.

November 7.

I hope that this letter can go to-morrow. It ought to have gone the 3d, but the person was delayed by his affairs, and I preferred to wait, to be sure it was safely delivered This person, who starts to-morrow morning, returns soon I think the opportunity is safe.

Is it true that the King of Sweden has sent a minister to the princes at Coblentz? I am much afraid they will force the king here to write a letter to the King of Sweden with his own hand on present affairs; if that happens, it will be only another proof of his non-liberty. No ministry yet Mme. de Staël is bustling much for M. de Narbonne. I have never seen a stronger or more intricate intrigue.[1]

The answer of the emperor to the acceptance contains, they say (I have not yet seen it), a very good phrase, which may prepare the way for the congress, provided he keeps to it, and makes haste to announce it, for in spite of the appar-

---

[1] The Russian ambassador in Paris, M Simolin, writes of this appointment thus "No one in society has a more brilliant mind than this new candidate; he spent his youth with men of letters, whom he surpassed in the piquancy and wit of his poems He had a stormy youth, and Madame Adélaïde covered his follies several times with great liberalities Mme de Stael, the Swedish ambassadress, long possessed M de Narbonne's heart, she quitted him two years ago for the Bishop of Autun, his best friend M de Narbonne, audacious in character, and ambitious on principle, will certainly not fail to upset everything in the department they are going to confide to him; all the legations, the embassies, the bureaux will be made over new, and his ministry may perhaps prove an epoch of extraordinary changes in French politics" (Letter of M de Simolin to Mme. de Sullivan November 4, 1791) — Tr

ent quiet at Coblentz, heads are much excited and it is to be feared that the princes cannot control them much longer. I must give my letter to-morrow morning, so I must finish it. Adieu.

My sister has shown me a letter from *Monsieur*, dated from Brussels, to justify the one that he wrote to the king, in which he says that you had announced to him that the king wished to charge him with everything during his imprisonment   I warn you of this in case the same thing should be said where you are, as for us, we know very well all about it.   Adieu.

Queen Marie-Antoinette to Count Fersen.

November 7, 1791.

Be perfectly easy; never will I let myself go to these madmen, we must use them to prevent great evils, but as for good, I know very well they are not capable of it   Adieu; I am tired out with writing; never have I done such work, and I am always afraid of forgetting, or of putting in stupidities [*line missing*]. . . . I see that all the aristocrats and democrats are rabid against the Baron de Breteuil, I am uneasy at seeing you with him   It is to Coblentz and the *émigrés* that we owe this cruel persecution, they have said so much about our acting solely by the baron's advice, declaring that he has all our secrets, that the ministry and the madmen here are beginning to talk of it.

Count Fersen to Queen Marie-Antoinette.

November 11, 1791

The bishop [of Pamiers] goes to Paris.   I will send you by him a long detail of your position and of what I imagine there is to do.   It is very necessary that you should write to Spain and Russia to claim their help, and convince them that you do not abandon yourself wholly to the Constitution Your letter to Russia can go through Simolin, that to Spain by Breteuil. One word to Sweden would be well, and I will send it By this means, you will prevent those Powers from letting themselves go to the princes when they see that you wish to act for yourselves It would be well to speak of the congress which you have asked the emperor to call, and tell them that you will explain more in detail your projects, in which you hope they will concur.

Send me word if you have sufficient confidence in M. de Laporte for the bishop to send letters by him as if they were from the baron

I cannot sufficiently tell you how important it is that you should write as soon as possible to Sweden and Russia confidentially, to prevent them from giving themselves over to the princes under the conviction that you will never do anything. This first letter to the king would be only to say that you hope for the friendship and interest he has already testified for you, which you trust he will continue to testify, that your position requires the greatest caution, but that you will shortly let him know with confidence what your plans are, and that, knowing his noble and generous way of thinking, you do not doubt he will second them with all his power, and employ his influence with the empress to decide her in your favour, and with the princes to prevent them from committing any rash act which might thwart your plans. Your letter to the empress could be the same, flattering her a little. In this way they can be made very useful to you. Before writing the other letters wait until the Bishop of Pamiers brings you the memorial. I am writing of your position outside of France, you can then judge better what there is to do, and of the plan of conduct

which I shall propose to you.   Never write to me through
M. de Mercy; he can decipher all your letters.

Staël has just received a furlough of three months, with
orders to leave Paris immediately.

Do not forget to tell me to say something amiable from
you and from the king to M. Crawford, he deserves it so
much !

Queen Marie-Antoinette to Count Fersen.

November 25, 1791

I await the bishop with much impatience.   Here is a note
for the Baron de Breteuil; it is an extract from a long
memorial the king has written to render account to himself
of all that he has done in these days.   The paper is very well
written, but besides having arguments in it which are not
necessary, it is much too long to put into cipher.

Our position at this moment is terrible, the factious are
ceaselessly at work, the people are ready at any moment to
rise and commit horrors, the republicans employ all means
to excite them.   I believe, nevertheless, that if we are wise,
we can gain much, and sooner than we think, from this very
excess of evil; but great prudence is needful.   Without
foreign help we can do nothing [*six lines missing*], . . . but
the paper I mentioned will go to-morrow, by another opportunity, I prefer that, being afraid to make too thick a packet;
inside you will find two letters in white ink, one for Spain,
the other for Sweden, we do not dare write otherwise.   You
must bring out the writing; the baron can take charge of the
one for Spain.   If you think them bad, burn them and let me
know; also let me know what we ought to write.   The word
of the cipher is *cause*; I do not know if it is in all its letters,
for I was obliged to get some one to write it   There is nothing for you in it, so Breteuil can decipher it.   M. de Staël

has not gone.   He comes every day to Court.   Adieu; it is nearly two o'clock.

Annexed to the foregoing.

Extract from the memorial of King Louis XVI

All policy should be reduced to setting aside the ideas of invasion which the *émigrés* may perhaps undertake alone; it would be a great misfortune for France if the interests of the *émigrés* were put forward on the first line, and if they had the assistance of only a few Powers   Who can say that others, like England, would not furnish, secretly at least, aid to the other side, and take advantage of the unhappy state of France, which is rending itself to pieces.

The *émigrés* must be convinced that they can do no good between now and the spring, that their interests as well as ours demand that they shall cease to cause uneasiness.   We feel that if they think themselves abandoned they will rush into excesses that ought to be avoided; we must therefore give hopes to some of them for next spring, and provide for the wants of the others.

A congress would attain the desired end; it might contain *émigrés*, and alarm the factious   The Powers should agree together on the language to hold to all parties.   A combined action among them could only redound, not be injurious, to the interests of the king — besides their personal interests.   Occasions may arise when these interventions would be necessary; if, for instance, an attempt were made to establish a republic on the ruins of the monarchy. Neither is it possible that they should see without uneasiness *Monsieur* and the Comte d'Artois not returning [to France], and the Duc d'Orléans the nearest to the throne: what subjects for reflection!

The firm and uniform language of all the Powers of

Europe, supported by a formidable army, would have most fortunate results, it would temper the ardour of the *émigrés*, whose rôle would then become secondary, the factious would be disconcerted, and courage would revive among good citizens, friends of order and of the monarchy.

These ideas are for the future and for the present. The Powers have many reasons for wishing to have an understanding with each other, these reasons are given in the memorial sent six weeks ago to M de Mercy.

The king cannot, and will not retract of himself what has been done, the majority of the nation must desire him to do so, or he must be forced to it by circumstances; in this case, he must acquire confidence and popularity by acting in accordance with the spirit of the Constitution By causing it to be executed literally its vices will be recognized, and, especially, the anxiety caused by the *émigrés* will be removed. If they make an irruption without an overwhelming force France and the king will be destroyed. The Baron de Viomesnil, who has been spoken to on this subject, can develop the general ideas contained in this memorial.

Memorial of Count Fersen, written for Queen Marie-Antoinette.[1]

BRUSSELS, November 26, 1791

From all that I have written you of the slowness of the emperor and his want of active good-will for you, of which I am convinced by all that I saw myself in Vienna, and by the means that he never ceases to employ to paralyze the goodwill of the other Courts and prevent them from acting (of

[1] This memorial is very long and is shortened here, the parts omitted being indicated in the text It will be found in " Le Comte de Fersen et la Cour de France," vol i, pp 233-256. Firmin-Didot et Cie, Paris, 1878. — TR.

which I will some day give you positive proofs), I think it
necessary that you should adopt another plan of conduct;
but before proposing it I ought to give you a correct idea of
your position outside of France

The Powers which sincerely desire to help you, such as
Spain, Russia, Sweden, and, possibly, Prussia, see as yet in the
king's acceptance [of the Constitution] and in all his conduct
only weakness, above all, in his subsequent conduct, for
which they do not feel the necessity, even granting a necessity for the acceptance.   They fear that your intention is to
do nothing and continue to go on feebly, and always by the
Constitution; they feel the danger of that example, and, as
the restoration of the monarchy touches their own political
interests, they will ally themselves with the princes rather
than allow so monstrous a government to be established in
France.

The other Powers, such as the Empire, Holland, and England, to whom the debasement of France may be of some
advantage, will seek under different pretexts to prevent the
effect of the good dispositions of the others, but without
declaring themselves.   It is useful to them that disorder and
anarchy should continue, and that the kingdom should thus
become weaker without their seeming to have any hand in it,
and without its costing them anything

The King of Spain is very well-disposed; all his interests
unite to come to the help of the king, and the assurances
that he gives are positive.   The emperor alone chooses to
doubt them. . . .   The conduct of the King of Spain at this
moment, and the assurance which, I am informed, he has
given to Vienna, that he will never recognize the king's
acceptance, will show you that you cannot doubt his good
intentions.   It will suffice if you direct them, and make them
concur to a common end concerted with you.   The Kings of

Sardinia and Naples will follow the lead of Spain. I have
positive assurances of the favourable way of thinking of the
King of Poland, but, whatever be his good-will, his political
position does not allow him to act in any way.

After what took place at the interview at Pillnitz, and
after all that M. de Bischofswerder told me in Vienna and
has never ceased repeating to the emperor in the most earnest
manner, namely, that his master [the King of Prussia] was
all ready to act in your favour, that 50,000 men were prepared to march at the first requisition, on condition that the
emperor did the same; that he would act in harmony with
him in all the steps he might indicate, and that the treaty
just signed between them would assure the emperor of his
intentions, and finally, after what the King of Prussia himself sent you word by M. de Moustier, we certainly ought
to count upon him; at any rate enough not to fear that he
will be against you, or that he would oppose what the other
Powers may try to do in your favour. . . .

The inclinations of the Empress of Russia are not equivocal; they are even too pronounced, and might be dangerous
if influenced by others than yourself, and unless you can
bring them to concur in a plan of operations formed by you
and concerted with her   The two millions she has given to
the princes, the letter of authorization which she gave Count
Romanzoff to treat with them (for it was not a letter accrediting him, merely a simple cabinet letter letting them
know they could rely on what he said to them from her),—
all this proves the desire that she feels to help you, but not
being in any way informed of your projects, she takes the one
means that seems to her proper, and the only one that remains
to her. The emperor's slowness has inspired her with distrust as to his desire to serve you. . . . The warmth she
puts into succouring you is extreme; it is only necessary to

temper it a little and show her the ways and means of serving you.   For that, you should write to her, claim her assistance, let her know your plans and concert them with her.

You have long known the friendly dispositions of the King of Sweden and the ardour that he puts into serving you But his spirit is eager and restless and needs to be calmed; it is solely occupied with the means of succouring you, and nothing will seem to him too costly to reach that end.   You know the sacrifices that he made for it in his treaty with the empress, and all his actions tend to that object.   Here are some quotations from his letters: " Rumours are flying about as to the sentiments of the Court [of France] towards the princes, which are very unjust to them and very injurious to the common interests, so that I cannot believe those tales, give me weapons with which to defend that Court, especially to the empress, on whose mind I fear these things may make a fatal impression   If every one would only believe me, we should not wait till spring to act; it is merely, as I think, giving time to the factious to strengthen themselves."   And he ends by thus speaking of the king: " Even if he abandons the rights of his son, of his family, of his equals, I shall not abandon them; I shall use the same ardour in serving his brothers that I have been ready to use in his service, and I share this feeling with the Empress of Russia "

The King of Sweden cannot conceive the reasons which prevent you from trusting to the good-will of the princes, he needs, in order to feel that necessity, a closer and more detailed knowledge of your position than he has.   It is to give it to him, and convince him of the necessity of your conduct, that we are bending all our energies; but a friendly and confidential communication of your situation and your projects would have the desired effect; it would bring him

back to calmer ideas; it would keep him from acting with
the princes and induce him to concert with you; and in that
position his zeal and that of the Empress of Russia would be
very useful to you   You could even use the influence he has
on the princes to guide their conduct, through him, without
their suspecting it, and to make their actions tend to a common end concerted with the other Powers.   Denmark can
have no other will than that which Sweden and Russia
dictate to her.

England sees with pleasure the evils that are devastating
France.   The disorder and anarchy which reign there promise her, more and more, the degradation of that Power.   It
is to her advantage that they should continue, and whatever
may be the private sentiments of the King of England and
the general horror of the English for the means that have
been employed, he will never do anything to check them.
But, at the same time, there is every reason to believe that
the English ministry will never contribute to foment the
trouble, or to hinder the effect of the good-will of the sovereigns who desire to succour the King of France; on the
contrary, there is every appearance that the King of England is awaiting the moment when the other powers declare
themselves in favour of the king to do so himself, but without that preliminary he will always remain in his present
passive state   This, at least, is the opinion of a man who,
by his mind, his knowledge, and the relations he has with
his own country, is better prepared than any one to see
its true intentions: I mean Mr. Crawford; and in the journey he has kindly made to England, out of attachment to
you and to your service, he convinced himself of these
dispositions . . .

Holland is absolutely dependent on England, nevertheless, it is for her interests to see the germs of democracy

smothered, or they will reach her territory and destroy the work of the Stadtholder.

The emperor deceives you.   He will never do anything for you, and under the specious pretext of your personal safety and of fulfilling your wishes in not acting with the princes, he abandons you to your fate and allows the total ruin of the kingdom to be consummated.   He delivers you up to the hatred of the nobles, whom he reduces to despair and drives in that way to some desperate action, — equally dreadful for you if it succeeds, by throwing you absolutely into dependence on them, if it fails, by taking from you all means of action and exposing you still further.   Already you can see the effect by the decree just hurled at the *émigrés* and by the letter of Vicomte d'Agoult, which the Baron de Breteuil sends you.   The emperor is personally well-disposed, but he has neither vigour, nor means, nor character to take a course and carry it through against the opinion of his ministry. He is weak and kind, he does not know how to resist his Council, which is slow, feeble, undecided, timid, — afraid of compromising itself   Besides which, the humiliation of France enters into its policy as a means of obtaining for Austria a greater preponderance in Europe.

The indiscretion with which the emperor has made known to the whole world that he receives letters from you, and the little effect he has given to his good-will, make it generally concluded that you write to prevent him from acting.   Your enemies use this to spread about that you are opposed to all enterprises, that the desire to rule, and the fear of being ruled made you prefer to accept the Constitution and side with the factious, rather than owe the restoration of your authority to the princes and the *émigrés*.   They assert that you would rather lose the kingdom than a part of that authority,— with a thousand other tales, one more absurd than

the other.   These ideas are spread among the nobles and are
believed by them ; very sensible men, to whom you were
attached, are inclined to adopt them   Baron de Bieteuil is
regarded here as your agent for this purpose, and since his
arrival the great majority of the French will not see him.
I feel, as you do, how little notice should be taken of such
injustice, and you are unfortunately accustomed to worse ,
but in the position in which you are, in the uncertainty as to
events which may arise, we must try to destroy these
rumours, and let the result of what you will have done for the
émigrés prove to them and to all Europe, at a future day, the
falsehood of these tales.   For this, a plan should be adopted
and followed with all possible activity ; and here is the one
I now propose to you : —

If it is true, as I believe, that you cannot rely upon the
emperor, you absolutely must turn your hopes another way,
and that way can only be the North and Spain — which
ought to decide Prussia, and so compel the emperor.   Of all
the Powers of Europe those are the ones on whose disin-
terestedness you can most rely.   Their geographical position
precludes all views of conquest, and their political position
binds them to the maintenance of the French monarchy.
They should be asked (1) not the recall of their ambassadors from France, but their departure on leave of absence.
(2) the immediate assembling of a congress, the pretexts
to be those you have already suggested to the emperor,
(3) the despatch of troops to support the congress and
make its deliberations respected ; or, if the season does not
admit of the assembling of troops, then to make such
arrangements as shall prove the intention to march them as
soon as possible.

This action of the Powers of Europe, which you will not
appear to have instigated and which cannot expose you, will

inspire great alarm, the effect of which will probably be to
fling France into the arms of the king; and the king, being
the sole person with whom the congress could treat, will
find himself naturally the mediator between his people and
the Powers; he will obtain from his people the means of
acting, while indicating to them the course they ought to
follow under the circumstances. The princes and the
émigrés would then become useful, their conduct and actions
being regulated by the congress.

But as it would be impossible without a leader of some
sort to obtain any result, and as the king, not being free, cannot be that leader, the King of Spain should be invited to
take that rôle; as head of the House of Bourbon he has more
right to it than any other; and the refusal he has given to
recognize the king's acceptance of the Constitution gives him
great facilities. Russia and Sweden will easily adopt this
idea, which has already been broached to them, and by indicating to the Court of Madrid, in concert with those two
powers, the course to follow, you will have less to fear from
Spanish slowness and indecision.

I do not think it desirable, however, to break with the
emperor or startle him; he should be managed and treated
circumspectly, also, in spite of the just grounds for distrust
which you have as to the sincerity of his interest for you,
you must not let him perceive that distrust, and preserve an
air of confidence in him always.

If you adopt this new plan [1] it will be necessary that you
should yourself inform all the well-intentioned Powers
whose assistance you decide to claim, such as Spain, Russia,
and Sweden. Perhaps, too, a letter to the King of Prussia
might be useful, judging by what he said to the King of
Sweden. You ought, after thanking the King of Spain for

[1] It was adopted

13

all that he has done for you, for the manner in which he
received your protest in 1789, for the firmness he shows at
this moment, to make him a picture in brief of your present
position, and show him the impossibility of remaining as you
are; you should then communicate to him the plan you
adopt; ask him, in virtue of the friendship and interest he
has already shown you, and those you have a right to hope
from him through ties of blood, to take charge of your
interests before the Foreign Powers and support the demands
you may be in the way of making to them; say to him that
no one has more right than he to be the head of the league
which will restore your authority and repair the insults
offered during the last two years to the House of Bourbon;
and that you would rather owe the obligation to him than to
any one Inform him that you have asked the emperor for
the assembling of a congress, and request the king to propose an armed congress and point out to him the pretexts.
Say that you will make the same communication to Sweden
and Russia, whose dispositions are known to you, and ask
him to concert with those two Powers as to the steps to take,
and say that you wish to use the influence that those Courts
possess over the princes to guide their conduct. Beg him to
rouse the zeal of Prussia, which has given you positive
assurances of interest through M. de Moustier, and, if
you decide to write to the King of Prussia, tell him so.
You should end by representing to the King of Spain how
necessary it is not to lose time, but to adopt prompt measures. Ask him also to use his influence with Portugal,
Sardinia, and Naples; or, perhaps, charge the Baron de
Breteuil to speak with the Neapolitan ambassador who is
here then, after a few compliments, add that you do not
doubt he will consent to give you these proofs of a friendship on which you have always relied. It will be well

to add that Baron de Breteuil remains in charge of your
correspondence. . . .

Your position is becoming daily more and more critical;
France is advancing with great strides to its ruin. The
factious are working incessantly to make you lose the little
popularity you were beginning to gain, and the *veto* of which
the king has just made use is a means they will not fail to
lay hold of. You already know the rumours that are spread
about you outside of France for the purpose of alienating the
nobles from you; they are trying to degrade you at the
Courts by representing all your acts as the result of weakness; and if you do not quickly issue from the state in
which you are, you will be abandoned by all parties and
delivered over wholly to the mercy of factious persons and
republicans, who will then have no further obstacle to the
execution of their guilty projects. The steps which I have
just indicated towards the Powers of Europe can alone save
you; they will restore to you outside of France the consideration you deserve; they will prove to the Courts the falseness
of the imputations against you, and they will give you an
opportunity of acting by yourself and of calling back to you
the nobles, alienated by a hundred foolish tales which your
present inaction seems to warrant.[1] . . .

By all that I have now said you will see how necessary it
is to take a course as soon as possible and inform me of it.
You cannot stay in the position in which you are; and
you have everything to fear from Coblentz and the *émigrés*,
some of whom act in good faith, others in bad. Baron de
Breteuil behaves very well; he is entirely devoted to you.

[1] It is of course quite plain that in writing thus to the queen Count
Fersen was really addressing the king; his sense of Louis XVI.'s weakness
and lethargy pierces through these sentences. — Tr.

As for me, have no uneasiness; I am no longer anything to
the French; I serve the King of Sweden and I have no dealings with them; the only way in which I can be pleasantly
and safely among them is to be always a foreigner. They
treat me extremely well and with distinction; they fear me
because they know I have no need of them; I run no risk
whatever. But I think it necessary that you should take a
course, and a course which cannot be charged in the eyes of
Europe with weakness — otherwise the Powers will be forced
to turn away from France and have nothing more to do with
her but by very distant intercourse.

As for my departure from Brussels, whatever desire I have
to satisfy and tranquillize you, it is impossible. I am here
by order of my king and I cannot absent myself I am
charged with his affairs, he has ordered all his ministers
and ambassadors to correspond with me here and to be
guided by what I may convey to them. You see therefore
that I cannot leave my post. But you can be tranquil, I
run no risk.

Answer me, I beg of you, at the earliest moment as to what
course you mean to take · it is absolutely necessary to write
to the different Courts; it must be as soon as possible, there
is not a moment to lose. You will risk nothing in writing
to Prussia, and it is necessary Except the letter to Spain,
you can send all the others here by a safe man to me, or to
the baron, and we will send them on by courier. But all
this requires the greatest promptitude, for the season is
getting late. I received your long letter yesterday; but M.
de Mercy, thinking it was for him, read it before he gave it
to me. It would be better not to send again through him, or
at least to make a second inclosure and write him a line to
say to whom it is to be given

What you tell me of your home grieves me, but does not

surprise me; you are doomed to bear all evils at once! I understand very well what you say about the cipher; we will use it thus we will put one full stop [ ] at the beginning; and when there is a letter skipped we will put two full stops [:] There is another manner, which is less long, and of which we had better make use, namely, to squeeze the juice of a lemon into a glass and write with it, the writing should be between the lines of a gazette or pamphlet; which can be sent to me, addressed either to " Rignon " or simply to me. I will write to you in the same way and send the pamphlet to the Comte de Coigny, the Duc de Choiseul, or to Goguelat, inform them of this If you have confidence in M. Laporte it would be safer and more convenient to send through him, and to use the three others only occasionally. Answer me as to this. You must be careful that the printed lines are far enough apart and that the paper is good enough not to blot. This way is brought out, like white ink, by warming it.

You have no money in Brussels M. de Bouillé remitted to the princes the five or six hundred thousand francs which remained. As for that which I sent into Holland for you, I will send you the details as soon as I have a moment to look them up. You will lose at least one quarter; for two thousand they give me here but fifteen hundred.

You see by the refusal of the emperor what you have to expect; I am not content with him or with M. de Mercy. He is very well for me and for you in words, but results do not follow, and it is absolutely necessary that you should act for yourself, or else renounce doing anything and decide to stay as you are. I do my best to restrain the King of Sweden, but it is not easy, for he has the empress with him; if he is once assured that you will do nothing it will be impossible to restrain him.

Sunday the news was spread that you had escaped and had arrived at La Marck's house at Raismes. All the French were wild, many started; all who doubted were regarded as bad citizens. Baron de Viomesnil had you on his arm with the dauphin; the Duc de Choiseul had the king, disguised as a woman No one ventured to give me the news or even speak of it, or ask me if it were true. They never speak to me of affairs, nor I to them; I keep them at a great distance. It is a horror to have spread this story; and they are now endeavouring to find out whence it came M. de Nicolai and M. de Simon were the first to spread it here, it is thought it came from Coblentz or even from Paris, to prevent your departure, if such were your intention.

Answer me as to the possibility of my going to see you, entirely alone without a servant, in case I receive an order from the king to do so, he has already said a word to me about his desire for it

Baron Thugut told Mr Crawford that you implored the emperor with clasped hands to keep quiet and do nothing for you, consequently he could not act.

Count Fersen to Queen Marie-Antoinette.

BRUSSELS, December 4, 1791.

I have received your letters of the 25th and 26th. We will send those to the Kings of Sweden and Spain in cipher. They are admirable. If you decide to write the second letters we will send both in the original. The Note is perfect. I have given it to the baron.

I deeply feel the horror of your position, but it will never change without foreign assistance, or by excess of the evil. The present evil may give place to another; but you would be always miserable, and the kingdom would fall into dissolution. Never will you win the factious; they have too

much to fear from you and your character. They feel their
wrong-doing too much not to fear vengeance and not to keep
you always in your present state of captivity, even preventing you from using the authority given you in the Constitution. They will accustom the people to no longer respect you
and love you. The nobles, believing themselves abandoned
by you, will think they owe you no duty; they will act for
themselves, by themselves, and with the princes, they will reproach you with their ruin, and you will lose the attachment of
all parties, some of whom will accuse you of having betrayed
them, others with having abandoned them. You will be
lowered in the eyes of the Powers of Europe, who will accuse
you of cowardice, and the weakness for which they blame
you will prevent them from allying themselves to a ruined
cause which can never be of any utility to them. In the
fear the King of Sweden now feels that you will do nothing,
but await all from time and from events of which you can
foresee nothing, being unable to control them and unwilling
to make use of the princes, he writes me as follows · —

"The Empress of Russia is very much dissatisfied with
this conduct, especially because the Queen of France writes
letter after letter to the emperor to prevent him from acting
while she, the empress, is using all her influence on his mind
to induce him to take active steps. The empress herself
writes this to me."

In speaking of the dissatisfaction that such conduct inspires he says: —

"Judge yourself what would be the position of the queen
if the king should die, and she saw herself at the mercy of
her two brothers-in-law and of a *noblesse* who could reproach
her with having sacrificed them and with being the sole
cause of their ruin and their proscription."

The king gives me positive assurances of the good intentions of Russia and Spain, hopes as to those of Prussia, and about the neutrality of England.

From all this you see that both for interest and for honour, it is indispensable that you should take a course. Pardon the zeal and the attachment that I have vowed to you, and which will never cease to inspire me for you, if I show you hard truths; but I know you are capable of hearing them, and nothing can stop me when it is necessary to serve you. Besides, I think it is a duty to hide nothing from you.

I think it certain that M. de Mercy returns to Paris. This is a great misfortune for us. It ought to prove to you once more all that I have said to you about the emperor, and how little you can rely upon him.. If you accept the plan I have proposed you should write a letter to the emperor at the earliest possible moment. Perhaps, learning of your action towards the other Courts, he may change his course, this is all the more important as one of the reasons of M. de Mercy's journey to Paris is doubtless to influence your conduct and direct it according to the desires and interests of the Court of Vienna.

Queen Marie-Antoinette to Count Fersen.

December 7, 1791

Here are our last two letters. I do not know if you will be satisfied with them   I have tried to put in all you told me, but it is very difficult for one who has not the habit of writing. On re-reading your papers I see that in our two long letters we forgot a great quantity of things; happily, they were not the most essential.

You could not believe the pleasure I have had in seeing the bishop; I could not leave him   I desired so much to write you by him if only a word, [*line missing*] . . . but I could not find a moment. He will tell you many things from me;

especially about new acquaintances and intimacies [*liaisons*]. I found him very severe; I thought I had already done a great deal, and that he would admire me. Not at all, he told me point blank that I could not do too much. — But, joking apart, I am keeping for you, in the happy days when we shall meet again, a volume of very curious correspondence, and all the more curious because one must do justice to those who have taken part in it, no one in the world suspects it, and if it is spoken of, it is so vaguely as to be thought one of the thousand absurdities that are told daily.

I did not need the letter of the *sans torts* ["blameless one"] to hold him in horror, the bishop will tell you what right I have to detest him, he is the most dangerous one of all, and perhaps the only one really to fear. It is absolutely impossible that you should come here at this moment; it would be to risk our safety, and when I say this I may be believed, because I have an extreme desire to see you. — I have just received a letter from M. de Mercy, who complains bitterly of the conduct at Coblentz against the emperor. He says "They are trying to excite all Germany against him; they inflame Sweden, and above all, Russia." He himself proposes that I shall write to the latter Court to enlighten it, and strengthen its good intentions by regulating them. I am going to answer him that we have already written to thank Russia, without entering into other particulars with him. The bishop will tell you that in consequence of the emperor's extreme indiscretion I think he ought not to be told of the other correspondences. M. de Mercy has an air of wishing to come here; I think he is urged to it by my friends the madmen here   His coming would do great harm at this time, and could do no good, on the contrary, it would cause a hundred thousand more tales about me. Moreover,

such a step would sharpen still further the anger of the
émigrés against the emperor and me.

You must have received the Baron de Viomesnil. I do
not know what M. de Breteuil will have said *to* him; but it
is becoming rather embarrassing. I think we must throw it
all upon the slowness and delays of the emperor, which prevent us from saying anything positive   The indiscretion of
Coblentz is too great; nothing can be confided to them; I
was confounded by receiving, a few days ago, a letter from
that stout d'Agoult saying: "We await with impatience the
fat Lorraine baron, so that the union may be perfect between
here and where you are." — Can you conceive of it ! Oh !
this accursed nation ! how unfortunate to have to live among
them and owe them service !

Our position is rather better since the bishop left   It
seems that all which calls itself constitutional is rallying to
make a great force against the republicans and the Jacobins,
they have drawn a great part of the Guard to their side,
especially the Guard on pay, which will be organized and
formed into regiments in a few days. They have the best
intentions, and are burning to make an example of the
Jacobins. The latter are committing all the atrocities of
which they are capable, but at present they have only
brigands and scoundrels with them: I say "at present"
because from one day to another everything changes in this
country, and none can tell where they are. The department
is to bring, to-day or to-morrow, its address to the king against
the decree of the priests; I am delighted, because, even if it
does no good, at least it declares war among the parties and
forces this one by this very step to rally to the king and
sustain him. The address is composed by a M. Garnier and
put in shape by Duport and Barnave, but this is a secret.

Count Louis de Narbonne is at last minister of war; what

glory for Mme. de Staël! and what pleasure she will now take in having the army — hers! He could be useful, if he chose, having intelligence enough to rally the constitutionals and quite the tone in which to speak to the present army. In other respects, he seems inclined to attach himself to M. Bertrand in the Council, and he is right, for that is the only member of it who is worth anything. Can you conceive my position and the rôle that I am obliged to play all day long? Sometimes I do not recognize myself, and I am obliged to reflect and see if it is really I who am speaking. But what else can I do? it is all necessary. Believe me, we should be much lower than we now are if I had not taken this course at once, at least we gain time by it, and that is what we want. What happiness if I could one day become able to prove to these wretches that I was not their dupe!

The baron must press our cause on Russia and Spain. What a misfortune that the emperor has betrayed us! If he had served us well, merely from the month of September when I wrote to him in detail, the congress might have been established next month, and how fortunate that would have been for us, because a crisis is advancing with great strides here; perhaps it will precede the congress, and then, what shelter shall we find? — Beware of Prussia, M. de Schulembuig writes constantly to M. du Moustier, and if M. Heymann discovers anything he will let M. de Giliers know of it.

The address of the department has come; it is perfectly good as to the discussion of the decree of the priests, but the wretches are frightened and have put in a mass of impertinences. M. de Narbonne made his entrance to the Assembly in a speech of almost unbelievable platitude for a man of intelligence. I am waiting for Mr Crawford with impatience; but I am sorry for you that he leaves you; I

hope they will not pass the winter here, and that he will go
back to Brussels, for you need distraction.   I am impatient
for your secretary to arrive   How is your health ?   I will
wager you do not take care of it, and you do wrong.   As
for me, I bear up better than I could expect under the immense fatigue of mind I have incessantly, and seldom going
out of doors; I have not a moment to myself, what with
persons I must see, and the writings, and the time I am
with my children.   That last occupation, which is not the
least, is my only happiness . . . and when I am very sad I
take my little boy in my arms and kiss him with all my
heart, and it comforts me for that moment.

Adieu.   The idea of the chocolate is excellent; it is
doubly useful to you, and I shall use it with prudence, but
sometimes this winter.   Adieu, again.

Friday, 9th.

I have just received your letter inclosed in an image.   I
am delighted that you have received mine.   I hope our letters to the Powers will calm them and show them our true
natures.   What they say of my letters to the emperor is in-
comprehensible, for some time past I have suspected that
my writing is being imitated to deceive him; I will clear
this up.   M. de Mercy will do very wrong to come here;
but I think that I must write him a word about our letters
to the Powers.   Send me a line at once when you receive
this packet.   I have not been able to finish the letter to the
king in a better manner, for twenty-four hours I have
turned it in every way.

I think, as you do, that evil alone cannot work for good;
and for that reason we must have the help of a foreign and
external force; but when you think that Frenchmen reflect
and are capable of following a system you do them too much
honour; I assure you that, for the mere pleasure of change,

they will return as quickly as they have been rabid for the new order of things   Meanwhile, I believe we are going to declare war, not against a power which has means to fight us — we are too cowardly for that — but against the Electors and a few princes of Germany, in the hope that they cannot defend themselves.   These imbeciles cannot see that if they do such a thing they serve us ; because if they begin the war, all the Powers must unite to defend the rights of each   But, if so, the latter need to be well convinced that in this we are executing only the will of others, and that the best way of serving us is to fall upon us bodily.— The bishop will have told you the difficulty there is in writing to me. . . . Adieu.

Count Fersen to Queen Marie-Antoinette.

BRUSSELS, December 12, 1901

The letters to Spain and Russia have arrived, they are perfect.   I await those for Sweden and Prussia.   There is still another step which is very necessary ; it is to write yourself to the Queen of Spain a letter of politeness and confidence, referring to the one to the king, and making her feel the necessity for the greatest secrecy, on account of Paris   You know the influence she has, and this step cannot be too quickly taken.   You can send it to me by diligence, in a box of Bouc tea, addressed to MM Daniel Danoot, Sons, bankers.

M. de Viomesnil has passed through Brussels.   The emperor is trying to make a close alliance with Prussia, Holland, and England.   It is thought that England will refuse.

CHAPTER VIII.

1791-1792. Proposal of the King of Sweden to rescue the King and Queen
of France declined by the King — Louis XVI compelled to declare war
against the Princes of Germany — Further Negotiations for a Congress

[THE scheme of the King of Sweden for a descent on the
coast of Normandy having failed for this year, he generously
meditated another plan of escape for the unhappy royal
family, which he submitted to the King and Queen of France
in a very interesting document (dated December 22, 1791),
which he charged Count Fersen to deliver to Their Majesties
in person. The count, who had been proscribed in France
since the flight to Varennes, went to Paris disguised and under
a false name. He arrived there February 11, 1792, saw Their
Majesties, gave them the document and letters, and discussed
with them the question of another escape. The king decided against making the attempt, and the count left Paris
February 21, reaching Brussels safely on the 25th.

The correspondence between the queen and Fersen continued as before; plans for organizing the armed congress,
and for concentrating the armies of the Powers along the
frontiers of France went on, the King of Sweden still pursued his idea of invading Normandy, carrying off the king
and queen and their children and taking them to England,
when all was brought to a sudden end by the death of the
Emperor Leopold, March 2, 1792, and by the far more
disastrous death of the King of Sweden, who was shot by
Ankerstrom, an ex-captain of his Guard, March 16, 1792.

The death of the brave and chivalrous king was an
irreparable blow to the cause of Louis XVI. The Duke-

Gustavus III
King of Sweden

regent (Gustavus IV. being a minor only fourteen years of age) was not willing to carry out the plans of Gustavus III. He refused to join his troops with those which the Empress of Russia still desired to send into Normandy. It is said that history may some day show that the Jacobins had a hand in the intrigues that stopped Sweden from giving its promised assistance to the unfortunate royal family of France.]

The King of Sweden to Count Fersen.

STOCKHOLM, December 22, 1791

The memorial for the King of France which I send you herewith, together with letters which I have written to T. V. C. Majesties, will put you completely *au fait* as to all that regards the affairs of France, and will serve for your instruction regarding the conduct you have to follow in the commission with which I have charged you I will add only that I regard as the most essential thing for the success of our projects that the royal family shall escape from Paris at the earliest possible moment. I request you, therefore, and before all else, to use your influence to make the king take that course, on which all the rest depends, and without which the measures of the other Powers and those of the princes can advance very little towards the end proposed.

You will see in the memorial itself what action I think should be taken to avoid, as much as possible, the dangers attending the execution of such a project. You will develop, better than I could do in writing, the expedient of a disguise, which I have only indicated as a safe means , and you can speak to the king and queen of the necessity of sacrificing on this occasion, and for such paramount interests, comfort and conveniences, the momentary deprivation of which cannot be put into comparison with the object of this step, on which the whole future fate of the kingdom and the royal family depends. But for this it is absolutely essential that the king shall take another route from that of the queen with the dauphin and Madame Élisabeth; if the king will go, as I think most useful, to England, and the rest of the royal family see nothing better than to take an opposite direction, we must, at any rate, fix their point of reunion only at the spot whence they embark for England. Without this precaution the scenes of Varennes may easily be renewed, and so cause to vanish for a very long time the hopes their friends found upon the king's flight, if he succeeds in escaping with his family the slavery in which factious men now hold him.

I have charged Baron Taube to write you at full length in relation to the details of this project The knowledge you have of the country and the personages make you more capable than any other to judge of what is, or is not practicable, and I rely on the zeal, activity, and skill of which you have already given such marked proofs. I thought at first of proposing to the Queen of France the courageous course of remaining herself in Paris with the dauphin, to facilitate the king's escape; but on further reflection I thought that such resolutions are good only when one takes them one's self; it is difficult to advise them. I do not, however, regard the step as very dangerous for the queen, the king saved, no one would touch her, and as for the dauphin the worst that could happen to him would be to be proclaimed King of France in place of his father; his life and person would become too precious to them to hurt. The queen would give by this act a great proof of courage and generosity, which would impress not only her friends, but would make her so respected in the eyes of the people that she would greatly influence all minds. It would be only the first moment after the king's escape was known that could have any dangers for her; but besides taking all precautions and doubling the guard, or else going herself with the dauphin to the Hôtel-de-Ville and putting herself into the safe keeping of the municipality, she would captivate all minds and put them so to sleep that she could later save herself and the dauphin. I communicate these reflections to you that you may use them or keep them to yourself, according to occurrences.

Another and easier plan would be for the queen and her children to escape from Paris and conceal themselves somewhere for a few days till the king is safely out of France, when they could take another route and escape easily. It is the quantity of persons who assemble round them and travel with them which retards the flight and leads to discovery. For this reason, it is essential to insist that the king and queen take different routes, for I feel sure that that will be the point most difficult to obtain.

As for what concerns the congress, you will have seen by my former letters the reasons I thought myself obliged to oppose to it so long as there was hope of bringing the emperor to conduct more analogous to the circumstances. At present the congress seems, on the contrary, the only way to reach that end. I intend, consequently, to write to the Empress of Russia, and after we have concerted together I will let you know the result, which will serve you for instructions in the matter. Meantime I refer you to what I have said about it in my memorial to the King of France, and to what I have already said to you, — namely, that all emissary from the self-styled National Assembly must be excluded, and I even think that the presence of an envoy from H. V. C. Majesty, in his present position, inadmissible to a congress for which the rights of the people of Avignon and the injured rights of the Princes of Germany are made the pretext.

14

I send you by this courier the passports you asked for, and also a letter, accrediting you to the Queen of Portugal, which will screen you more completely from all insult in France. For this reason I have directed to the Queen of Portugal the packets here inclosed for the King and Queen of France. On which I pray God to have you in His holy keeping, being

Your very affectionate

GUSTAVUS.

Postscript. I add herewith copies of my memorial and of my letters to T. V. C. Majesties. You will keep these copies for your private instruction, and when you start for Paris you will leave them locked up in Brussels; so that you may have recourse to them in case some accident should oblige you to destroy your papers on the road. Of the two letters for the queen, you will see that the longest is the most voluminous, and after what you find [in Paris] you will decide to make use of one or the other, you will then decide which of them should be given to the queen. I leave you to choose the one which you find to be written in the manner most analogous to the circumstances.[1]

Last Paragraph of the King of Sweden's Memorial to the King of France.

The king has now placed beneath the eyes of his friend and ally all the reflections that his zeal, and the truest friendship, and the most sincere interest have inspired in him. H M hopes that the King of France will recognize these sentiments; and the king will regard it as the finest day of his life if he can, by his person or his counsels, contribute to

---

[1] The memorial is very long, and goes over ground already known to us; it closes with the words that here follow in the text, and the whole will be found in the Appendix to vol i. of "Le Comte de Fersen et la Cour de France," pp 281–292. — TR.

draw the King of France and the French monarchy from the fatal condition into which they are plunged The sight and the enlightenment of men are limited; they can judge only by experience and the examples that history furnishes, and often fortuitous incidents upset the best-laid plans But kings are born to command, and by their firmness to rule events when they threaten their States; and duty calls them to sacrifice themselves for their posterity; they ought not to hesitate; in such cases the most perilous course is the safest.[1]

From the King of Sweden to the King of France: Autograph Letter.

HAGA, December 17, 1791

MONSIEUR, my brother and cousin :

The interest which I do not cease to take in Y. M, of which you will find proofs that are not equivocal in all the steps I have taken hitherto, has prompted me to write a brief memorial on your present situation I beg Y. M. to read it alone, and to consult none but your own heart, your august wife, and that sister whose devotion renders her so interesting and so estimable. You ought to come out of the state in which you are, and you cannot doubt the zeal of your friends. It is with these sentiments that I am, Monsieur, my brother and cousin,

Your Majesty's

good brother, cousin, friend, and ally,

GUSTAVUS.

Postscript. This letter was written and about to be sent when I received that of Y. M. of November 26th. You can-

---

[1] The tone of the brave king shows plainly his sense of Louis XVI's weakness, if not cowardice Perhaps his advice to separate the king and queen, which at first sight seems harsh, may have been dictated to his gallant heart by a fear of the king's nervous folly, which did much to stop them on the road to Varennes — TR.

not doubt for a moment that all that depends on me is devoted to you, but I cannot answer for events if the length of delays reduces your faithful subjects to despair. Y M. will see by my memorial the warm interest that the Empress of Russia takes in your cause. I will write to her to-day, following your instructions, and I await with impatience the second letter which Y. M. is good enough to announce to me.

Copy of Autograph Letter No. 1 from the King of Sweden to Queen Marie-Antoinette, sent to Count Fersen.

STOCKHOLM, December 22, 1791.

MADAME, my sister and cousin:

I send to the King of France a memorial relating to present circumstances. I beg Y. M. to read it and, if you think it useful, to further what I propose. It is the truest friendship and an experience of popular movements which I have gained in the course of a long life which have dictated it   I beg Y. M. to consider well that it is only by violent remedies that violent ills can be cured; and that if moderation in the current of ordinary life is a virtue, it often becomes a vice when used in public matters. The King of France cannot re-establish his kingdom except by recovering his former rights, all other remedy is illusory; all other conclusion will only open the door to endless discussion, which will increase confusion instead of ending it. It is with the sword that the king has been robbed of his rights; it is with the sword that he must regain them.

But I pause. I ought to remember that I am speaking to a princess who in the terrible moments of her life has shown a most intrepid courage.

Y. M., in reading the memorial, will at least do justice to my sentiments for you, and to the interest inspired in me by your sorrows and your constancy.

Copy of Autograph Letter No. 2 from the King of Sweden to Queen Marie-Antoinette, sent to Count Fersen.

STOCKHOLM, December 22, 1791.

MADAME, my sister and cousin:

It is nearly two years since, in the midst of the war in which I was then engaged, but profoundly touched by the misfortunes that were overwhelming Y M. and the King of France, I expressed to the latter my sincere regret at not being able then to come to his assistance. Sincere in my protestations and constant in my principles, you cannot doubt, Madame, how much I feel the difference in my position, now that the peace which restores the union of Russia and Sweden enables me to offer you my help at this moment when your troubles are increasing.

Y. M. is not ignorant of all that I have tried to do to save you since the misfortune at Varennes, and if at that moment the treaty of alliance between the empress and myself had been concluded, and if that princess had then had her peace made with the Turks I do not doubt she would have united her forces with mine to go to your assistance; and Y. M. will see by the memorial I send to the King of France what zeal and ardour the empress is now putting into your cause. I present to the king all the reflections that my friendship and the interest I feel for you both dictate to me Your situation is violent, and you must issue from it by violent means. Whatever be the peril that confronts you, it will always be less great than that of abandoning your fate to events and leaving to others the merit and the opportunity of saving the kingdom.

But I am not duly reflecting that it is useless to speak of peril and try to diminish it in the eyes of a princess who, on the 6th of October, showed herself with such intrepidity to the

eyes of a furious and misguided people, and who has since
been fed, so to speak, on peril. But I believe, as a true
friend of Y. M , that I ought to insist strongly on the absolute and imperative duty of making the king leave Paris and
France   Not that I have any doubt of the fidelity of his
brothers, or of the greater or less obedience they would pay
to him if he were restored to the throne by them alone.   On
the contrary, I am convinced by the very words of *Monsieur*
and the Comte d'Artois, and still more by the feelings they
showed at our interview, that not only would they never
presume upon the advantage that service would give them
over their unfortunate elder brother, but that those by whom
they are surrounded would have no power to persuade them
to evade the perfect obedience which their duty towards their
king and brother imposes upon them.   Neither do I fear for
the life of the King of France, nor for yours, Madame, in case
of an attack by the princes.   I am convinced that the factious
regard the person of the king and yours as the sole means to
save themselves, and I believe that you will be more impor-
tuned by the negotiations they will open to recover favour
then alarmed by their threats.   But, unless the king be at
liberty, I believe it to be almost impossible to make the other
sovereigns act, especially the emperor; and if the princes
undertake an attack alone and fail, all hope is lost, the discouragement of your friends will increase the audacity of
your enemies, and in that way your danger becomes incalculable.

By the picture I have made to the king of the disposition
of the crowned heads, Y. M. will see that all depends upon
himself. I have, out of regard for you, Madame, softened
as much as I could the proceedings of the emperor, but I
think I owe it to Y. M and to the true friendship that I
profess for you to tell you the truth without alloy. It is

essential that you should know the conduct of your brother, in order that you may remedy it and force that prince, so to speak, within his own intrenchments. He has done nothing but embarrass and stop the progress of negotiation. After the capture of the king at Varennes, he put himself forward as head of the league of sovereigns which he proposed to form. He lost time in negotiations, though fully able to march his troops in the Low Countries at once into France, where, guided by M. de Bouillé, they could, in the state of confusion in which all France then was, have reached Paris easily. Though he had promised you to send orders to the archduchess, governor of the Low Countries, to march those troops at the moment of your attempted evasion, she never received them, they did not arrive until three weeks *after* you had been taken back to Paris. At the interview at Pillnitz, the King of Prussia offered to march his troops instantly. The emperor would not consent. He wished to wait until he knew the answer of the Empress of Russia to his propositions, — although that princess had never disguised from him her sentiments and the zeal she put into your cause; and when Prince Hohenlohe was sent by the King of Prussia to Prague to settle the operations and the marching of the troops, he obtained neither an audience of the emperor nor an answer. And finally, when the news of the acceptance of the Constitution came the emperor would not see in it, as the rest of us did, the effect of compulsion and tyranny He received the French ambassador, and induced the King of Prussia to do the same and to make a reply which that prince would not have done had he followed his own feelings supported by letters from the Empress of Russia. But what is still more fatal is that the emperor makes use of your letters, Madame, and thus, covering himself with the aegis of your name, he embarrasses even your most sincere friends, and I have long trembled lest these representations should cause the King of Spain to weaken and abandon the firm conduct he has hitherto maintained. Happily, that prince, being, as a Bourbon, personally interested in your cause, has continued up to this time immovable in right principles.

There, Madame, is the truth that I owe you, given at the risk of displeasing you; it is in the discretion of Y. M. that I confide. You will feel that if ever your brother should be informed of what I have just written he would never forgive me for it, and a misunderstanding between us might be injurious to your affairs, — all the more because I am persuaded that, by the urgent solicitations of the Empress of Russia, and provided the king be once more at liberty, the emperor may return to good feelings and join your defenders.

But you see by all this how essential it is to put the king in a position to speak the language that becomes him; to put yourself, Madame, in the way of urging your brother to succour you, — a succour all the more to be desired because the territories of the emperor surround France and it is through them or by the sea that we can reach you. The pains he has taken to set aside the proposal for a congress, which by its results, might have led him farther than he wished; the pains that he took by his last note, to induce us to make a declaration which, though the terms were threatening, was, nevertheless, in recognition of the present state of things as accomplished in France, — all this ought to prove to Y. M. the indispensable necessity of drawing your friends from error, or, to express it better, to give them weapons with which to plead your cause.

The measures which I make bold to propose to you for your escape are also essential. The passage to England is the shortest and least suspected, and I implore you in God's name to make the king adopt it, and to employ all the ascendency you have acquired over his mind to induce him to take this step. I have instructed the person who will give you this letter in all that I do not venture to confide to paper, in order that he may give a detailed account of it to Y. M. You know his devotion, and the unequivocal sign that he now gives of it in bearing to you this packet through great perils is no slight thing. It is a proof of such great attachment that it rouses all my gratitude and my admiration, for I should never have resolved to command him to go had he not offered it himself. I will not doubt that a zeal so rare will have its reward in the fortunate success of his commission. For myself, Madame, I count myself happy in proving to Y. M. that in whatever position you find yourself I will never abandon you, and never cease to be, with those sentiments, Madame, my sister and cousin,

Your Majesty's
good brother, cousin, friend, and ally,
GUSTAVUS.

Queen Marie-Antoinette to Count Fersen

No 1   December 22, 1791

I received your little letter yesterday. I should be uneasy at your not having received our letters if the date of yours were possible, you have dated it 19th and I received it 21st; no post can go so quickly. I had already received four printed sheets; I warmed them, and wet them with the liquid, but found nothing.

I am very uneasy at getting no answer to the last letters. It has been impossible to send any one to Vienna; I could find no one strong enough, or sufficiently safe and discreet for that errand. I am sorry, it is very important that the emperor should know our true intentions, and that I should at last know what we can count on from him, for without it

I shall be daily dragged into taking false steps, my language and my manner to the people about me ought to change according to what we ought and may expect from without. I am strongly inclined to send you M. Goguelat, if only for three days, that he may talk things to the bottom with you. I have not yet spoken to him of this idea Send me word what you think of it. He knows nothing of my correspondence with the persons the bishop named to you, he must not be told of it.

There is talk here of a loan of forty millions which the *émigré* nobles want to raise upon their property; this is madness, and it will end by the pillage of their estates. If the baron has the means of doing so, he must let our brothers know, and we authorize him to do it, that we cannot approve of this idea, which will be the ruin of those good people

I have missed the opportunity to send this letter. Beginning with this one I shall number them all that go by the post either in white ink or in cipher. Do the same. We must keep a bit of paper on which to mark them down and see that none are missing. Adieu.

Count Fersen to Queen Marie-Antoinette

December 22, 1791

I hope you have received the letter in which I proposed to you to write to the Queen of Spain. I think that step important. Also it will be well in the end to write to the King of England and the Stadtholder; but the time for that has not come. Send me word if you will decide to do it Baron de Breteuil has invited M. de Brautzen, who is very well-intentioned for you and whom it would be good to treat well, to write to the Stadtholder [the archduchess Marie Christine], with whom he is reconciled, asking her to induce the King of Prussia to come out more firmly, and also to make a definite proposal to the emperor, which would prove to all Europe the falsity of the doubts the latter casts on his good-will and show that the inaction comes only from the emperor   These propositions will not compromise him, for he is always master of acting only as much as the emperor acts

It is very important that you should put your papers in a safe place where they cannot be discovered, for you ought to be prepared for everything.

M. de Toulangeon — the one who came from Franche-Comté — was hurt by the coldness with which his good intentions were received.   Do you not think that, without too highly distinguishing them, it would be well to show to persons of good-feeling and good-will certain marks of kindness?   No one knows better than you how to use that money.

The Duke of Brunswick is a man of intelligence, talents, and a great ambition   Do you not think it important to win him?   He has always liked France; and the French service is the one he would have chosen by preference in which to place his son, of whom he is very fond.   An advance toward him might do great good and promote your affairs in Prussia   He could be made to hope something for his son.   If you think this useful, a rather distinguished man, who would please him, should be sent to him.   The Marquis de Castries would be good for that, or failing him, M. de Bouillé   Let me know if you adopt this idea   I have not yet spoken to the baron about it, but I am sure he will approve   Your letters for Sweden and Prussia have not yet arrived, and I feel uneasy. Sending by diligence is the safest and surest way.   Your letter for Spain went by the Comte de Seuil by way of England, the Marquis de Bom-

belles, who is to carry the one to Russia, has not yet arrived
here.

Monday.

We learned yesterday of the step the king has taken; as I
am ignorant of the reasons and the object, I must own to you
that it astounds and grieves me [1] I fear that they have given
you treacherous advice   I fear that you have taken hastily
a step, good in itself, and which might have been useful to
you at another moment if concerted with the Powers, and if
the latter had been ready to act for you by seeming to sustain the German princes.   I think the king ought to have
let himself be forced by the Assembly, and then, yielding to
their desire, have represented to them how embarrassing such
action was at a moment when peace was needed for the
establishment of the Constitution, for the restoration of the
finances, for the security of the public debt, and to avoid
increased taxation upon the people.

As it is now, I see only a source of embarrassment for you,
additional dangers, and the bad effect that this will have in
Europe   It will be attributed to the weakness already laid
to you; discouragement will take hold of the friendly Powers;
in fact, what idea can those to whom you have just addressed
letters and on whom you have sought to rely have when they
learn from the public newspapers so important a step, without knowing its motives or being warned of it by M. de
Breteuil ?   They will be tempted to believe you have only a

---

[1] The decree of the Legislative Assembly against the *émigrés*, compelling
their return to France under penalties of death and confiscation, was
vetoed by the king November 14, 1791 ; he also vetoed, November 27th, a
decree of the Assembly forbidding all priests who had not taken the civil
oath to exercise their ministry   On the 14th of December the king, to mod-
ify the effect of his vetoes, went in person before the Assembly and made an
explanation, ending by virtually threatening to declare war against the
princes of Germany.   See Thiers' " Histoire de la Révolution Francaise,"
vol. ii , pp. 20-39 — TR.

half-confidence in him ; and that belief will make his negotiations more difficult ; they will even suspect, and with some
foundation, your intentions, and the confidence you appeared
to place in them will seem doubtful   Having adopted the
plan proposed, no important step should have been taken
without consulting them ; or, at least, without consulting M.
de Breteuil, who, being better informed as to the disposition of
those Powers would have told you the effect such a step
would have ; or, at least, he would have been in a position
to give them the reasons that led you to take it, and so prevent the bad impression it will produce.

I know there are circumstances in which you might be
obliged to decide and act promptly ; but as you can always
foresee the possibility of this, we ought to be informed and
the step delayed long enough for letters to reach us before
the public papers, and thus enable us to guide the first im-
pressions to the side most favourable to you.   I know that
confidence cannot be given, and I am far from asking more
than you wish to grant to me ; your interests alone guide
me and will ever guide me ; and even if you could doubt the
views and projects of M. de Breteuil, I have the vanity to
think that my past conduct ought to take from you the
possibility of doubting mine , it ought, rather, to convince you
of their purity, and of the zeal, attachment, and devotion I have
consecrated to your service.   My sole desire is to serve you ;
my sweetest recompense, the only one to which I aspire, is
the glory of succeeding in that — I want no other.   I should be
but too much rewarded if I could know you were happy and
think that I had been happy enough to have contributed to it.

I hope to receive a word from you which will guide me in
what I must write to the King of Sweden, and give me the
possibility of justifying and defending, to his eyes and those
of the empress, the step that has just been taken.

Postscript. All that I have now written becomes useless for your letter to the baron and M. de Mercy has just arrived. Nevertheless, I must observe that it was very important to have received them earlier in order that the Powers should have been warned by you and not have learned your action from the public papers.[1]

Queen Marie-Antoinette to Count Fersen.

No 3   December 28, 1791.

De Narbonne [minister of war] has a crazy idea, which I thought had fallen through · to invite the Duke of Brunswick to come here and command the army. The idea is so out of common-sense that I supposed nothing more would be said about it. Yesterday I heard that they were going to send the little de Custine to the duke to negotiate the affair. Comte de Ségur may have been commissioned to speak of it without our knowledge. I tell you of all this so as not to be scolded, and also that the baron and you may take your precautions. I have no doubt the duke will refuse; and that will be serving us. Adieu I have not yet received the packet of M. Crawford. . . . [2]

Queen Marie-Antoinette to Count Fersen.

                                     January 4, 1792.

I can only write one word. . .   The person who will bring you this will tell you and make you know our position just as it is I have entire confidence in him and he deserves it for his attachment and his good sense [Count Fersen writes

---

[1] It will be observed that this letter is of the same date as the King of Sweden's memorial and letters to the King and Queen of France, which did not reach Count Fersen till the 8th of January, 1792 — TR

[2] This autographic letter was written in "white," or "sympathetic" ink, addressed on the outside to "Monsieur l'Abbé de Beauverin, Poste restante, Bruxelles" Count Fersen notes on the margin, "Reçu Jan. 3 Rep Jan 5" See fac-simile. — TR.

reçu le 3 Janv: 1792. — rue de Jan. ce 9. ce 29 xbre

De narbonne en ait que j'ai écrit que je croyois Tonible, Jen
gage le Duc de Briensuich a venit commender l'armée
cette idée est si fort hors dezens que j'ai cru qu'on
n'en parleroit plus hier j'ai appris qu'on l'avoit envoyé
le petit de custine pour traiter cette affaire, Le Duc de
sigur pourroit bien être chargé d'en parler aussi je
sens que nous le sachions je vous previens de Tout
cela pour n'être pas gronde et que le Baron et
vous puissiez prendre vos precautions je
ne doute pas que le Duc refuse et c'est mieux nous
servir; Adieu je n'ai point encore le paquet e

mrs: evertdordt .

reçue le 8 Janv: par g.g: ce 7 Janvier

je ne vous écris qu'un mot ~~expedie~~
~~————————————————————~~ la personne
qui vous porte celle-cy, vous dira
tout et fera connaître notre
position Telle qu'elle, est j'y ai
entiere confiance, et il la merite
par son attachement, et sa raison
il porte un mémoire absurde
mais que je suis obligé d'envoye,
il est essentiel, que l'imp.
soit bien persuadé qu'il n'y a
pas la un mot, qui soit de nous
n'y de notre maniere de voir les
choses, mais qu'il me fasse
pourtant une reponce, comme
si il croyoit que c'est la ma
maniere de voir, et que je puisse
montrer; car ils sont si méfians
icy qu'ils exigeront la reponce

le porteur de tous ces papiers
ne sait pas, par qui ils me sont
venus, et il ne faut pas lui
en parler le memoire est bien
mal faite et on voit que les
geux on peure mais pour notre
sureté personnelle il faut
encore les menager; Et surtout
leurs inspirer confiance par
notre conduite icy. on vous
expliquera tout cela, ainsi que
les raisons pourquoi souvent je
ne peu pas vous avertire d'avance
de ce qu'on va faire... mon
homme n'est pas encore revenu
je voudrois pourtant bien avoir
des nouvelles d'ou vous etiez
que veut dire cette declaration
subite de l'emp: pourquoi ce

silence profond de vienne, et
meme de brua.- envers moi, je
m'y perd, mais ce que je sais bien
c'est que si c'est prudence ou politique
qui fait qu'on ne me dit rien, on
a bien tort, et ont m'ea pose beaucoup
puisque personne ne croira que je
sois dans cette ignorance, et il seroit
pourtant necessaire que je puisse regler
mes propos et ma conduite d'apres
ce qui se passe, c'est ce que je charge
la personne de dire a m.: de mercy.
je vais finire ~~~~~~~~~~~~~~~~~~~
~~~~~~~~~~~~~~~~~~~~~~~~~~~~~~~~~~~~~~
~~~~~~~~~~~~~~~~~~~~~~~~~~~~~~~~~~~~~~
~~~~~~~~~~~~~~~~~~~~~~~~~~~~~~~~~~~~~~
~~~~~~~~~~~~~~~~~~~~~~~~~~~~~~~~~~~~~~

" Goguelat " on the margin]   He carries with him an absurd memorial, but I was forced to send it.   It is important that the Emperor should be convinced there is not a word of our own in it, nor of our manner of seeing things, but he must make me an answer as if he believed it was my way of seeing things, which I can show, for they are so distrustful here they will exact an answer.   The bearer of these papers does not know by whom they are dictated to me and must not be spoken to about them.   The memorial is ill-written and shows that these wretches are in fear, but for our personal safety they have to be managed, and, above all, we must inspire confidence in them by our conduct here. All that will be explained to you, also the reasons why I often cannot warn you in advance of what they are going to do here.   My man has not yet returned; I wish I could have some news from where you are.   What is the meaning of this sudden declaration of the Emp. ?   Why this profound silence of Vienna, and even of Brussels towards me ?   I am lost in conjectures, but what I know well is this: if it is prudence or policy that makes them say nothing to me, they are very wrong and expose me much, because no one believes that I can be in such ignorance ; and yet it is necessary that I should regulate my words and my conduct on what is taking place : that is what I have told this person to say to M. de Mercy   I must end. . . .

Queen Marie-Antoinette to the Queen of Spain.

MADAME, my sister and cousin .   January 4, 1792

I desired much to be able to write to Y. M. at the same time that the king wrote to the King of Spain, but time then failed me, and we are forced to be so circumspect in all our actions that I have had to await an opportunity to send this letter to the Baron de Breteuil in Brussels, who, as you know has all our confidence. I write to you, Madame, with all the more pleasure, to connect myself with the letter the king has already written, because the nobleness of your character and the double tie of blood which unites you with us leaves me no doubt of the interest you will take in regard to us. Be so kind, therefore, as to maintain the King of Spain in his good-will towards our interests. The letter he has received from the king will explain to him our true sentiments, and we can have no others. It is unnecessary to say to Y. M. that the greatest secrecy is necessary; your prudence and our position make it obvious enough As for me, Madame, I shall be charmed to owe you an obligation, and to add that sentiment to the friendship and attachment I have so long, and for my life, vowed to you.

MARIE-ANTOINETTE.

Count Fersen to Queen Marie-Antoinette.

BRUSSELS, January 6, 1792

An aide-de-camp of M. de Jaucourt has brought to Ath [near Brussels] an order for the assemblage of *émigrés* there collected to take itself to the frontiers of the Elector of Trèves. You will readily see the annoyances of this operation, and how disadvantageous it may be. 1st, it increases the embarrassment of the Electors and forces you to put yourself on the defensive, which it was desirable to delay until there was better preparation made outside; 2d, it is one means the less of compromising the emperor, and 3d, it is giving the Assembly the facility to represent this departure as the result of the king's threats. It may excite the Electors to the same conduct; they will no longer be able to reply that they conform in their States to the course of the Low Countries, and from the knowledge I have of the emperor's intentions I should not be at all surprised if he supports this

demand. I know that he is determined not to furnish to
the Electors and princes of the Empire more than the con-
tingent he is forced to send as a co-State.   He fears war, he
fears to be mixed up in your affairs; and having now no
assemblage of the French in his own States, he may exact
that there shall be none in those of others   Baron de
Breteuil has written to the Marquis de Castries to stop, if
possible, the departure of the *émigrés*; I have written the
same to Baron Oxenstjerna.

The answer of the king to the emperor seems to me a
little too strong, do you not think it best to hold one's self
in readiness to make war, but to delay the moment of beginning it until a concert is established, with sufficient force to
be a support to you?   Do you not think it would have been
best to say that, if at a fixed epoch the Elector of Trèves has
not dispersed the assemblages, the king will rely on the good
offices of the emperor to compel him to do so. I think it
important to grant the Elector of Trèves a second period —
till the 1st or 15th of February, if possible; this delay would
give us time to receive answers.   Could not the king derive
some benefit from the desire he has to preserve peace and
avoid war, always ruinous, but especially so at this moment
when the finances require such great attention?

The King of Prussia to his Very Christian Majesty the King
of France.

MONSIEUR, my brother.   January 14, 1792

I have just received the letter that Y. M. wrote to me
December 3d, and which the Baron de Breteuil forwarded.
I recognize with keen sensibility the confidence you testify
in me, and I beg you to be fully convinced that M. de
Moustier expressed to you my true sentiments in speaking
to you of the sincere interest I take in your situation and

that of the queen, your august wife, and the desire which animates me to be useful to both, in order to bring about a state of things more in conformity with your wishes

As a result of these dispositions I am much inclined to enter into the views of Y. M in regard to the establishment of an armed congress, and I shall in consequence sound H. M. the emperor immediately on that subject, having so far followed a confidential concert on the affairs of France with him, to whom Y M. informs me you have made the same proposition. In spite of the slowness and difficulty which the arrangement of an armed congress will necessarily meet with, I like to think that its effects and the impression which will result will answer the expectations of Y M. But, with all the good-will with which I feel myself inspired for your interests, I cannot at the same time refuse to consider the very considerable expenses to which this measure will give rise, and, father of my people, I shall say, with frankness, to a king who has given such strong proofs of the same sentiments, that a just indemnity for those costs seems to me indispensable to conciliate the services which I hope to render to Y. M. in conformity with my cares for the welfare of the State I govern.

I shall take pleasure in communicating, through my minister, Count Schulemburg, with the Baron de Breteuil, whom Y. M. honours with your confidence and who so justly deserves it, on all that relates to this important object, but I shall be charmed at the same time to receive direct news from Y. M. as often as you judge that you can give them to me in safety; as for the secrecy you ask of me, the great necessity for which I feel perfectly, I will guarantee you that it shall be religiously and strictly observed by myself and by those to whom the matter must be confided by me, but you will feel, without difficulty, that I cannot answer

for the secrecy of the other Courts which must concur
in it.

I end this letter by reiterating to Y. M. the ardent and
sincere desires that I form for you and your royal family,
and the assurance of the invariable sentiments of consideration and attachment with which I am, Monsieur, my brother,

Your Majesty's good brother,

FREDERICK WILLIAM.

Baron Taube to Count Fersen.

STOCKHOLM, January 17, 1792.

The courier from Hamburg arrived last Saturday evening,
and everything came safely. The King of Sweden is perfectly satisfied with the letter of the Queen of France to him,
and with the one she has written to the empress; but he is
not as much so with the one that the King of France has
written to the King of Spain. The King of Sweden thinks
that the help and succour he wants of him are not strongly
enough defined, and that the king has not said to the King
of Spain that he desires no compromise with the rebels and
not to have a mixed government, but to see the monarchy
restored with the royal power in all its plenitude. The
King of Sweden charges me to tell you, my friend, that
if the King of France does not persist in those sentiments
all foreign help will be useless to him, and his power will be
equally useless to his friends and allies The King of
Sweden strongly approves of the conduct the King of France
is holding at the present moment towards the rebels, they
cannot be too much lulled into security, but with his friends
he ought never to talk of, or propose, anything but the re-
establishment of the monarchy in its entirety, such as it was
before the revolution.

As for the proposal to take Denmark into the league, that

is impossible; for the twenty years that the King of Sweden has reigned, Russia has tried in vain to force him to make a triple alliance between Russia, Denmark, and himself, without ever being able to succeed. Therefore that idea must be totally left out of the projects of the king and queen if they want his support. Between ourselves, my friend, if it had not been for the foolish consideration which France has shown from all time for Denmark, contrary to the interests of Sweden, we should to-day be much more powerful, and consequently more useful at the present moment to France.

The King of Sweden has written to the King of Prussia to warn him of Ségur's arrival, so that he may send him away. The King of Sweden will also write to the empress on the subject of the congress, about which Baron de Breteuil is urgent in the name of the King and Queen of France.

The King of Sweden to Count Fersen.

The little castle of new HAGA,
January 20, 1792.

I received on Saturday last the packet that Reutersvaerd brought to Hamburg My departure for Gefle, and the numerous occupations which the opening of the Diet occasions me, prevent my writing to you at length, but the annexed paper will prove to you that I have adopted the measures that the King of France asked of me. I beg you to tell this to the Baron de Breteuil, and though I hope nothing from such a congress, which will serve more to embroil the sovereigns than unite them, and am convinced that the emperor will refuse it, still I wish to show the King of France that I conform to his wishes before the answer of the emperor can be given If the Assembly goes on with its present rapidity we shall be obliged to have recourse to methods much less slow than a congress.   Meantime, I *insist on the necessity of getting the king out of Paris.*

On which I pray God to have you in His holy keeping, being

Your very affectionate

GUSTAVUS.

Count Fersen to the King of Sweden.

BRUSSELS, January 22, 1792.

SIRE, — According to the letter which your Majesty did me the honour to write to me December 30, I hastened to send to the queen the details on the disposition of the Empress of Russia which concerned her and would prove to her the necessity for a firm and persistent line of conduct and plan.   I hope before long and as soon as they think it suitable, to explain everything more in detail to the king and queen and to learn more positively their resolutions.

The Queen of France has been forced to send to the emperor a memorial written in her name by MM. Barnave, Lameth, and Duport, without the knowledge of the present Assembly and in which it is very ill-treated.   In this memorial, which is very bad and ill-written, they endeavour to frighten the emperor as to the results of a war with France ; suggesting to him the seductions which will be offered to his soldiers, and the propagation of the new doctrines of equality and liberty which will be spread in all the countries where the French army may go.   They next attempt to prove to him, by very false arguments, the interest it is to him (even for his Belgian provinces) to ally himself with France and to maintain the Constitution such as it was decreed by the former Assembly.   One can see in every line of this memorial that fear dictated it, and that it is only a means attempted to detach the emperor from the general league, and especially from the idea of a congress, — a step which they seem to dread above everything.

The queen thought that she ought to consent to send this memorial and have the air of adopting it, she even desired that her brother should make her an ostensible reply to it, which she could show to its authors to convince them of her simulated sincerity, and I have the honour to send Y. M. a copy of a private letter which the queen wrote on this subject to the emperor, also passages from the one she did me the honour to write to me about it. When remitting these papers to M de Mercy I informed Baron de Breteuil about them, and in the conversation which they had about them on the following day M. de Mercy said that he did not think the memorial bad, that there were several good things in it which he thought quite reasonable. Y. M. can judge of the surprise of M. de Breteuil and his indignation; and finally, seeing that he was unable to convince M. de Mercy, he ended by representing to him that the King and Queen of France, regarding the matter from another point of view and asking of the emperor a reply analogous to their opinion, had the right to hope for it. This conversation with M de Mercy, joined to what M de Sémonville said to General Wrangel, has made me suspect that Mercy had already knowledge of the memorial, and that it was made in concert with him; for I have long suspected and I have several indications of a correspondence between him and the factious part of the former Assembly, of which the emperor was aware. Baron de Breteuil has been of my opinion, and believes as I do. I have thought it necessary to inform Y. M. of these details, in the belief that the emperor will seek to make a further bad use of the sending of this memorial.

The dispersion of the *émigrés* [warned out of the States of the princes of Germany] is no doubt a misfortune for them, but I do not think it harmful to the cause. To succeed, all must advance together, the within must not go faster than the without. In fact, what aid would the king have at this moment to sustain a movement made by the *émigrés* in his favour? These movements, whatever they are, can never have a great effect without the aid of some foreign power; and the season does not allow Y. M. or the empress to furnish at this moment the assistance you are determined to give. . . .

The reason why the queen cannot inform us in time of what is about to be done is the rapidity with which determinations are made and executed. That of the summons to the Electors [princes of Germany] and the going of the king to the Assembly was decided at eleven o'clock at night, the speech was made up during the night and delivered the next day. And so with other matters.

Count Fersen to Queen Marie-Antoinette.

January 24, 1792.

You will see by the letter of the King of Prussia that his inclinations are good, but that he will do nothing without the emperor. There is nothing, therefore, to do but to push the King of Prussia into making propositions to the latter.

I have received a perfect letter from Spain, of which I will send you the details Those of Russia are the same. The empress writes to the King of Sweden: "Perhaps the Queen of France will herself feel the necessity of claiming the assistance of her brother. Y. M ought to know better than I if it would be difficult to induce her to do so." The empress will be entirely convinced as to that by your letter. She says, farther on· "The more the cause we plead is worthy of all our care, and the more we neglect nothing that will enable it to triumph, the more we shall have, my dear brother, with our contemporaries and with posterity, the merit of not having desisted from so noble an enterprise without making every possible effort to surmount the difficulties which we encounter."

But the king and empress both insist on another flight, as to which I shall bring you a memorial and the letters of the king. His project is that it be executed by sea and by the English, of whom only two will be in the secret. I shall also bring you new proofs of the emperor's conduct. They say the Queen of Portugal is well-disposed; she has a great deal of money, and they think she would give it. I think it would be well to write to her; it might decide her.

Mme. de Vaudemont is in Paris to prevent the seizure of her house or to obtain an indemnity for it, but as she carries with her the resignation of MM. de Lambesc and Vaudemont, you will believe no doubt that they are not obliged to give her anything, nor yet to grant the pensions those men are now demanding, especially not to M de Vaudemont, if M. de Lambesc gets 20,000 or 30,000 francs it is all he can hope for. Also, as you can suppose, he will not be allowed to sell his office He proposed to do so to Baron de Breteuil's son-in-law for 300,000 francs. The latter refused it, saying he thought the king ought not to fetter himself in that way, and that he should no longer tolerate the sale of offices But the baron asks the king's kindness to give that office to his son-in-law some day, adding, when he mentioned it to me "He thinks well, and he is too rich to ask the king for anything, and enough so to keep up a great state"— besides which, he is too stupid ever to be troublesome or meddle in public matters. I will pay the baron the 22,000 francs that are due to him, but I must be authorized to remit to him 20,000 or 30,000 more (for which he will render an account), outlay on couriers, etc., which it is indispensable he should make.

The loss on money is terrible, it is 40 per cent; that is to say, of the . . . which you have in Holland you will only get . . . I will send you an exact account. I have decided to draw it all out and deposit it, for fear the loss may increase I have the same loss on all that I draw myself.

I shall make all my arrangements to arrive on the 3d at six in the evening.

Count Fersen to Queen Marie-Antoinette.

February 6, 1792.

It is absolutely necessary that you be drawn from the state in which you are, and only violent means can do it. . . .

The little archduke told the officers at the Order that all must be ready by March 1, that 6000 men had already started, that 14,000 more were ready to follow them, and that war with France seemed certain. M de Metternich says that they are going to change their language at last, that he was only awaiting the decision of the council of Brabant (about the persons lately arrested) to send a very strong note on that subject to M. de la Gravière. He added that we should soon hear news from Prussia more important than that of the suicide of M de Ségur. In spite of this I shall believe in nothing from the emperor until I see its effects.

It is said here that they want the king to veto the decree on passports Those who advise this act will try to make it seem an act of liberty. I think the king ought to sanction. The factious would represent his veto as a proof that he wants to go away and preserve the means of doing so Besides, this decree is a vexatious thing which bears hard upon the people, on account of the stamped paper, and it is well to let them feel its weight. Moreover, in spite of the king's veto, the Jacobins, by their influence, will continue to harass travellers. The veto will be good for nothing; people will still be obliged to get passports.

Count Fersen to Baron Taube.

BRUSSELS, February 14, 1792.

MY DEAR FRIEND, — All is once more changed, and I start for Paris in an hour. It may be necessary, to avoid suspicion, that I should make a turn towards Spain In any case I shall be back here by the 23d or 25th.

M. de Simolin [private envoy of the Empress of Russia] is here; he goes to Vienna from the queen, to tell the emperor their true position and their desires, and to urge him to act. In the conversation he had with her, the queen said: "Tell the emperor there is nothing to fear for us: the nation has need of the king, and that his son shall live, they must be rescued, as for me, I fear nothing. I prefer to subject myself to anything rather than live longer in the state of degradation in which I am; anything seems to me preferable to the horror of our position."

My friend, those words are significant, and Simolin has written them to the empress. The queen has also written to her about Simolin's journey: and she wrote the same to the emperor, and a charming letter to Prince Kaunitz, begging them to put entire confidence in Simolin. I hope for good effects from that step.

Baron Taube to Count Fersen.

GEFLE, February 16, 1792

The King of Sweden writes by post to-day to Staël [his ambassador in Paris] an order not to return to Sweden, it ought to meet him at Hamburg in case he took the course of returning here, which is against the king's orders.

The king is very well pleased with the letters of the King of Prussia, but he is in despair at the memorial which the queen let herself be forced by Barnave and others to write to the emperor, — especially after the letters she had just written to and received from the other sovereigns   In the first place, she is the dupe of the scoundrels who have wrung this memorial from her, for they will betray her; then it has shown them that she has means of communication, which they will now spy upon and intercept in the end.   We may also be certain that the emperor will make a bad use of that paper, in spite of the private letter that the queen wrote to him.   The King of Sweden has just warned the empress of this, in order that she may not be misled by the emperor

I disapprove strongly of what the queen has done in this matter; for who or what forced her to enter into negotiations or speak with Barnave and consorts?   Besides, my friend, he who undertakes to deceive too many persons at once, deceives no one.   The queen has but one rôle to play, so long as she remains shut up in Paris. which is to never trust herself to a Frenchman while she lives in France, not even if she believes him well-intentioned ; but she ought to make every one, and every new-comer believe that she desires to live according to the Constitution on all its points.   That is the only way to put those rebels to sleep.

I feel, my friend, how impossible it will be to separate the King of France from the queen and the dauphin ; I think it is a necessity that they shall stay together   But as for Madame Élisabeth and the little girl, I do not think it necessary that they should go too, or be even notified of the going ; all confidence in this matter is too risky.   Besides, they risk nothing in staying behind , the fury of the rebels will not be turned against them.

That which distresses me most is to see that nothing advances; that all is hemmed in by intrigues and negotiations which have no result. The king hears nothing more of pecuniary succour from Spain; and without money it is absolutely impossible to march his troops or send his ships to sea. Another misfortune is, that the winter is very severe this year, so that our ports will probably not be open before the end of May. Otherwise, the army by land and sea is in a complete state to advance. It only needs money to set it in motion, provide the commissariat, and purchase horses for the artillery and baggage-waggons.

16

CHAPTER IX.

1792 Count Fersen's Diary — His fruitless Mission to the King and
Queen in Paris — Death of the Emperor Leopold — Death of Gustavus III. King of Sweden — Advance and repulse of the French army
under the Comte de Rochambeau — Efforts to induce England to assist
in the rescue of the King and Queen — The 10th of August. — Imprisonment of the Royal Family in the Temple — Fatal retreat of the
Duke of Brunswick — The Duc de Choiseul's Account of August 10th,
and of the Arrest at Varennes

January 1, 1792. Brussels. The Elector of Cologne has
given orders to all the French refugees at Andernach to leave
his State. He asked the archduchess for protection by the
troops of the emperor. She replied that she had no orders
for that.

2d. Memorial of the queen to the emperor; detestable;
made by Barnave, Lameth, and Duport, intended to frighten
the emperor and prove to him that his interest is not to
make war, but to maintain the Constitution, for fear the
French may propagate their doctrines and debauch his
soldiery. Letters from the queen to the emperor, the Queen
of Spain, and to me   Memorial and letters to King and
Queen of France [from King of Sweden] well done.

11th   Letter from Crawford; he has seen queen and
talked with her. They want to send the Bishop of Autun
[Talleyrand] to London to negotiate, little Custine to
Brunswick; they expect to gain all by money.

14th. The Abbé de Limon, just returned from Paris,
says that minds are amazingly changed; that the people
desire a change, and that some one should come to
their relief; they want the Constitution, but with great
changes.

18th. M. de la Galissonnière says that two or three hundred of the bourgeois of Paris are going in parties of ten or twelve to Kehl, where they have rendezvous; thence to the princes. Two came to his house and asked him the way. They each had twenty-five louis.

21st. The queen consents that I shall go to Paris.

24th The Princesse de Tarente has arrived. News from Paris of a riot about the dearness of sugar, which costs three livres, five sous. They pillaged the hotel of the Americans, it is said, and several grocers' shops. Sugar was sold in the market for twenty-four sous. My departure for Paris is fixed for the 3d of February.

29th. Letter from the queen, begging me to defer my journey until the decree about the passports is given, and tranquillity is more established in Paris. Much is being said about the departure of the king, and the newspapers indicate by way of Calais. This is the fruit of French indiscretion, those who imagine a project tell it to everybody, and spies are sent to the spot.

February 1. Dined with La Marck. Much talk of Mirabeau and all his intrigues with Lafayette. La Marck is an intriguer. The Prince of Nassau wrote to the Comte d'Artois that he was very well pleased with the emperor, who would act. The Comte d'Artois wrote it to the Prince de Condé, and the Prince de Condé sent the original letter to be read by all the gentlemen in his service.

3d Letter from the queen, says it is impossible, on account of private passports, that I should go, and I must renounce it. Bad for me and for affairs They feign to suspect the king's escape, and the rumour is spread in Paris to prevent the new guard of the king from entering upon its functions, which is for the 10th, and the decree on passports is made to prevent his departure, the means are not bad.

6th. I have determined to go to Paris on a letter from the queen telling me that the decree on the passports will not be sanctioned, Frenchmen who have passed in very well write to say so.

9th. Simolin arrived from Paris at eleven o'clock without any obstacle. Dined with him at Breteuil's. He is going to Vienna from the queen to inform the emperor of their position, the state of France, and their positive desire for succour. He saw them secretly ; the queen said · " Tell the emperor the nation has too much need of the king and his son for them to have anything to fear ; they are the ones it is important to rescue   As for me, I fear nothing, and I would rather run all possible dangers than live any longer in my present state of degradation and unhappiness " Simolin was touched to tears as he spoke of it   He told me of the queen's charming letters to the emperor and the empress and Prince Kaunitz   M. de Mercy, whom he had seen, held the usual language. Simolin reproached him for his conduct, so different from that indicated in his declarations at Padua ; he told him he had deceived the Powers, and he forced him to admit it.

The orders of the Empress of Russia to Simolin were : to make the declaration at Padua, to rally always to the most vigorous measure that was proposed, without waiting for new instructions, and to leave Paris at once if the other ministers left.

10th. All my arrangements are made to start.

11th. *Saturday.* Started at half-past nine in a courier's chaise with Reutersvaerd, and no servant. We had a courier's passport for Portugal under feigned names. The letters and memorial of the king [of Sweden] to the King of France, addressed to the Queen of Portugal, I put into an envelope of the ambassador of Sweden to Paris, with a false cipher to which I counterfeited the signature of the king, and another cipher, also false, for Bergstedt, chargé d'affaires, the whole sealed with arms of Sweden, made here. I had also, for my own safety, a letter accrediting me to the Queen of Portugal

By eight o'clock we were at Tournai, where we slept.

12th. Left at half-past three in the morning Reutersvaerd went in the evening to see M. d'Aponcourt, commandant, to get the gates opened. He took him for a Swedish courier, and told him he would not get to Paris in fifteen days, and would be stopped everywhere. At Orchies nothing was said to us : we breakfasted at Bouchain, dined at Bonavis, and slept at Gournai, our chaise broke down at Péronne and we were there four hours. Reached Gournai at half-past one in the morning. I kept myself hidden ; I had a wig Everywhere they were very polite, especially at Péronne, — even the National Guard.

13th, *Monday.* Fine and mild. Started at half-past nine Stopped two hours at Louvres for dinner ; reached Paris without accident at half-past five in the evening, without a word being said to us. Left my officer at the Hôtel des Princes, rue Richelieu, took a fiacre to go to Goguelat, rue Pelletier The coachman did not know the way. Another fiacre told us. Goguelat was not there ; waited in the street till half-past six. Did not come Felt uneasy. Went to join Reutersvaerd. He could not get a room at the Hôtel des Princes and they did not know where he had gone. Returned to Goguelat. Not in. Decided to wait in the street. At last at seven he came. My letter had only arrived at midday that morning, and they had not been able to decipher it earlier. Went to the queen ; took my usual way ; afraid of the National Guard ; did not see the king

14th. Very fine and mild. Saw the king at six in the

evening.   He will not leave, cannot, on account of extreme
vigilance ; but the truth is, he has scruples, having so often
promised to remain — for he is an honest man.   He has,
however, consented that when the armies arrive, he will go
with smugglers, always through woods, and let himself be
met by a detachment of light-troops   He wants the congress to concern itself at first solely with his demands and
if they are granted then to insist that he shall leave Paris for
some place chosen for the ratification   If this is refused, he
consents that the Powers shall act, and he submits to all
dangers   He thinks he risks nothing, because the rebels
need him to obtain the terms of a capitulation

The king wore the *cordon rouge* [Order of Saint-Louis]
He sees that there is no resource except in force ; but, in
consequence of his feebleness, he thinks it impossible to recover all his authority   I proved to him the contrary ; told
him it could be done by force and that the Powers desired
to do it   He agreed.   Nevertheless, if he is not constantly
encouraged, I am afraid he will be tempted to negotiate with
the rebels.

After a time he said to me · " *Ah, ça !* here we are alone
and we can speak.   I know that I am taxed with weakness
and irresolution, but no one was ever in my position.   I
know that I missed the right moment ; it was July 14 ; I
ought to have gone then, and I wished it ; but what could
I do when *Monsieur* himself begged me not to go, and Maréchal de Broglie who commanded said ' Yes, we can go to
Metz, but what shall we do when we get there ? ' — I lost
the moment, and since then I have never found it ; I have
been abandoned by all the world "   He begged me to warn
the Powers that they must not be shocked at anything he
was obliged to do, for he was obliged, — it was the effect of
compulsion.   ' They must,' he said, ' put me entirely aside

and let me act as I may.' He desired also that it should be
explained to the Powers that he had sanctioned the decree
on the sequestration of the property of the *émigrés* solely
for the purpose of preserving it, otherwise, it would have
been pillaged and burned; but that he would never consent
to have it sold as national property. He also wished to veto
the decree on passports.

The queen told me that she saw Alex. Lameth and
Duport; that they told her incessantly there was no remedy
but that of foreign troops, without them all was lost, that
this state of things could not last, that they themselves had
gone farther than they wished; that it was the folly of the
aristocrats which had made their success, and the conduct
of the Court, which could have arrested all if it had joined
with them. They talked of aristocrats, but she thought it
was really the effect of their *hatred* to the present Assembly,
in which they are nothing and have no influence; they are
frightened, seeing that all must change, and they wish to
make themselves a merit in advance But she thinks them
bad, does not trust them; but uses them, finding it serviceable
to do so. All the ministers are traitors who betray the king.
M. Cahier de Gerville is the worst, and threatens constantly
to leave the Counil and denounce his associates Bertrand
[minister of the navy] is good, but alone he can do nothing
Narbonne and Lessart [war and post] will do everything to
preserve themselves, and nothing for the king. Cahier de Gerville was a little lawyer at seven hundred francs a year. —
Mlle. Rocherette [the dauphin's maid, in fear of whom the
flight to Varennes was delayed] was Gouvion's mistress and
told him everything. She had nothing but suspicions
Questioned on the day after the departure, she said horrors
about the queen; being asked if she had not heard passing
through that door, and whether, as she did not give warning,

she was afraid, she said she heard passing so often after the
king had gone to bed, that it seemed nothing new to her. —
For some time, the guard was often tripled, it was so on the
afternoon of June 20.   M. de Valori, who had been told he
would be sent as courier with his two comrades, repeated it
to his mistress, who was also the mistress of M . . one of
the fanatics. — As the queen crossed the Great Carrousel she
sent M. de . . . , who accompanied her and who did not
know the way, to ask the sentinel on horseback where the
Little Carrousel was.   At Chalons they were recognized; a
man warned the mayor, who took the course of telling him
that if he were sure he had only to make it public, but he
must be responsible for results.   The body-guard good
for nothing   On the way back [from Varennes] M. de
Dampierre, who came to see them, gave his arm to one of
the dauphin's maids to help her into the carriage.   She
warned him to go away, as they were all against him.   He
said no.   He mounted his horse, and fifty paces on they shot
him like a rabbit on the plain; when he fell from his horse
they massacred him and came back to the carriage with
their hands all bloody and carrying his head. — The queen
gave a piece of beef-à-la-mode, which I had put into the
carriage, to a man, a voice cried out: "Don't eat it, don't
you see they want to poison you?"   The queen immediately
ate some and gave some to the dauphin. — Latour-Maubourg
and Barnave behaved very well   Pétion was indecent.   The
first would not get into the carriage with the king; he told
them they might feel sure of him, but it was important to
win over the two others.   Pétion told them he knew everything; how they had taken a hired carriage close to the
palace driven by a Swede named — here he pretended not
to know my name and asked the queen to tell him.   She
replied: "I am not in the habit of knowing the names of

hackney-coachmen." — Mlle. Rocherette presented herself in full dress; she expected to be their chamber-maid. Before the departure she had several times searched the queen's desk. — They were from six o'clock in the morning till seven at night from Meaux to the Tuileries, without daring to let down the blinds of the carriage. — During the next six weeks officers were in the adjoining room. They wanted to sleep in the queen's chamber. All she could obtain was that they would keep between the two doors, two or three times during the night they came in to see if she was in her bed. Once, when she could not sleep and lit her lantern, an officer came in and established a conversation. A camp beneath the windows kept up an infernal uproar. Every night the officers in the room were relieved every two hours [1]

21st. At six o'clock went out; found Reutersvaerd, with whom I made all arrangements for departure at midnight. I accompanied Goguelat to take leave of the king and queen. The queen sent me word that the answer to the bad memorial she had sent to the emperor, written by Barnave, Lameth, and Duport, had just arrived and was detestable. I took tea and supped with them. At midnight I left them. Frantz let me out by the great gate. I did not find Reutersvaerd, which made me uneasy. At the end of a quarter of an hour he came; we went to his inn, where the landlord, though Protestant and a democrat, had loaded him with kindness, as did every one.

At one o'clock we got into the carriage, — a light one with three horses.

22d *Wednesday.* Passed Senlis at half-past three without difficulty At Pons, though the National Guard were already

---

[1] Further particulars of these interviews with the king and queen will be found in Count Fersen's report to the King of Sweden, February 29, 1792 — TR

afoot, nothing was said to us. We breakfasted at Gournai; it snowed there for an hour rather hard, then fine and cold. We were much delayed by the slippery roads. Reached Bonavis at seven in the evening. Supped badly and slept in our clothes, in the cartmen's room.

23d. Fine, very cold. Started at half-past six, roads dreadful as far as Cambrai, stayed there one hour and a half, the postilions would not start, on account of the roads, and the post-master told me that in times like these he could not force them to go. At last, one of them, in view of the lightness of our carriage agreed to do so. We passed Bouchain very well, but at a little village of a dozen houses, half a league before Marchiennes, I was awakened by the stopping of the carriage, and some one asked Reutersvaerd for his passport. I pretended to be asleep. After studying it five minutes, the man said it was worth nothing, it said " by the order of the king," and not " by order of the law;" besides, there was no description of our persons, it was not good. Reutersvaerd got angry and said: " But it is a passport from the embassy, they ought to know how to write them, and our minister would never have given it to us if it was not all right." The man said : " It does not conform to the model we have, it is worth nothing" Then the postilion, who saw the courier's badge, said : " But, monsieur, don't you see that these gentlemen are couriers ? You have no right to stop them." " Of course not," said Reutersvaerd, " and Swedish couriers, too, that is in the passport; and here is that of our minister." The imbecile had never discovered this and at first, when he saw that Reutersvaerd was polite, he was insolent. After reading the paper a second time he let us pass, saying that we must not be surprised if they stopped us at Marchiennes, which was done at the only gate there was to the town by a sentinel in a gray jacket.

The officer, in a brown coat, let us pass on our telling him we were couriers and showing him our passports. . . . By four o'clock we were at Tournai, where we dined well and in the same chamber where we slept on our way. What a difference! We reached Brussels at three the next morning. My joy was great in having succeeded and being once more at home.

27th. Baron de Breteuil warns me that M. de Mercy complains of the dissatisfaction the queen shows with the emperor, and believes that I am the cause of it; he gave the baron to understand that he had discovered this. It could only be through my letters, and I do not believe he could decipher them, for the Swedish cipher is very difficult, and as for my letters to Paris, all are written in white ink, and they would not have reached their destination intact had they been washed and read. This is a mere suspicion on their part because they find that the King of France has himself addressed the Powers. M. de Mercy let M de Breteuil know that I was much suspected and very inconvenient, and he begged him never to tell me anything that he confided to him That does not trouble me; it only proves that they did not think me so clear-sighted. I went to see M. de Mercy; he talked to me of affairs, of the annoyance the princes were, he said they must be got away, and had much better be in the South. I was of his opinion, except as to sending them wholly away; they could be made useful on the second line and by directing their conduct

5th. Dined with M. de Breteuil. Thugut and Browne launched out against the emperor, in displeasure that he would not act. The first added that he was sure of it. He also doubted whether the emperor desired to restore things as they were in France, and said that, to make sure of this, we had better ask M. de Mercy whether he expected that

the management of the finances would be restored to the
king as before the revolution.   Thugut believes, and I am of
his opinion, that the emperor wants to avoid acting; if
forced to do so he wants to be stiong enough with Prussia
to exclude the Northern Powers and give France a mixed
government which would make her dependent on him and
take from her all her strength and influence in Europe.
For this reason he has consented to the fifty thousand men
promised by Prussia in order to represent that force to the
Northern Courts as sufficient, and so prevent them from
sending troops; and if he cannot succeed in that, at least
to have a great superiority in deciding matteis.   But with
the influence of the Empress of Russia, the good-will of Prussia, and the ambition of the Duke of Brunswick, that
plan can easily be foiled, and then the princes must be put
forwaid, made to make demands (concerted with the king),
to which the Powers would have the air of yielding.   He
advised the baron not to bind himself towards de Mercy for
any repayment of money until the king was restored to his
full authority.

8th. The Bishop of Pamiers came at half-past seven to
tell me that the emperor had died suddenly; the perfoim-
ance at the theatre was interrupted, the actor announced the
news, and theie were two or three applauses. I knew already that a courier had arrived. The archduchess was
ignorant, she even sent M. de Metternich after dinner to
inquire if there were any letters for hei. Later in the evening she sent for all the generals and spoke to them very
well and firmly. —The Vicomte de Véiac, who came to see
me in the evening, told me the people were saying about
the streets: "The emperor is dead; well, that's good!" He,
the bishop, and many others think this will change and delay
everything. I am not of that opinion; I showed them why,

and I felt that Baron de Breteuil agreed with me.   I decided
to write my opinion to the queen and send it the next day
by post.

9th. In all societies last night the emperor's death had
little effect and did not upset the various parties.   The generals did not show the slightest regret, but almost the contrary   Thugut told the baron he was glad.   In the city the
news made no sensation, the officials were even pleased
Papers were scattered about inciting the people to revolt,
saying this was the moment to rise, they must profit by
it and seduce the soldiery.   The gates of the town were
closed after eleven in the morning, but nothing riotous appeared in the streets — Some say the emperor died of con-
gestion of the lungs, others, among them the chancellor and
M. de Metternich, that he had an attack of colic, was bled
three times, the attack returned at midday and he died in
horrible vomitings.   By which they mean that he was poi-
soned.   So much the better, if it proves to them the necessity
of exterminating those French monsters   But the chancellor's purpose in crediting that tale is, on the contrary, to
prove the danger of interfering in the affairs of France.

13th. M. de Narbonne is dismissed from the ministry
[of war] by the king in consequence of his base conduct
towards M Bertrand, minister of the navy, whom he endeavoured in every possible way to ruin, and also because of
letters which he made the generals Rochambeau, Luckner,
and Lafayette write to him to preserve his ministry.   The
Chevalier de Grave, a young democrat, twenty-eight to thirty
years of age, succeeds him.   This is a triumph for the Jacobins   It was MM. Duport, Barnave, and Lameth who
wanted the dismissal of M. de Narbonne; they were dissatisfied with him, and said he deceived them.

18th. Letter from Crawford, which makes me all the more

uneasy because the Chevalier de Coigny had sent me word
of a project of the Jacobins to put the queen in a convent or
take her to Orléans to be confronted with M de Lessart,
and a few days ago March 10, M. Vergniaud said in the
Assembly "Terror must now enter that palace from which
it has issued so many times, let all those who are in it
tremble, there is but one person there who is inviolable."

22d. Letter from Mme de Lamballe to Baron de Breteuil
saying that they want to denounce the queen in the affair of
M de Lessart [late director of posts] and separate her thus
from the king to put her in a convent. This confirms my
letter from Crawford. I believe in the project, but I doubt
its execution. The Abbé de Saint-Albin says he thinks the
queen will go away. I do not believe she will ever separate
from the king · and where could she go? it would be difficult to go anywhere, on account of Coblentz.

23d. Found Goguelat when I came home; he passed
through Calais, Dover, and Ostend. He left them eight days
ago. Their position is horrible. I give the details in my
letter to the king of the 24th. He heard the deputies say.
"Lessart will get out of this, but the queen will not." Goguelat had a little paper [to the new emperor] which read
thus: —

"I beg you, my nephew, to have confidence in all that the
bearer may tell you from us.

"MARIE-ANTOINETTE"

"I join your aunt, and think absolutely as she does.

"LOUIS."

We went to see Baron de Breteuil. He had the air, I
thought, of not approving this step; but he said nothing

25th. Dined at home with Baron Thugut. He thinks
wonderfully well. He told me there were fifteen thousand

The Princesse de Lamballe

men in the Milanese provinces to protect the King of Sardinia   He disapproved of the emperor's reply which caused the dismissal of Lessart   He wanted an insignificant one, and the immediate despatch of fifty thousand men, after which a firm answer.   He blames Mercy and those who made the answer; wished they would act with vigour at once and enable the king to leave.

April 3d   The Duc d'Uzès, at the head of one hundred and fifty French gentlemen, came to see me to ask news about the assassination of the King of Sweden.   Letter to the queen

12th   Received letters from Sweden of the 23d and 27th. The bulletin bad.   In Brégart's envelope a paper was added on which was written that the king died on the 29th towards midday.   I was horror-struck   Baron Hopp, the Dutch minister, said the same thing   I tried to hope it was false, but I could not, the details on his condition were too bad I am tortured.

17th. Dined with Breteuil. Thugut told him that the King of Hungary [1] had written here that he was weary of what was going on in France, and had decided to act and put an end to it, that he should march his troops at once, and the French must be amused for two months until the troops arrived, then, whether the French attacked him or not, he should attack them.

25th   An engineer officer, named Obredi, who was sent to reconnoitre the country, the French, and the disposition of the inhabitants, reports that M. de Rochambeau is encamped, since Monday at Maubeuge, opposite to Mons, in a very fine intrenched position, and that nothing hinders the

---

[1] Francis, son of the Emperor Leopold succeeded his father in his hereditary dominions as King of Hungary and sovereign of Austria, but was not called Emperor of Germany until his election, July 5, 1792 as Francis II — TR.

French from entering the country and coming to Brussels; that no precautions are being taken to prevent it, that the troops are so placed that they can be cut off with no chance of reuniting, that absolutely nothing is being done; that this is horrible, and there is not a moment to be lost. When he made this report to the archduchess she burst into tears, and said she was lost   He thinks the inhabitants about the frontiers are very ill-disposed   In short, he thinks their position [that of the government of the Low Countries] very dangerous, and their inertia and apathy extreme Nothing has been done.   The jealousy of General Browne against General Bender is excessive and will spoil all.   The former has never been to reconnoitre the country.   A faithful man in Namur, who has been a patriot, asked two months ago, through M. de Breteuil, to be called here to give important information to the government.   M. de Metternich forgot it, and he has not yet been called or heard.   When important affairs are talked of to the archduchess she weeps; Duc Albert [her husband] chatters; Mercy says there is nothing to be done, but he will talk of it with Metternich, who forgets it — it is all abominable.   If they suffered alone it would not be so bad.   Bender wanted to form a cordon from Ostend to Luxembourg fine stupidity ! They are going to encamp and take a position.   General Ferrari, a man of merit is indignant.   He is not employed, but he has pointed out several positions important to guard, which they had never thought of.

26th.   Dined at Court; the archduchess did not speak to me.   Rochambeau's camp has only 100 cannon and 1200 men.   He writes from Valenciennes to General Beaulieu at Mons, his letter is dated "Year IV. of Liberty."   In it he deplores the evils of war and asks, to spare blood, that no hostilities shall take place on either side until the *guerre franche* (?) has begun. He says he is not authorized to make this proposal, but he hopes that the general will convey it to the general government, and if they have not confidence in him, he will send a courier to Paris and obtain the king's orders. He speaks in his own name. His aide-de-camp reached Mons as the parade was beginning, they let him see it, and then sent him back.

30th. Received news in the morning that there had been an affair near Tournai, where the French were repulsed. The Austrians had been very uneasy all day about Mons. At two o'clock I met M. de Metternich, he told me that they had just heard of an affair at the outposts of Mons; he added that he had felt the keenest anxiety lest the troops had not assembled before the French attack, but that now he was easy on that point. "At any rate," he said, "it would not have been my fault; for I have warned them for the last three weeks, and never ceased to urge them about it, but they did nothing." Returning from a drive at eight in the evening, I heard that the French had been repulsed and well-beaten at Mons, that at least is what Count Metternich wrote me.

May 10th. The princes have written to the archduchess offering her all the Frenchmen who are under their orders, and they wrote the same to Vienna. She answered she could decide nothing without the orders of the king [of Hungary]. She did this by the advice of M. de Mercy, who told M. de Breteuil they had decided not to use Frenchmen, and not to admit them to participate in anything. He told Thugut that his chief fear was that the Baron de Breteuil was mixed in this affair, and he must be excluded. He asked him to say in Vienna (where Thugut is now going) that although he had previously decided to retire, he should now stay on, because of these important circumstances in

17

which he might be useful, that he would continue to
negotiate affairs and desired to be charged with making
peace, but on condition that he had full powers to make it
as he pleased.   In all he says one sees his desire to negotiate
and come to some agreement, which could only be bad because he is allied, through La Borde, with the constitutionals
Barnave, Lameth, Duport, etc., and he has not spoken to
the Baron about the princes' offer.   I advised the baron to
repeat to him the same offer, and show him the advantage of
accepting it and the danger of refusing it at a moment when
they have not enough troops and when the *émigrés* could be
of use in enticing the French to desert, and if he refuses, to
request him to remember the fact that the offer had been
made.

26th.   Strücker has arrived.   Says that disorder at Valenciennes is at its height.   Rochambeau would have been
massacred like Dillon if he had not kept himself hidden
in the Abbey of Saint-Sauve for three days; where they
went three times in search of him   On Monday, Luckner
wanted to break camp; the troops refused, swearing against
that —— foreigner who wanted to lead them to butchery, and
threatening to hang him.   The Royal-Swedish refused to
go into garrison at Douai.   Three soldiers met the Duc
d'Orléans, they stopped him and insulted him, declaring
that if he made them start they would massacre him, that
it was he who was instigating all this, that he was a scoundrel, and his proper place was at Coblentz with the other
princes, but his behaviour had been so bad he dared not go
there.

June 7th.   Bergstedt [Swedish secretary of embassy in
Paris] arrived at 9 o'clock last evening; passed safely
through Valenciennes.   Says the Jacobins in Paris are quiet
since the king's body-guard has been dismissed; they want

to be masters of his person and carry him off with them; he thinks they could succeed, for those who wish to prevent it have no leader; and as the majors [*chefs de bataillon*] command the National Guard for two months, they cannot have any. Servan has quarrelled with Dumouriez, who wanted to rule every thing. . . . It was Mme. de Staël [wife of Swedish ambassador] who wrote the letters of the generals to Narbonne, and who got Lessart dismissed. All the constitutionals, friends of Narbonne, did not go to the Assembly to defend him, and in that way the Jacobins succeeded in arraigning him. It was an intrigue of Mme. de Staël. She always carries poison on her to take in case anything happens to Narbonne. She went, disguised as a man, to see him at Arras; her carriage was overturned on the way back; all that made talk. She was absent from Tuesday to Sunday.

24th. Received "Cosmopolite" of 21st. Frightful account of an attack on the Tuileries on the 20th; horrible! the consequences make me shudder.

July 8th. Lasserez has arrived with letters from the queen to me and to Mercy. She wants them to act and speak at once. It cannot be done until the forces arrive; for they must speak only when acting.

9th. Saw Mercy. He is of my opinion that they must be ready to act when they speak. The queen asked that in their manifesto they would hold Paris responsible for the king and his family. She asks if it would not be best to leave Paris. He answered, "Yes" if they were sure of persons to protect their departure, and if so, they should go to Compiègne, and appeal to the departments of Amiens and Soissons. He talked to me very well about the manifesto; said hope must be left to all, except the factious, in order to save the king; the Constitution not to be mentioned; make war upon it, but say nothing, and so annihilate it. He complained of those who surrounded the Baron de Breteuil and prevented him, Mercy, from confiding in him; and said that the king could not recover his authority at once, — that was impossible, — only little by little. Said he himself was calumniated, accused of coldness to the interests of the queen; that his correspondence would prove the contrary; but that he dared not trust the French, who, one and all, even the aristocrats, were worth nothing. he had always written urging action to Vienna, but could never bring anything about. — He said all this with temper and impatience. He was indignant at the conduct of Spain, which covered her, he said, with mud.

10th. Sent Lasserez back with letter to the queen. In the "Gazette Universelle" of the 7th a horrible speech by M. Danton to the council-general of the Commune of Paris. It is frightful. Wrote to the queen by post.[1]

14th. I have received from Paris a pamphlet entitled. " Le Cri de la douleur" — The "Cry of Pain, or the Day of June 20th." It is written by Mercier, very well done and worthy of preservation.

23d. Received four letters from Paris. Their situation is alarming, they ask for the issuing of the manifesto and the entrance of the armies. They think they will be removed into the interior. The queen would not yield to the proposal of the constitutionals, with Lafayette and Luckner, to go to Compiègne, fearing to fall into their hands and give

---

[1] From this point the Diary contains a great deal relating to the condition of the Low Countries, the movement of troops, the endless negotiations and intrigues of diplomatists, princes, émigrés, in which Fersen, after the death of Gustavus III, was more of a trusted spectator than an active agent In this volume only those parts of the Diary and letters which relate more particularly to the fate of the King and Queen of France are given — TR.

the Powers, who have so little willingness to act, a pretext to negotiate.

26th. Four hundred federals from Marseille passed through Lyon, the municipality invited them to the theatre, where they sang horrible songs against the queen, the honourable citizens silenced them, the next day those citizens were accused by the municipality.

31st. The emperor and the King of Prussia have a great aversion to the *émigrés*. Mercy has no influence. Schulemburg says the troops ought to be brought into action at once, for both officers and soldiers are beginning to grumble at their fatigues and their expenses for the affairs of France.

August 3d. A violent affray has taken place in Paris with the National Guard on the arrival of the Marseillais, those of the Guard who are stationed in the palace were returning from dinner in the Champs-Élysées when they were insulted by the populace who were joined by the Marseillais, the National Guard drew their sabres and fought. Three guards were killed, several wounded. The mayor arrived and quieted the people. The National Guard demand justice and will take it.

7th. Dined with Sullivan. The municipality of Paris demand the fall of the king. Very anxious. Mme Sullivan, who is deeply distressed, never ceases to concern herself with the fate of the king and queen; she is even ill from anxiety, and urges me to send some one to England to entreat the king to take some step to save their lives, and to make him declare he will not allow those lives to be attacked, or he will take some startling vengeance. He could be shown that this would not affect their system of neutrality because it is only in the event of an attack upon the life of the king and queen that they are asked to do anything, and besides, it binds them to nothing; for if the king and queen were massacred, England would still be the mistress of doing nothing   I thought the idea good, but a thousand obstacles in its way, — Pitt's embarrassment lest such a demand should be discussed in parliament, and the question as to what point a nation has the right to dethrone and condemn its king; also, the short time there was, and the known ill-will of the English.   She answered that, admitting all that, we might at least try it, that the point was to save their lives, and we must not regret the useless pains we take, for even if they came to nothing we should at least have the satisfaction of having tried everything.   I had nothing to reply to this, and I decided to induce M. de Breteuil to undertake it.   Mme Sullivan talked with Simolin, who agreed with her and thought the thing might succeed, she begged Crawford to be the one to go to England, and he consented.

In the evening I spoke to the Baron de Breteuil; he was entirely against the idea for the same reasons as mine in the morning; and he added his fear of ill-will in Pitt, who might betray the whole thing and by informing the factious in Paris expose the king.   That was exaggeration and I proved it to him.   However, he persisted in his refusal, adding that in politics a useless step is always injurious.   I gave him the arguments that Mme Sullivan had given me in the morning, and begged him to reflect over them that night, and I would see him in the morning to know his decision.   Meantime I have agreed with Crawford that if Breteuil persists in refusing, we will send a man with letters to the Duke of Dorset and try to induce him to get this action taken.

8th.   I went at 8 o'clock to Baron de Breteuil; he had entirely come round to my idea, and his letter to Pitt was already written, he wished to send it by courier, but I represented to him that it was better to send some one who

could speak and show the interest that was felt in it, he
wished Crawford to go. I went to see Crawford, and he consented; but said a Frenchman, such as the Bishop of
Pamiers, the baron's confidential agent, would have more
effect, for they could tell him, Crawford, that this was only
an idea of his; and that as an Englishman he ought to have
dismissed it. I represented this to the baron, and the
bishop was decided on. At two o'clock Crawford and I
were at the baron's I begged him to write also to Lord
Granville, minister of Foreign Affairs, and to Lord Camelford
to get him to introduce the bishop It was agreed to avoid
speaking on a single thing but this one object, namely, to
secure the safety of the king and queen, and to prove that
that object could not in any way injure the neutrality.
Crawford and I wrote letters to the Duke of Dorset, and
before night all was ready

10th. News from Paris is reassuring, but how can we
count on anything with those scoundrels and cowards? The
palace is still threatened, and the king and queen sleep only
alternately; one or the other is always up.

13th. Terrible news from Paris. Thursday morning the
palace [of the Tuileries] was attacked, the king and queen
escaped to the Assembly. At one o'clock the populace were
fighting in the courtyards and the Carrousel Blood flowed
in streams, many killed and hanged, the palace forced on
all sides, eight pieces of cannon levelled and firing upon it.
Romainvilliers killed; Daffy also; a thick smoke makes
people believe they have fired the palace. My God, what
horrors! — Mercy came to Breteuil; suggests sending a man
to Lafayette to propose to join his army with that of the
Austrians folly; for if the object is to succour them, it is
too late; if to negotiate with the constitutionals, it is worth
nothing and cannot save them in the end. Mercy said in

the evening that the Assembly had surrounded itself with cannon, and that step awed the factious The king had either been deposed, or had abdicated of his own accord

15th. News from Paris. The Royal family in the Hôtel de Noailles, watched day and night, not allowed to see any one. Talked to Breteuil about inducing the King of Prussia to persuade Lafayette and the generals to come over with their armies and dissolve them, etc., etc. . . .

17th. News from Paris. The king and his family imprisoned in the Tower of the Temple. Mmes. de Lamballe and Tourzel imprisoned with them. Lameth arrested at Rouen on his way to Havre to escape to England with his wife. He begged for all favour not to be taken back to Paris, where he would be massacred.

19th The King of Prussia has written to Vienna to propose the regency of *Monsieur*, on condition that Calonne be dismissed, and Baron de Breteuil be put at the head of affairs. Vicomte de Caraman [Louis XVI's envoy to Court of Berlin] writes that the king desires much that M. de Breteuil should go to see him. The baron does not wish to go, but as the King of Prussia is a yielding man and lets himself rely on the last who speaks to him, they might give him prejudices against the baron and his "intractability," so it may be better that he should go for a moment and return here at once. All this is an intrigue of the devil. The baron got M. de Metternich to write to Vienna and discourage this idea of a regency

21st. The Bishop of Pamiers has returned, satisfied with the Duke of Dorset. Pitt spoke well, more interested in the affairs of France than he wishes to show. The bishop took upon himself to say that it was by order of the king that the baron took this step He insisted on a more decided expression at the close of the despatch to Lord Gower, but

could not obtain it. He thinks they all desired to be more
decided, but dared not, on account of the nation, which is
strongly worked upon by propagandists of all nations, with
whom London abounds. Pitt assured him that factious
persons should never be received in England, he said they
had a great deal of money there. — Letter from Dorset to
me, very good. Lafayette, Alex Lameth, Latour-Maubourg,
Baron de Perzy, with thirteen others, their servants, forty
horses, and a great deal of gold, arrested at Rochefort

27th. Duke Albert [husband of the archduchess, regent of
the Low Countries] wanted to keep Lafayette but let the
others go, opposed in this   Baron de Breteuil has talked to
the archduchess about the duke's inaction, he said it shamed
him, that he might have acquired glory by attempting to
take the places that confronted him, for which there was
great probability of success. She had the air of feeling this,
but, nevertheless, put forward fears on the internal tranquillity of the Low Countries; she took note of what he
said, however.

30th   News from Paris. The project of the Jacobins is
the agrarian law, and the National Convention will take it
up. The Princesse de Tarente, who was at the Abbaye
with two guards over her, is taken to the prison of La Force.
Maréchal de Mouchy is to be arrested. M. de Nicolai
writes me that the queen is not well. M. d'Affry [comman-
der of the Swiss guards] is absolved; he said he did not give
the Swiss an order to fire on the people, though the queen
had repeatedly requested it; and the proof was the few
cartridges he had issued, for they had but six: what infamy
for him! — Lafayette and company have left Luxembourg on
demand of the King of Prussia   Lafayette asked the archduchess to see him, he having things of the utmost importance to communicate to her; she refused, and sent him a

man to know what he had to say, telling him he could put
entire confidence in him, the man has returned, nothing has
transpired.

September 2d.   M. de Rivarol came to see me in the
evening.   He talked much and very well, but said little.
He told me that his brother, who was at the Tuileries on the
10th of August, wrote him that the king himself placed all
the posts. the Swiss Guard were on the Theatre side, four
thousand of the National Guard at the other end of the palace;
the queen accompanied him, encouraged every one, took a
pistol from the Duc de Choiseul and gave it to the king.
They returned to the palace.   The brigands, who were arriving, fired six shots and cried out that they were surrender-
ing.   Five of the artillery went over to the side of the crowd
and turned their cannon on the palace, the rest were faithful.   It was then that they induced the king to take refuge
in the Assembly.   The Swiss and the National Guard fired,
and every one fled.   Then they came and told the Swiss
they were wrong to defend the palace, for "the bird was
flown," — the king was not there   The Swiss replied it was
a trap set for them, they knew very well he was there.   They
told the same thing to the National Guard, who abandoned
the Swiss and surrounded the Assembly   M de Rivarol here
said that the king did wrong to abandon the palace and put
himself under the blade of the Jacobins of the Assembly,
had he stayed where he was, the *canaille* would have been
repulsed and the constitutionals would have had the upper
hand, which would have been well, — for at least, the king's
life was safe.   Rivarol was right, but to judge, one must
know all the circumstances

5th   News from Paris awful.   They say the Princesse de
Tarente has escaped   They say the people condemn and
execute at once. — Verdun was taken on the 1st at seven in

the evening, after a bombardment of four hours. The commandant blew out his brains. The garrison sent back to France disarmed.

6th. Dreadful details from Paris. Manuel said to the king, when they forced him to see the dead body of Mme. de Lamballe: " Look at it! there may be a counter-revolution, but you shall not profit by it; there's the fate that awaits you." — All these details make me fear for the king and queen; I decide to send a courier to M. de Breteuil and write to him. I believe it is necessary to adopt another course; I have never feared so much.

7th. Saw the Prussian minister, Baron Beck; he talked well on French affairs. He thinks the king lost. He urges Duke Albert to act, but finds little good-will and much slowness and indecision. He seems to say pretty freely what he thinks, and disapproved loudly of delaying at Thionville and not exterminating the Jacobins in every town they passed through; too much mercy was shown. He added that too many persons meddled with advice. — News from Paris; all is calm at present; I am not. I wrote also to the Duke of Dorset.

10th. Letter from Baron de Breteuil at Verdun, 8th. Arrived the 6th, in the evening. Had seen the King of Prussia; much satisfied with him and with the Duke of Brunswick; both very right for the king [of France]; great desire to reach Paris. Will propose to *Monsieur* to keep his title and put himself at the head of affairs with M. de Breteuil only. The latter will act as a machine; for that he will call upon several persons; it is not yet known if *Monsieur* will consent. Calonne goes to Naples; he has dilapidated their finances; has repaid himself all his advances, and two days ago he presented a note to the princes informing them he had no money, not enough even to pay the troops. Twenty thousand francs had to be sent to them. *Monsieur* openly expresses displeasure with him. The Comte d'Artois is forced to admit he has been the dupe of his own good heart. The Duke of Brunswick hopes Duke Albert will act at last. — Nothing new in Paris; all is quiet. The Duc de la Rochefoucauld massacred near Roche-Guyon.

15th. M. de Mercy came to see me. Tried to get him to speak to Lord Elgin [British minister in Brussels], with whom I had already arranged it, and ask him to represent to Mr Pitt how shameful it would be for England if, being able to save the royal family of France without arming a single vessel, and able to do more with a single word than all the combined armies, she would not say it, also to ask him to promise them safety, asylum, protection; and even rewards to those who contributed to save their lives. M de Mercy would not advance so far, nor would he let the archduchess do so, — 1st, because he had no orders; 2d, because he feared that England might use the request as a means to meddle in the affair and try to play a leading rôle, 3d, because the ministers of Vienna and Naples had taken upon themselves to make a similar demand, to which Mr. Pitt had replied very coldly. He said he would speak to Lord Elgin that evening at Crawford's, but only historically, and represent to him how much the honour of England and her advantage urged her to that course; also that he would write a very strong letter on the subject to M de . . . , the emperor's ambassador in London, and would arrange to have it read there, which would have more effect than what he might say to Lord Elgin. — The bishop came to read me his plan; which seems to me good.

17th. M Dumouriez, knowing that General Clerfayt was at Grandpré, started with six thousand men and turned the Croix du Bois to attack him. Clerfayt detached four battalions to attack the French at Bouc-aux-Bois, defeated them, took their cannon, and drove them back. Prince Charles de Ligne was killed. They lost five killed, eleven wounded, among them four officers. — Lord Elgin sent off a courier to London and reported in a very strong manner his conversation with M. de Mercy; he offered to go to Paris if the ministry desired it. He had received a private letter from Lord Granville in which the latter expressed the anxiety of the British ministry about the royal family of France, and their desire to contribute by all and every means to their safety.

18th. News from Paris. The Duc d'Orléans has changed his name and taken that of Égalité; and he calls the Palais-Royal [his residence] the Palais de la Révolution. Great massacre at Lyon and at Besançon. They have arrested all the relatives of *émigrés*.

20th. Much is said of the frugal life of the King of Prussia five solid dishes, no dessert, no coffee; that is his dinner. He usually has thirty at table. He is always on horseback; he said to M de Breteuil, who praised this frugality, "It is by such economy that I feed my army"

24th. News from Paris on 21st: "Paris very tranquil yesterday, seems to be so to-day National Convention, to the number of 217, assembled in the Tuileries News of the day makes little sensation, but that from England much, it will probably secure the lives of the royal family, the desire of the sections for that object is more and more marked, meanwhile *each* is fairly well."

On a request from Count Stadion, the emperor's minister, and M. Castelcicala, the Neapolitan minister to Mr. Pitt, that steps be taken by England to secure the life of the king by declaring that those who should commit the crime of killing him would find no asylum in England, Mr. Pitt replied that the King of England had decided to take that step, but as he had no means of sending the notice authentically to Paris, he took the course of sending it to all the foreign ministers, requesting them to forward it, if they had means of doing so. He gave assurances of the desire of the king to contribute in all ways to the preservation of the French royal family. This declaration is not sufficient; he ought to have added some active measure.

25th   Dined with M. de Mercy. He told me that much severity was needed; it was the only means; all four corners of Paris should be set on fire. — Duke Albert has marched with his army; he made a proclamation. M. d'Orsay has circulated a paper in which he says that the King of France ought to be sent out of the country, and allowed to go; that a king driven away is an object of contempt, and can never recover his rights, but if he is assassinated he inspires both pity and interest. That would be very well if we could know by which way they would send him out, so that we could take him, and if they did not murder him at the frontier. — I expected to go to the army to join M. de Breteuil. I should have been glad to be a witness of the operations, and more at hand to give advice and urge to what ought to be done

October 1st. Letters from Paris to the 27th, the commandant at Valenciennes held them back. They say nothing of Dumouriez's position; but the evening " Journal " says that the Duc d'Orléans presented a letter to the Convention which proposes an agreement on the part of the King of Prussia; the Convention decided not to receive it until the armies should have evacuated French territory. If this is true a clumsy blunder has been made, it is not in this way, nor through the Duc d'Orléans, that they ought to negotiate.

4th   At midnight Lord Elgin's courier brought news that

the Prussian and Austrian army retreated October 1st to
Grandpré, and thence to Verdun.   The courier was an officer:
he says the combined army is worn-out with fatigue, want of
everything, and disease; seeing no arrival of their supply
trains, the fear of being surrounded began to spread among
them, the French made a bold front, they never ceased
throwing up breast-works; they were much fired upon without answering or ceasing to work; their sentinels scoffed at
the Prussians when they departed.   He says the inhabitants
of the country were detestable; they brought nothing to the
camp; they fired upon every one and gave nothing to travellers even if paid for.   He was forced to follow the army to
Grandpré for fear of being captured.   He accuses the Duke
of Brunswick of timidity, and says he could, on the 25th,
have attacked Dumouriez and defeated him.   In England
they have the same opinion of the Duke of Brunswick's
character, they say he prefers to negotiate.

5th.   Received a letter from Baron de Breteuil.   This
retreat is horrible in its consequences.   All is ended, it
seems to me, for this year, — unless the army can be put in a
state to act and a new plan be formed, which I doubt.   I
must see the Duc de Choiseul, who has just arrived.   He is
perfect for the king and queen

6th.   Lord Elgin thinks it certain that it was the cabinet
of Vienna which induced the retreat of the Duke of Brunswick and the project of going into winter quarters.   That
cabinet desires to disgust the King of Prussia with the enterprise, so as to leave the emperor sole master   This is not
the personal disposition of the emperor, but that of his
cabinet

11th.   The Duc de Choiseul departed.   He gave me details as to all that has happened in Paris, also about the
affair at Varennes.   By what he told me of Paris, it seems

that after June 20th [return from Varennes] the constitutionals, foreseeing their fall and the impossibility of strug-
gling against the Jacobins, resolved to get the king out of
Paris, willingly or by force, assembling and patrolling troops
along the road, and thus take him to Compiègne. Lafayette
and Luckner prepared the spirit of their armies towards this,
and had their addresses ready. At one time Lafayette came
to Paris to try his influence, but though the National Guard
received him well he could never get four hundred of them
to agree to fire on the Jacobins. The king revolted at the
idea of departure; the queen even more, though she told the
Duc de Choiseul and others that she had no opinion and it
was for the king to decide. Lafayette went away to maintain his army in the same disposition, and always with the
hope of getting the king to go to Compiègne. Then came
the federation; there was one party for Pétion, and another
for Lafayette The ministry was good. The minister of
war would not send away the Swiss Guard. They all in-
trigued, and the Jacobins foiled their intrigues repeatedly.
The individuals who were to have formed the army in Paris
arrived, but without any order or any discipline. Lafayette
had a scheme to hold a review, and to profit by that assembling of troops to fall upon the Jacobins. The affair was all
arranged. Pétion [mayor of Paris] suspected it and for-
bade the review. Luckner went before the military committees and said and did a hundred follies, compromised
Lafayette, etc., etc. — At last the Jacobins made the scene
of August 10th and all was lost. That event had been predicted Everybody had urged the king to go away, but he
would not. M de Sainte-Croix [one of the ministry] behaved very well, he predicted to the king and queen all that
happened. He read to them a paper in which all the details
were given, and clear information as to the project, one

thing he did not read, namely, that the queen was to be put
in an iron cage and exposed to the sight of the people   The
cage was made.   Two days earlier the ministers had urged
the king to start with relays for Compiègne.   He could have
got into a carriage in the morning while taking his walk by
the Pont Tournant, crossed the bridge at Poissy, which they
would have destroyed behind him, the Swiss and 600 or 700
gentlemen on foot and on horseback would have covered the
march, and (to take from this departure the look of a flight)
he was to send a note, when he got into the carriage at eight
in the morning, to inform the ministry that in virtue of the
Constitution he had gone to Compiègne   But the king
refused everything.   During the day of August 9th they
were informed of the rising among the people, the guard
was doubled; it was faithful; all the Swiss, to the number
of a thousand, were there.   M. Mandat, commanding-general
of the National Guard was there; M. Rœderer came; three
hundred private gentlemen were in the palace; no one went
to bed.   Reports came in constantly.   M. Mandat obtained
from the municipality an order to repulse force by force.
At midnight M. Pétion arrived, he was very ill-received by
the National Guard; they put his carriage in a corner of the
courtyard and resolved to keep him and make him give
orders for the defence.   He assured the king that all would
calm down   On going downstairs he observed the arrangements of the guard and made no attempt to go away, he
walked about the courtyards and garden talking with
Rœderer, who, under an appearance of devotion, betrayed the
king   The municipality, uneasy at the non-return of Pétion,
notified the Assembly of its fears that he was arrested in the
palace   He was summoned to the bar to give account of the
facts, and denied that he had been prevented from leaving
As soon as he was out he sent reinforcements to the palace

18

of the very worst kind, National guards and men with pikes. They mingled with those in the courtyards, but posted themselves chiefly in the garden along the terraces. The Swiss lined the staircases; they were also in the courtyard with the National guards.

At three in the morning shots were fired from time to time; an artilleryman fired a cannon in the courtyard under pretence of awkwardness, but there is reason to think the shots were signals. At six o'clock the king went to visit all the posts of the gardens and courtyards. He was insulted in the gardens and ran some risk; muskets were aimed at him, he was threatened with pikes, and closely pressed by two men with pistols. A National guard who accompanied the king returned all pale and trembling. At seven o'clock M. Mandat received an order to go to the municipality, under pretext of concerting plans of defence, but in reality to evade the order for repulsing force by force and to disorganize the National Guard by removing its commander. Mandat did not go, and a second order came Rœderer advised him to obey. He went and was massacred on arriving From that moment no one commanded. They organized the gentlemen; M. de Viomesnil, Maréchal de Mailly, Pont Labbé, and d'Eveilly were put in command. The National Guard took umbrage The king and queen talked to them kindly and forcibly; they were convinced, mingled with the gentlemen, and were posted with them in the apartments. The king had already been talked to about going for safety to the Assembly. The ministers had warned him that this was in the plan. Everybody, especially M. de Sainte-Croix, dissuaded him, he was induced to remain, and the queen said to the Baron de Viomesnil and M. de Clermont-Gallerand· "If you see me going to the Assembly I give you leave to nail me to this wall."

Queen Marie Antoinette

At eight o'clock M. Rœderer returned at the head of his bureau. He asked to speak with the king in private, and passed with him, the queen, and the ministers into the king's cabinet. M. Rœderer requested him to go to the Assembly as the only course to take. The queen opposed it strongly. M. Rœderer asked her if she would take upon herself the responsibility for events, for the massacres that might take place, — that of the king, that of her children, and of all the gentlemen in the palace; he told her that more than twenty thousand men were marching against the palace, etc. The queen said nothing, and the king decided to go. M Rœderer requested him to go alone with his family, for fear of danger to him if he were seen with many persons about him. The king then ordered every one to remain, and went out through the apartments, the grand staircase, the middle iron gate, and the garden, and mounted the steps of the terrace opposite to the Assembly. There was no one with the king but the queen, the children, Madame Élisabeth, the Princesse de Lamballe, Mme. de Tourzel, and M de Brigé As they passed through the apartments the National guards and the gentlemen wept and tried to stop them, the king consoled them, saying he should soon return. As soon as he was gone discouragement fell on every one. Half an hour later the palace was attacked; the artillerymen opened the great gates, the *canaille* rushed in, but a volley from the Swiss Guard and the National Guard swept them back, they seized two cannon. Meantime all who were in the palace, National guards and gentlemen, escaped as best they could, but the Swiss, surrounded on every side were all taken and massacred.[1]

[1] The well-known lion cut into the rock at Lucerne, from a design by Thorwaldsen, is Switzerland's memorial to the twenty officers and seven hundred and sixty men of her soil who died faithful to their duty on this occasion — Tr

By the details which the Duc de Choiseul gave me I
see clearly that he had reason to quit his post at the bridge
of Sommevesle with his detachment [this refers to the
flight to Varennes], for the country was rising on account of
certain villages belonging to M. d Elbœuf, which had refused
to pay taxes   The peasants were to be compelled to do so by
force, and they believed that the hussars (under young
Bouillé) had come for that purpose.   The tocsin was sounded
and the peasants were gathering on all sides.   Many came to
see the hussars; uneasiness was spreading as far even as
Châlons.   The detachment had good reason not to repass
Sainte-Menehould, where it had been very ill-received on its
way   Still, in spite of all that, and the delay of five hours
between Paris and Châlons, and the king's thoughtlessness
in talking and letting himself be seen at Sainte-Menehould,
where the post-master recognized him, he could have got
safely through Varennes if the hussars had been mounted
outside of the town, and if there had been some one there to
tell him where the relay was, for the town was quiet.   The
post-master entered the town as the king was stopping to
ask where the relay was, but the hussars were in the stables,
or drinking in the town, the horses were not saddled, and
young Bouillé was in bed.   He was awakened by the Duc
de Choiseul's groom, who told him there was trouble and a
carriage had been stopped which was said to be the king's.
He ran to saddle his horse, and when the Duc de Choiseul
arrived, half an hour after the king was arrested, he found no
one in the barracks but the horses, not saddled, and the
stablemen, not an officer and not an hussar.   He assembled
as many as he could.   The municipal officers came and
ordered him to surrender to the municipality   For all answer he marched his detachment to the house where the
king was.   There was then a crowd of about three to four

hundred persons ill-armed. He went up and found the family all in one room. . . It was proved to the king that with the hussars he could go on, that M. Bouillé was certainly on the march and they would meet him, the advice was difficult to follow, for all had to go on horseback and there was no answering for musket-shots. The king preferred to remain and await M. de Bouillé, for up to this time there was no talk of making him return to Paris. Some people in Verdun wanted him to go there, saying he would be safe, they spoke to Sauce, the mayor, and showed him the credit he would have if he saved the king, and on the other hand, the certainty of vengeance when M de Bouillé arrived. Sauce seemed shaken, the municipality also. Matters were thus when Lafayette's two aides-de-camp arrived, with a decree from the Assembly Then everything changed aspect, it was resolved to take the king back to Paris. The king, under various pretexts of illness and fatigue tried to delay; but the people cried out that he must go; they must put him into the carriage by force, etc., etc., and at eight o'clock in the morning he was taken away without hearing anything of Bouillé. Thus it appears that the fault was, 1st, the carelessness or ignorance of young Bouillé at Varennes, 2d, the fact that his father, instead of being at the centre of the expedition, was at one end of it, 3d, the delay of five hours on the road to Chalons; 4th, the king's imprudence in showing himself at Sainte-Menehould.

CHAPTER X.

1792-1793.   Diary continued — Battle of Jemmapes — Evacuation of Brussels and Flight of the Austrians and *Émigrés* — Trial and Execution of
Louis XVI — Dumouriez proposes to the Prince de Coburg to dash
on Paris with 50,000 Men and rescue the Queen   Scheme defeated
by Dumouriez's Army revolting against him — The Queen removed to
the Conciergerie — Last fruitless Efforts of her few faithful Friends —
Her Death.

Brussels, October 22d, 1792.   Letters from France, delayed
since the 2d, have arrived.   The last gazettes are to the
18th   The royal family are reunited; the king's trial is
put off for four months.   At the time of the separation the
king was put in the big tower in the middle of the Temple,
the room had iron gratings and was lighted from above.
The farmer of M. de Nicolaï, a National guard, was witness
of the parting of the king from his family, which, he said
was dreadful.   The queen and the others were also separated
for some days.

25th   News of the taking of Mayence by Custine with
thirty thousand rebels; after thirty hours' bombardment the
town capitulated; the troops came out with arms and baggage.   They say the French are marching on Frankfort.
Longwy surrendered by capitulation; they re-established the
magazines and captured artillery.   The baron [de Breteuil]
adds· "This amazing conduct casts great blame on the
Duke of Brunswick; he is a man in the mud."   The letter
is dated 21st.

November 1st, 1792   It seems that the Duke of Brunswick is a man beneath his opportunity, who is afraid of a
little resistance where he expected none; who wished to

negotiate, and was fooled by Dumouriez, who wanted to gain time to intrench. The Prince of Nassau desired to speak to General . . . , the latter came with his suite to the outposts, where the two generals talked from a distance. The Frenchman spoke in a very arrogant tone, suddenly his horse seemed to bolt forward in spite of himself quite close to the Prince of Nassau, to whom he said in a low voice: "*Mordieu!* why don't you act? To-morrow we expect a convoy from Châlons, if you take it we are lost." Then, riding off, he said: "Monsieur, if you have nothing else to say to me, it was hardly worth while to bring me to the outposts" The Prince of Nassau immediately reported this, they hesitated, and arrived an hour too late to seize the convoy!

The King of Prussia is in despair; but he assured the baron that nothing was really lost, as they would now claim the help of all the Powers and make preparations to begin a campaign with more vigour in the spring The Duke of Brunswick told the baron that if it were not cowardly he would blow his brains out. He maintained, however, that it was impossible to attack. Nearly all the Prussian generals were against the expedition, especially Kalkreuth.

7th. Baron de Breteuil came to tell me that the Austrians have been defeated before Mons by eighty thousand Frenchmen with one hundred and fifty cannon [Dumouriez's victory at Jemmapes], that retreat from Brussels is decided on, that the government and the archduchess are starting to retire to Ruremonde, and Metternich had advised him to go Their troops have suffered greatly. The baron told me that he should leave for Ruremonde in three hours. At nine o'clock the news was made public; consternation and fear general. One would have thought that the French were at the gates of the town; nothing was seen but people running about in search of means to get away All the unhappy *émigrés*, without money, without resources, were in despair. Not a single hackney-coach could be found. All were engaged to go to Antwerp or elsewhere, and the whole day nothing was seen but departures, also equipages coming from the army.

For two days there had been orders to give no post horses without permission; that was alarming. I went to tell the news to Crawford and get them to pack their things. I packed mine and we arranged to go together, with Simolin, by Antwerp to Breda. I went to see Mercy to ask him if proper care was taken of the diamonds of Joséphine[?]. He had the face to tell me he did not know there were any; he had certainly received a box, but he gave the key to the archduchess on her arrival, whereas it was I who had written him the letter and sent him the box[1] I tried to give him courage and prove to him that all was not lost, that the forces scattered through the country must be collected, a strong position taken up between Mons and Brussels, there to wait for the French and attack them. By this means we should get them away from their supplies and beat them easily. He said he had written and said all that, and should do so again, but with a man like Duke Albert there was nothing to hope, and the only thing to do was to go, for the French army would certainly be in Brussels within a week, possibly the next day The archives had already gone, and they were emptying the treasury. Terror, astonishment, and fear were on all faces. I met Maldeghem; he told me they had fought hard; the Austrians attacked several times and were repulsed; they lost heavily. The whole road from Mons

---

[1] Possibly, even probably, these were Madame Élisabeth's diamonds which she intrusted for safe-keeping to the Duc de Choiseul She stated this on her examination before Fourquier-Tinville on the day preceding her execution. See Life of Madame Élisabeth in this Historical Series. — TR.

was covered with war equipages and carts with wounded; all the squares were filled except the Place Royale.

I was engaged to dine with the Neapolitan ambassador; he sent to excuse himself. The Court carriages and equipages were starting constantly. We had fixed our departure for the next day, but M. de Mercy, who came in the evening to see Mme. Sullivan, advised us not to be in a hurry, we had still three or four days, he said he was not going to Ruremonde, a vile, unhealthy place, but to Düsseldorf, and begged us to come there too. So we decided to go, and postponed our departure.

8th. Lord Elgin received notice last night from M. de Metternich that the government had started for Ruremonde. La Marck came and told us that Metternich was also leaving in the night, and Mercy with him; that the council of Brabant was dissolved and they were about to open the prisons; he was starting at midnight and advised us to do the same, for probably the troops posted along the road to protect the departure would soon be withdrawn. Crawford wanted to start last night, I tried to reassure them and make them wait till the next day, swearing at Mercy for his selfishness in not warning those he lived with daily, and leaving them exposed to danger   Lord Elgin came repeatedly to tell us there were plots in the town and other nonsense, for the place was perfectly tranquil   It was decided we should leave the next day . . .

9th. Simolin, who took charge of getting horses to hire, could find none. I bought four for the fourgon, and found eight for the carriages; I had my own. They charged twenty-two *louis d'or* for four horses as far as Maestricht. — The news of the insurrection at Antwerp was made public, and it was said that one carriage Lord Elgin had sent there was toppled into the canal by the rascals. . . . They urged me to burn the portfolio containing the papers of the queen; but I did not do so; I placed them with mine in Simolin's carriage. The night before I had resolved to send them to England in charge of Lord Elgin, but the insurrection at Antwerp made me change my mind.

At last at midday we started, — Simolin and I in his carriage, our valets in mine, the two women and Crawford in another, and the lady s-maids in a third; with the fourgon, two cabriolets, and my saddle-horses. In spite of what I had said, I was not without fear of trouble in Brussels or on the road, but all was quiet; every one had a look of fear and consternation. A lamentable spectacle was that of the unfortunate *émigrés* along the road. Young men and old men of the Bourbon corps were left behind, scarcely able to drag themselves along with their muskets and knapsacks There were even women of elegance, with their maids or without them, going on foot, some carrying their children, others little parcels. I longed at the moment for a hundred carriages to pick up those unfortunates; I felt horror and pity. . . . We put up for the night at Louvain. . . .

11th. Reached Maestricht at one o'clock. Not a lodging to be had. We stopped for dinner at an eating-house and the master gave us two rooms. Simolin and I got a room near-by; both of us in a cellar room. I went to see the baron and found him at dinner with twenty persons well-known in society Nine thousand persons had arrived in two days. Some had slept in the streets.

14th. Dined with the Prince of Hesse, Mme. de Brionne, Breteuil, Prince Camille de Rohan, Dangevilliers, Archbishop of Rheims, etc., etc., there. As we decided to start the next day for Aix-la-Chapelle, I sent a man on to engage lodgings. . . .

December 15th. Reached Cologne at three o'clock. I

lodged with Simolin at the Court of Cologne; the two ladies at the Domhof. Letter from Paris, sent to me by Mr. Blair, gave me pain.

17th. Started at ten and reached Ophiden at two Badly lodged.

18th. Started at eleven and reached Düsseldorf at six in the evening.

23d. Talked with Breteuil. The King of Prussia told him he knew all the democratic talk that went on in his army and against himself, it was always so in the antechambers of his uncle, who paid no attention to it, neither did he.

January 2d, 1793. The king [of France] was summoned to the bar on the 26th. Delasèze read his justification, which is strong in points. The king added with feeling that what hurt him most was to be accused of having wished to shed the blood of his people — he, who throughout his reign had sought only their happiness The king retired, and they adjourned the discussion from day to day until it was decided.

12th. Mr. Murray passed through Düsseldorf on his way to join the King of Prussia and remain with him. He says that Pitt has fully decided to declare himself, that they are working to save the royal family, and they want to win Dumouriez, for he has given himself over, with Danton, Sainte-Foix, Robespierre, and Marat, to the Orléans party. The latter want to exterminate the royal family and substitute that of Orléans; and if they cannot establish the father [Égalité], at least they can the son [Louis-Philippe]. Roland and Le Brun are against it.

27th. Received last night at half-past ten o'clock, from the Archbishop of Tours[1] the sad details of the death of the

[1] See Appendix.

King of France.   Though I was prepared for it, the certainty
of so awful a crime renewed all my sufferings   The most
heart-rending memories returned to my imagination.   I sent
off a courier that evening to the regent [Duc Charles of
Sudermania, Regent of Sweden during the minority of Gustavus IV.].   The despatch cost me heavily.

30th   Louis XVI.'s will superb.   Nicolai offers himself
to defend the queen.   He has written to the queen to make
this offer, and has sent his letter to the president of the
Convention.

31st.   Letters from Paris say nothing of the queen's trial;
she is still in the Temple.   La Marck proposed to Mercy to
ask the emperor to take a very simple step, and solely to save
his aunt.   I opposed the idea   The step is not a useful one,
and could not save her; nothing can influence those villains,
and it might be dangerous by stirring up the question of her
trial, hastening it perhaps.   A step that cannot be useful
should not, it seems to me, be taken.   Crawford, Simolin,
La Marck, and I consulted the whole evening over this

February 3d.   They have written M. Quitor, who is here,
that it is proposed to declare the dauphin a bastard, degrade
the queen, and shut her up in the Salpêtrière.   One dares
not think of it from horror — but everything is possible.
Young Bouillé says that the Prince of Wales had a scheme
with the Duc de Choiseul and others to carry off the king
That gave me an idea for the rest of the family; but Englishmen
alone could undertake it, and I see a thousand difficulties.   Still, I fasten to the idea

Monsieur's declaration for the regency has come, the
Archbishop of Tours brought it to me this evening.   It is
well written, but he ought to take that title only according
to circumstances, without specifying " until the majority,"
and he ought to have been silent as to pledges.   The docu-

ment will be printed at Cologne; other printers have not dared to do it, they tried to get it printed at Frankfort. Cardinal de Montmorency, who is charged with notifying the *émigrés*, wished to assemble them in a court and read it to them; but it was represented to him that, the French being here by fact only, not by right (inasmuch as there is an order for their expulsion), it would be imprudent. He wanted also to make them take an oath of allegiance; but the bishops all opposed that. Not even at a coronation are individual oaths taken   Every Frenchman is born a subject Already there are parties among the *émigrés*. Some approve of the regency of *Monsieur;* others remember the rights of the queen, and it is much to be feared that this division of opinion may have bad results some day. The princes are already beginning to commit follies.

6th. The death of the king does not seem to have had a great effect upon the *émigrés;* they console themselves with *Monsieur's* regency. Some have even been to the theatres and to concerts.

13th. News from Cologne that France declared war February 1 on England and Holland, that a manifesto is to be issued with an appeal to the people; that eight hundred millions of *assignats* have been decreed, twenty millions to buy grain in foreign markets, that wood is to be brought from Corsica to build ships at Toulon immediately. Special protection given to the English and their property. If this were serious it would be laughable.

16th Letters from Paris through the Hague tell me that the queen is very thin and changed, but is well in health, that the dauphin is charming, that his guards weep over him. Kalkreuth says that the secretary of M Pache, who came with him to Mayence and is the most violent fanatic of them all, told him that the Duc d'Orléans asked to be the executioner of the king, he said if they drove him from France he should demand to be guillotined, for he would not be received in any other country

26th. News from Breteuil to the 17th that he knows the queen and her family are well in health. They tell that Dumouriez said on leaving Paris that in six weeks he should return and find a king there, — apparently the Duc d'Orléans, whom they want to make consul with unlimited powers.

March 7, 1793. Nicolai writes from Paris on the 26th that a section deliberated in the Temple, and declared that Louis Capet [the dauphin] was born to be a bad man and they must make a good one of him by taking him from two incorrigible women. There is talk of petitions to condemn the queen. It seems certain that the Orléans party are working hard, it is thought they may profit by the riots caused by want and misery, that they even excite them, to prove the necessity of a sovereign and get the Duc d'Orléans nominated.

30th. Baron de Breteuil arrived to-night He is personally much satisfied with Pitt and the English ministers. He says that Pitt is a poor man on all external affairs, which he does not at all understand, and covers his mediocrity by silence; but he understands perfectly the internal affairs of the kingdom, especially intrigue to keep his office and his popularity. He thinks the ministry are working towards the total ruin of France, and are not much interested in the preservation of the royal family. The constitutionals have proposed to the baron to obtain a decree to exile the queen and her family, and for that they ask six millions payable when the queen is on foreign soil. The baron spoke of this to Mr. Pitt, with a view of obtaining the six millions, but Pitt saw great difficulties; such as dealing with people of

that sort, and the fact that they would boast of it ; he promised, however, to speak to the king of it.

30th. Dumouriez has written a letter under date of March
12, which is published in the "Brussels Gazette," the last
number printed ; this letter is very strong against the Assembly ; by it Dumouriez seems to wish to break with the
Assembly altogether. No report of this has been made to
the Convention, at least none is mentioned in any Paris
newspaper. It seems certain that Dumouriez has made proposals to the Prince of Coburg [he was defeated by the
Prince of Coburg at Neerwinden March 18] ; MM. La
Marck and Fischer went to his camp and were a long time
with him ; on their return, Fischer instantly started for
Vienna.

31st. Received a letter from the Duchesse de Polignac,
who tells me she has received news of the queen through a
physician ; he must surely be La Caze.

April 5, 1793. An express sent by the Vicomte de Caraman [French envoy to the Court of Berlin] to the Baron de
Breteuil brings the agreement made by Dumouriez with the
Prince of Coburg. I despatched it by express to Sweden.
The joy is very keen. It is all the greater to me because I
fear no longer for the queen. I asked Taube to write
me whether I was to regulate my actions according to the instructions I already have, in case the king [Louis XVII.]
were set at liberty, or whether I must await others ; in the
latter case to send them instantly, for things might go very
fast. As he knows the situation best, I thought it better
to leave the matter to his decision than to ask any questions
myself.

In the evening Maréchal de Broglie received information
that Dumouriez was marching alone on Paris with fifty
thousand men, all wearing the white cockade ; and that the

Prince of Coburg remained on the frontier ready to support him, if necessary.

7th I proposed to the baron to send some one who could see the queen at the moment of her deliverance, to inform her fully as to her position, and to give her advice on what she ought to do, in contradiction to that which Mercy would not fail to write to her. He liked the idea, and the Bishop of Pamiers is to start to-morrow morning; he is to approach the French army and endeavour, through Sainte-Foix, to see Dumouriez.

8th I was occupied early in the morning in writing a note to the queen when the Bishop of Pamiers came to tell me that Dumouriez's army had revolted against him; that he had ridden through Mons with his staff, nearly all the officers of the engineer and the artillery corps, and many troops of the line, and that others were following him. It was Dampierre who bribed the National Guard. When Dumouriez saw that something was plotted, he endeavoured to deliver over the artillery and the treasure, but this was prevented, and he could only make his escape alone. He was even shot at by one of his own detachments. At the first moment the news shocked me, my fears for the queen revived; otherwise the news would have been good; their army was disorganized, and Dumouriez, who, at the head of 50,000 men would have been a power, was no longer anything. The consternation among the French was as great as their joy had been, they now thought all was lost.

10th. The Maréchal de Castries [agent of the princes] passed through on his way to Brussels some days ago. He said he was going on pecuniary business; but it was doubtless to get nearer to events and to Dumouriez, and negotiate the regency. M. de Limon, who has seen *Monsieur*, assures me that, from what *Monsieur* said to him, he had reason

to believe that he would resign the regency to the queen as
soon as she was set at liberty. I told Limon how important
it was to induce *Monsieur* to write and send a letter to be
given to the queen at the moment of her deliverance; or, at
least, that *Monsieur* should take that step the moment he
received news of her freedom. I said that if he did not do
this of his own impulse and without consulting any one, he
would surely be dissuaded by his advisers; and that this re-
nunciation was important to avoid intrigues within the country, and prevent disunion among the Powers. Limon felt the
truth of this reasoning, and offered to be the man to induce
Monsieur to take the step, provided he could be the first to
give him the news of the queen's deliverance, and so forestall the deliberations of *Monsieur's* council and their communications to the Powers. Breteuil approved of this, and
we agreed to try, through Metternich, that he should be the
first person informed of the event.

17th. Dumouriez arrived at two o'clock; I went with
Simolin to see him at the post-house. We struggled through
a crowd of people and found him in a lower room, the windows besieged by the people outside. He was alone with
three aides-de-camp. He recognized Simolin; I named myself; he made me a compliment, saying he ought to have
known me by my handsome face. I thanked him for his
courtesies to Berlin; he answered that if he had not done
more it was not his fault, but that of circumstances. I told
him that I was very glad to see him *here;* he answered that
he had long intended it. He told us that Sainte-Foix had
nothing to dread; that fear was in Paris and they would not
dare to do anything to him. I said to him: "Explain to
us, monsieur, what has taken place in relation to the Duc
d'Orléans." — "I can give you no explanation, monsieur le
comte," he replied, "for I have never had any relations with

19

the Duc d'Orléans, whom I have always despised, and considered a scoundrel.   I know, however, that much has been
said; and as this rumour is the only stain with which they
can blacken my conduct, I am going to issue a proclamation
which will prove that I have never had anything to do with
him "   He said much good of the Duc de Chartres, who, he
told me, did not resemble his father in any way. . . .   He
complained much of Dampierre, who had betrayed him, and
in whom he had confidence, being, he said, a man of quality
and born to think rightly   He said his plan had been to
capture and deliver up [to the Prince de Coburg] Lille,
Condé, Valenciennes, and Maubeuge, with the commissioners
who were there to serve as hostages, that this plan had
partly failed through the imbecility of those he intrusted
with it, but the proposal had already been made to exchange
the four commissioners against the royal family,[1] that his
opinion had been that everything should be granted to get
possession of the royal family; after that, no terms should
be kept with those wretches; and finally, he said that even
if the republic were recognized, the war should be continued
to see which were the stronger, it or the Powers. — On the
whole, I found him a true Frenchman, vain, confident, heed-
less; with much intelligence and little judgment.   His
scheme failed through excess of confidence in his strength
and in his influence with the army.   He did not sufficiently
prepare the thing.   I noticed that he was very uneasy and
nervous at the noise made by the crowd at the door and
windows; he seemed to be afraid of some mishap.   His
valet came in and complained of being insulted by an *émigré;*
he sent him away and said to us: "If those gentlemen push

---

[1] Eventually these commissioners were exchanged, in November, 1795,
for the last living member of the royal family, Marie-Thérèse, afterwards
Duchesse d'Angouleme.   See Life of Madame Élisabeth — Tr.

the thing too far I shall show them that I can still make myself respected." His man was in the wrong, he said that his master had always been a good patriot. The *émigrés* were very angry and wanted to knock him down. I left him with the fear that some hot-heads might make a scene

As he got into his carriage he was insulted. He told me, in order to justify the different proclamations he had made, that one had to talk to those fellows in their own language, for they could not pass from the state of anarchy in which they were to despotism without going through various gradations

25th   *Brussels.*   Our carriage broke down and obliged us to pass a whole day at Aix-la-Chapelle. Propositions have been made to exchange the royal family against the four commissioners captured by Dumouriez, but they demand, in addition, an unlimited suspension of arms, and the recognition of the republic. The Prince of Coburg has asked an explanation of the term "unlimited suspension," and also that the royal family be brought, to the frontier, where the commissioners would also be brought, and then they would negotiate. The answer to these proposals is now awaited. Metternich told Facius, the Russian consul, that he hoped the royal family would soon be here.

28th. The archduke made his re-entrance [into Brussels]. He was in a phaeton arranged like a car, drawn by over three hundred persons, — a cupid on the box. He was received with demonstrations of affection. He held a Court. All the apartments are devastated; in the salon the mirrors and tables on one side are broken, the chimney-piece also, the tapestries carried off. At the theatre they offered him congratulations, afterwards there was a ball and supper and an illumination. It was quite remarkable what order reigned among the crowds who were everywhere.

May 22, 1793. Dr. La Caze has been to the Temple: he

found the queen little changed, but Madame Élisabeth so unrecognizable that he did not know her until the queen called her "my sister." She was in the room, wearing a night-cap and a very common cotton gown. The little *Madame* had her body all covered with ulcers, and is threatened with consumption of the blood. Her youth and care may bring her safely through it. They write from Paris that the young king has been ill, and that the Commune refused the doctor the queen asked for on the ground that he was an aristocrat; they sent one of their own choosing. Louis XVII. has had a rupture.

June 28th, 1793 Mercy says that the queen has been very ill, but is now well, and that she was extremely well taken care of during her illness.

July 10th, 1793. A woman just from Paris says they are beginning to feel better towards the royal family. The queen walks in the garden, and the people applaud when they see her; they even cry out, "Vive le dauphin !"

12th. Bad news from Paris. The dauphin is separated from the queen by the [word omitted] and put in another room in the Temple, this seems to me very bad; what awful suffering for the queen; unhappy princess !

13th. The bad news confirmed. The separation of the dauphin and queen is inconceivable. One only thing consoles and gives me a little hope; it is that they speak more respectfully of the royal family. Letters from Paris say there is a project of taking them to Saint-Cloud, and that General Wimpffen is nine leagues from Paris — but this is doubtful.

25th. News of the taking of Mayence arrived this morning; it surrendered by capitulation on the 22d. Lord Elgin arrived last night; the details he gives as to the operations of the Duke of Brunswick are horrifying. He adopted an ill-chosen and disastrous defensive.

August 11th, 1793.[1] Having talked with La Marck on
the means of saving the queen, and agreeing that there were
none except to push forward at once a strong body of cavalry
to Paris, — which would be the easier to do at this moment,
because there are no troops before the city and the granaries
are full, — I went to see Mercy about it, and found him all
ice to the idea. He saw the impossibilities. He believes
the royal family lost and that nothing can be done for them.
He does not think the factious would negotiate; he believes
they will go to all lengths in order to so bind the whole of
France to their crimes that there will be no course for individuals to take but that of victory or death with them. He
ended by telling me there was no hope. I left him and urged
La Marck to speak to him. He did persuade him to write
to the Prince of Coburg, and promised to show me the letter
the next day — I went to the theatre to avoid what might
seem like affectation. I found the French all there as usual,
even the women   Great Gods, what a nation!

12th.   La Marck brought me the letter to the Prince of
Coburg, which he had himself written for Mercy; it was
very urgent and very well done. He proposes the march to
Paris. . . . Mercy exacts nothing, but the proposals are very
pressing, and if the Prince of Coburg does not yield to them,
he will be responsible for the evils that will happen. La
Marck had great difficulty in getting Mercy to take this
step, he was afraid England would not like it, and would
accuse them of continually changing their plans. Crawford
reassured him as to the earnest desire of the English ministry to save the family. Mercy begged him to write to
England and explain the reasons for the new plan, and he
promised the Comte de La Marck to send off the letter to
the Prince of Coburg by express last night.

[1] The queen had been taken to the Conciergerie.

13th Letters from Paris to the 6th say nothing of the queen, one from the Duchesse de Mailly to her daughter says, in a very involved way, that she is running great dangers

14th. Papers of 10th mention the queen only to refute a false report, but they assert that she is in the Conciergerie. Letters from Menin speak of news received there that the Convention had proposed to the queen to write to the emperor to withdraw his troops, and on that being done she and her family would be set at liberty; but she answered that the same promise made to the late king relating to the Prussian troops had not saved his life, and, moreover, that she could not negotiate with assassins.   All this seems to me false.

16th The reply of the Prince of Coburg is pitiable, it dwells on the idea of going with the whole army to Paris, and the impossibility of such an enterprise.   In his letter he considers nothing but the military side, and even the mechanical side of that; for it is plain that the proposed operation was the best of all to make if it had no other advantage than carrying off all the food supplies in Picardy, the horses, carts, etc, possess them himself, and prevent the others from having them . . . The Prince of Coburg covers himself with shame; he gives the measure of his genius and that of his right arm, Prince Hohenlohe, who is only a military routineer; the departure of M. de Mack is more to be regretted than ever, he was the man to have led this thing.

19th. At the solicitation of La Marck the Comte de Mercy has decided to send some one to Paris to know what is happening, and see if we could negotiate the release of the queen for money and the hope of pardon.   He has cast his eyes on Noverre, the ballet-master, who consents to go, and on M. Ribbes, a financier, who has always managed the various parties for his private interests; but who thinks well, nevertheless I went to talk of it with Breteuil, I found him rather opposed to it from the fear that instead of quieting their malignity it might increase it by showing them the interest taken in the matter. I have always thought that as long as the queen was in the Temple with her son, and was not threatened, she was safe, but now that she is threatened and is parted from her son, and especially since the refusal of the Prince of Coburg to march his cavalry to Paris, I think there is nothing but this one step to take, and that it may present advantages without dangers. The baron resolved upon it, and I promised to see Ribbes and propose the journey to him. — I showed La Marck, whom I went to see, that, in order to succeed, the queen must be isolated from all political questions, and made simply an object of interest to the Austrian family, it should also be shown to those men how useless this fresh crime would be to them, and how certain to bring down vengeance on their heads; and above all, they should be made to see that it could not stop the advance of the allied Powers. He was of my opinion, and the baron also. I advised that the step should not be taken without informing England and Prussia.

21st. The baron has seen M Ribbes, he agrees to undertake the commission; as he cannot go himself to Paris he will go to the frontier and send for his brother, whom he will instruct to see Danton, and, if necessary, ask him for an interview near Paris to which Ribbes could go.

22d The baron has seen La Marck, and they agree perfectly on the sort of commission to give M. Ribbes, though they do not agree on political points

25th The gazettes of Paris to the 20th say that the public prosecutor of the revolutionary tribunal has asked for documents against the queen, and it is decreed to give them to him. This makes me tremble; I am very sure there are none, but they will forge some.

In the Homburg Gazette there are details on the removal of the queen to the Conciergerie which have not been in any other paper; they are horrible. O'Connell, he who served in the Royal-Swedish and was so protected by Comte d'Artois and the Polignacs, and who remained in the revolution, being made a major out of his rank and before others, gave the following details. [These details are missing.]

29th. Ribbes has seen M. de Mercy; he thought the proposed instructions good; but made difficulties about promising money; thought that favours, safety, protection, and pardon should suffice. He gave in, however, or seemed to do so; but refused absolutely to let the overture be made in the emperor's name. He wanted Ribbes to speak to Danton as if from speculators interested in the political condition of Europe and anxious to know what to expect. A miserable method; and this change in M. de Mercy surprises and grieves me. La Marck, without saying so, seems to disapprove it. I am all the more distressed because I think I see in the second objection a doubt in Mercy's mind as to how far the Powers and even Austria desire the liberty of the queen. He added: "I must say it, although with regret, that even if the queen were on the scaffold, that last atrocity could not stop the Powers or change their course." The Baron de Bretcuil is extremely irritated against M. de Mercy, and is to have a conversation with him. I exhort him to moderation, to yield to circumstances, and try to get the best he can out of them.

30th. The baron has seen M. de Mercy; who, in spite of all the baron said to him, will not yield his ideas. Breteuil became angry and told him if that were so, Ribbes could not go and his mission was useless. M. de Mercy wished him

' to go and sound Danton, and promised that during that time he would send a courier to Vienna, so that by the time Ribbes returned he might be able to speak more positively. Ribbes came to me very discontented, he already thought himself an important personage, and regretted not being one. In that I thought him very French. I induced him to undertake the commission in the way M. de Mercy wished; and I persuaded the baron also by telling him that he ought to authorize Ribbes and give him greater latitude by naming the persons who sent him. The baron pointed out to M. de Mercy that the diamonds and the money captured at Semonville could be used for this purpose

September 3, 1793. Ribbes will, at last, start to-morrow; La Marck told him to ask Danton to send back with him a man in his confidence with whom we could negotiate, and to whom we could give all necessary securities. The baron sees in this a project to have a man near Danton with whom Mercy can negotiate without the baron's knowledge. I think this way of looking at it too suspicious; I see in the arrival of such a man a surer way of negotiating.

11th. The Abbé de Montesquieu has been to see me; he has just arrived from England. He told me that M. de Mercy must have in his possession, from the queen, fifteen hundred thousand francs which he, the abbé, took to him.

13th. The news from Paris which came last night is very bad for the queen. It is plain they intend to begin her trial. Ribbes has returned, he took the course of writing to Danton in a manner unintelligible to any but himself, and has sent him the letter. I fear it will arrive too late. What reproaches M de Mercy will then be forced to make to himself, — he who made us lose eight days by his stay in the country, and four more after his return by the difficulties he made. It is a horror to think of! God preserve her, and give me the satisfaction of seeing her once more!

26th. They write from Paris that the queen was subjected to an examination before the revolutionary tribunal. They asked her if she was the widow of Louis Capet; she answered. "You know that I am the widow of your king." To a second question she replied. "You can be my executioners, my murderers, but you can never be my judges." After that she was seized with a nervous attack which obliged them to take her back to her room.

October 5th. They have captured Drouet, commissary of the Convention, at Maubeuge. He is thought to be the post-master of Sainte-Menehould. I doubt it; I think that man was his brother. He is to be transferred here.

7th Drouet arrived at eleven o'clock. I went with Colonel Hervey to see him in his prison at Sainte-Élisabeth He is a man six feet tall, thirty-three or thirty-four years of age, who would be well enough in face if he were not such a villain. He had irons on his feet and hands. We asked him if he was the post-master at Sainte-Menehould who stopped the king at Varennes. He told us it was he who went to Varennes, but it was not he who stopped the king. He would not open his over-coat, lest he should show his chain, which went from his right foot to his left hand. The sight of that infamous wretch made me angry, and the effort I made to say nothing to him, on account of the Abbé de Limon and the Comte de Fitz-James, who were there, made me ill.

An officer captured with him said the queen ran no risk; that she was very well treated, and had all she wanted. The wretches! how they lie!— An English traveller who arrived in Switzerland says that he paid twenty-five louis to enter the queen's prison; he carried in a pitcher of water. She was in

a vault, where there was a bad bed, a table, and a chair. He
found the queen seated, her face leaning upon and covered
by her hands, her head wrapped in two handkerchiefs, and
she herself extremely ill-clothed She did not even look at
him, and he said nothing to her, which was agreed upon.
What a horrible tale! I shall try to be certain if it is true.

14th There was not a word of truth in what Count
Metternich told us last night. The traveller he spoke of is
named Aubré, a lawyer of this city who does business. He
came from Paris with goods, and never said a word of all that.
He is a species of Jacobin, that Aubré. He says, on the contrary, that the queen is not ill-treated, that her room was as
good as it could be in a prison, that her bed was iron with
cotton curtains, good mattresses, and the necessary covering,
all very clean Her dinner was that of a bourgeoise in con-
valescence, when they took away the jailer of the Conciergerie they also took away his wife, who waited on her and
was very respectful; since then the queen would have no one
serve her. He added that he could have saved the queen for
two hundred thousand francs which were proposed to him, but
she refused. This put it into M de Breteuil's head to speak to
this Englishman himself and offer him two millions if he succeeded I approved the idea, but only on condition that he
told us his means, so as to be sure he was not regarding the
queen's deliverance like a lottery ticket, and would not
expose her life to make two millions without great probability of success

16th I met the Prince de Ligne at Breteuil's. He is
much dissatisfied at not being employed, and consequently
blames everything that is done, in which he may be right.
He told us that the Emperor Joseph was extremely change-
able; sometimes kind, sometimes harsh to people, but he
always became kind when any one held firm against him.

20th. Grandmaison came to tell me that Akerman, a banker, had received a letter from his correspondent in Paris which stated that sentence on the queen was pronounced the evening before, and was to have been executed immediately, but circumstances had delayed it; that the people — that is to say, the paid populace — were beginning to mutter and say that " this was the day when Marie-Antoinette was to appear at the national window ! "

Though I was prepared for this, and ever since her removal to the Conciergerie have expected it, still the certainty overcame me; I had no strength to feel anything. I went out to speak of this sorrow to friends, to Mme. de Fitz-James, and Breteuil, whom I did not find, I wept with them, especially with Mme. Fitz-James. The gazette of the 17th speaks of it. It was on the 16th, at half-past eleven o'clock, that this execrable crime was committed , and divine justice has not yet descended on those monsters !

21st   I can think only of my loss , it is awful to have no positive details , to think that she was alone in her last moments, without consolation, without a person to whom she could speak, to whom she could give her last wishes. It is horrible. Monsters of hell ! — No, without vengeance my heart can never be content

November 6th, 1793.   The fate of Madame Élisabeth seems to be decided, and those unhappy children are abandoned to these infamous wretches ! *Madame* especially is to be pitied , she is sensitive, and has intelligence enough to feel the whole horror of her situation ; they are capable of everything towards her   As for the king, they will ruin his natural character, and his existence may become an evil to France, if ever he is king.   What a horror ! and why does not divine justice avenge such wrongs ?

17th.   They say that the coach which took the unfortunate queen from the Temple to the Conciergerie was full of blood. The coachman did not know whom he drove, but suspected it. When they reached the Conciergerie they were there a long time without getting out; then the men went first, and the woman last, she leaned upon his arm; and afterwards he found his coach all full of blood — but this is not authentic.

18th   I went this morning to see M. de Rougeville. I found a man slightly crazy, full of himself, of what he has done, giving himself airs of great importance, but thinking right and in no way a spy. Mme. de Maillé recognized him the other day from her window as a M. de Rougeville who spent his life in the queen's antechambers and followed her about everywhere. Here in substance, is what he told me of his last venture at the Conciergerie. —

He knew Mme. de Tilleul, an American, quite rich and right thinking, and together they formed a project of saving the queen. He made acquaintance with Fontaine, an honest man who sold wood, and through him with Michonis, formerly a lemonade-seller. They were both well-disposed. Michonis was struck to the heart about the queen, and refused the money Rougeville offered him, but he gave it to two others in the service. One day he accompanied Michonis into the prison, the queen rose and said. "Ah! is that you, Monsieur Michonis?" Then, seeing M. de Rougeville she was greatly overcome, and was on the point of falling into her chair, which startled the gendarmes; but he made her a sign to reassure her and tell her to take some pinks, among which was a note. She dared not; and he let them drop without being able to speak to her. Michonis left the room on business in the prison and he went too; the queen sent for Michonis to return and made him attend to the gendarmes, during which time she said to Rougeville that he

exposed himself too much   He told her to take courage;
she would be succoured; he would bring her money to bribe
the gendarmes.   She said to him: " Though I am weak and
broken-down, *this* (laying her hand on her head) is not." She
asked him if her trial would be soon, he reassured her.   She
said " Look at me, look at my bed, and tell my relations
and friends, if you escape from here, of the state in which
you saw me"   Then they went away.   They had gained the
concierge and his wife   Their plan was that Michonis
should go at ten o'clock at night with an order from the
municipality to take her back to the Temple, and then she
would escape   Thus, by signing the book of the concierge
no harm would come to him and they were free to go.
The two gendarmes for fifty louis would say nothing; a third
opposed the plan; Michonis told him he should have an
order from the municipality, but he threatened to call the
guard.   The plan failed and Rougeville escaped.

   Here are some particulars about the queen: her room
was the third door on the right after entering, opposite to
that of Custine.   It was on the ground-floor; the window
looked upon the courtyard, which was filled all day with
prisoners, some of whom gazed in through the window and
insulted the queen.   The room was small, damp, and fetid;
there was neither stove nor chimney.   There were three
beds: one for the queen, one beside it for the woman who
waited on her, and a third for the two gendarmes, who never
left the room, not even when the queen had wants or gave
herself natural cares.   The queen's bedstead, like that of the
others, was of wood, a straw bed, a mattress, and a blanket,
dirty and full of holes, which had long served other prisoners.
There were no curtains, but there was an old screen.   The
queen wore a black wrapper, her hair, cut short in front and
behind, was gray; she was so emaciated that it was difficult

to recognize her, and so weak that she could scarcely stand
on her legs. She had three gold hoops on her fingers, but
no rings. The woman who served her was a sort of fish-
wife, of whom she complained much. The gendarmes told
Michonis that Madame ate nothing, and in that way she
could not live; they said her food was very bad, and they
showed him a thin and nearly spoilt chicken, saying: "That
is a chicken Madame could not eat, and they have brought
it to her now for four days." The gendarmes complained of
their bed, though it was precisely the same as the queen's.
The queen slept always in her black garment, expecting to
be massacred at any moment, or led to the scaffold. Rougeville said that Michonis wept with sorrow; he confirmed to
him what was told of the queen's loss of blood and said that
when it was necessary to send to the Temple for the queen's
black wrapper and the necessary linen he could not get it
until after the Council had deliberated. Those are the sad
details that Rougeville gave me.

CHAPTER XI.

1792   Correspondence of Count Fersen with the King of Sweden until
his Death, and with Queen Marie-Antoinette until the 10th of August,
1792, when the Royal Family were imprisoned in the Tower of the
Temple, and all written Communication with them ceased. Brief Statement of Count Fersen's After-life and of his Death, June 20, 1810

[CARLYLE, in his fine account of the Flight to Varennes, remarks that from that day Count Fersen " disappears into unknown space."   We have now seen that, on the contrary, he was in the centre of European diplomacy, the trusted envoy of the one sovereign who was true to the King and Queen of France, and himself in the forefront of every effort to save them until the fatal day when the axe put an end to the object of his chivalrous devotion   After the death of the King of France, the Duke-regent of Sweden, in a confidential and autograph letter, appointed Count Fersen his ambassador to King Louis XVII., having already made him, in May, 1793, a major-general in the Swedish army.   But the honour that Fersen longed for was denied him.   In the midst of the Powers of Europe, all able to do the thing he had at heart, he was powerless to bring them to do it, and there is more of chivalry in the forlorn hope he then led than in the initial act of devotion for which his name is famous.

The last letters (in cipher and " white ink ") which passed between the queen and Count Fersen here follow, interspersed with some others of interest.   Fersen's general correspond-ence until the date of the queen's death is very voluminous, and will be found in the work already mentioned   " Le Comte de Fersen et la Cour de France," it relates almost wholly to the many fruitless efforts made by a few faithful men to save the royal family of France.]

Count Fersen to Gustavus III., King of Sweden.[1]

BRUSSELS, February 29, 1792.

SIRE, — Baron Taube must already have had the honour to lay before Y. M. the details of my journey; it would therefore be useless to repeat them here.

I carried to the king and queen the despatches of Y. M. which related to my mission. I found them greatly touched by the interest that you take, Sire, in their fate; they have charged me to express to Y. M. the liveliest gratitude, and to say how dear and precious the memory of it will always be to them. They fully feel the impulsion that their escape would give to affairs by facilitating the good-will of their friends, and also the advantages it would have for themselves; but however useful it would be, Their Majesties are too convinced that success is impossible at this moment to be willing to attempt it. . . . The queen, especially, feels deeply all the advantages, and assures me that the bad results of their first attempt does not prevent them from making a second; but Their Majesties, seeing for the moment no possibility of success, have refused the project absolutely. They have, however, consented to attempt it when the forces of the different Powers are united on the frontier and able to serve them as a point of support, or as a protection in case of an arrest like that of the month of June. The plan I have proposed to them for this purpose is to keep to the hunting forests and be guided through them by smugglers towards the frontier; there to be met (ten or a dozen leagues from the frontier) by a detachment of fifty of the light-horse

---

[1] This letter reports to the King of Sweden the result of Count Fersen's mission to Paris in February, 1792. — TR.

cavalry from one of the armies who could secure their issue, while the army itself would be ready to advance to their support, if need were   Their Majesties liked this idea, and consented to follow it, if they saw at any moment that such a course offered great advantages.

I next presented to the king the two methods of proceeding as to the congress, which are contained in the memorial. He preferred the second, giving as a reason that it offered him the best chance of himself joining the congress.   I represented to him, however, that it might happen that the rebels would consent to the demands of the Powers rather than have them meddle with the Constitution, and then that the good-will of the friendly Powers might find itself shackled by the bad faith of the emperor, who would say that having obtained all, there was nothing more to ask for   On which he replied: "But that would be the very time to insist upon my liberty, upon my freedom to leave Paris, and go to some indicated spot to sign and ratify the engagements I shall have made with the Powers; and if, as I believe, I shall not obtain that liberty, then the Powers will be free to act in my favour"

Another point on which I thought it important to inform myself was the latitude which the king was willing to give to the Powers to act so long as he was kept in Paris by the rebels, and the degree of caution he thought necessary for his personal safety and that of his family so long as he remained in their hands. I thought, however, that I ought to represent to him the dangers to which he might be exposed, I thought I ought to show him the possibility that he might be taken into the Cévennes and placed by the rebels at the head of a Protestant army, at the same time I told him I considered these dangers lessened by the necessity to the rebels of his preservation in order to secure better terms; and as for the Cévennes project, I proposed to him, in

case it were again renewed, to issue a pamphlet full of
demagogy and invectives against him and the queen, in which
the Cévennes project should be treated as a scheme of the
aristocrats to get him out of Paris and bring a foreign army
into France.

The king was of my opinion on all these points, and he told
me that, in case he could not leave Paris by flight or otherwise, he desired the Powers to take no heed of his personal
danger, that he saw his safety, as I did, in the interest the
rebels had in his preservation, that he should employ all
possible means to prevent his being taken out of Paris into
the provinces, that democratic pamphlets had already been
very useful to him, and if necessary, he would use the one I
suggested to him.   The king seemed to me quite decided not
to hinder the Powers in any way ; and the queen repeated to
me what she had already said to M. de Simolin · " Tell the
king there is nothing to fear for us ; the nation needs the
king and the life of his son, which must be saved ; as for me,
I fear nothing   I prefer to subject myself to all risks, rather
than live any longer in the state of humiliation in which I
am ; everything seems to me preferable to the horror of our
position."   The king repeated the same thing from himself.
The queen then spoke to me of one other point to be demanded by the Powers, namely, the disarming of the considerable forces which France now maintains, which are useless
if she has no hostile projects.   This point, she said, could
not be granted by the Assembly, even if it wished to do so ;
it was contained in the memorial which the queen had sent
in the month of September to the emperor, but M. de Mercy
never mentioned it to us.

I then declared to the king on the part of Y M that your
intention and that of the Empress of Russia was not to permit the establishment in France of a mixed government, not

to compromise with the rebels, but to re-establish the
monarchy and the royal authority in its plenitude. The
queen seized that idea warmly, but the king, though he
desired it, seemed to think it would be difficult to carry out,
but I had no difficulty in proving to him that by means of
foreign succour and with a firm determination (of which he
had assured me) not to compromise with the rebels, nothing
could be easier   He ended by being convinced, and assuring
me again that his intention was not to compromise with
the rebels, " for some," he said, " cannot do right, and others
will not do it" But he begged me, at the same time,
to represent to Y M the necessity under which his position
puts him to treat with the rebels at this moment, to make
use of them, and to do all they want, however repugnant it
may be to him. I assured the king that Y M. felt the
necessity of such conduct and approved it, but only as a
means to gain time and lull their minds. The king also
requested that Y. M be not surprised at any steps he might
be forced to take, and to see in them only the effect of his
misfortune and the constraint that he is under. All that
he said as to that, and as to the total abandonment in which
he was, deprived of counsel and separated from those on
whose attachment he could count and who might be useful
to him, touched me to tears. He was good enough to say in
return very touching and very flattering things for me. The
queen spoke to me with tender sensibility of the friendship
and interest that Y. M. and the empress showed for them,
comparing it with the conduct of the emperor — not to his
advantage, and she also compared their experience of
ingratitude from those of their interior who owed them
everything with the affection of those who owed them
nothing. The king charged me to tell Y. M that he sanctioned the decree on the sequestration of the property of the

émigrés solely to prevent its being pillaged and burned, — which would surely have been done had he refused; but he is determined not to consent to the seizure and sale of those estates as national property.

To sum up all, I found the king and queen very determined to endure everything rather than continue in the state in which they are; and from the conversations I had with them I think I can assure you, Sire, that they strongly feel that all compromise with the rebels is useless and impossible, and that there is no means of restoring their authority but force and foreign assistance.

The queen has just written to the Queen of Naples, and the Queen of Portugal; the latter is said to be disposed to furnish money.

Queen Marie-Antoinette to Count Fersen.

March 20, 1792.

M. de Laporte has received no newspapers for a month past. I fear you have written to me in that way, all the more as I saw in a letter to M. Crawford that you referred him to me for details. We cannot use newspapers any longer; there is reason to think they stop them.

The despatch from Vienna makes much noise: as for me, I do not understand it. I fear there is more ill-will; it is clear that he wants to gain time in order to do nothing M. Gog [uelat] will send you papers about all that. Adieu.

Count Fersen to Queen Marie-Antoinette.

BRUSSELS, March 4, 1792

I send you a note which Baron de Breteuil has given me for you. He is in pressing need of money, and I hope you will find his demand just. . . . It is very just; he is without resources and liable to lose all he has in Saint-Domingo.

It would be well to send him one hundred and fifty thousand francs for the current expenses, and thirty thousand for
his own expenses, this would be for six months. If you
like to remit this money to Périgord, as if for me, telling
him to send it to me, do so, but in that case you must send
at once, as the whole sum is wanted in full. Or, if you
choose, I will see if you can borrow it in Holland, where it
will cost you five per cent, instead of six or seven. As for
the sum I hold for you there, I will send you an account of
it in a few days; it is, however, insufficient for the above
expense, and it is best to keep it; it may be good to have it
in reserve some day. See if you can find any one in Paris
to procure you a loan of two hundred thousand francs, in
Holland or elsewhere, but out of the kingdom; if so, take it,
you will gain much [by exchange]; then you can remit it
to me here to the care of the bankers, Danoot, Son & Co.
I shall pay it to the baron on your order only.

M. de Mercy has complained to the baron of the discontent you show as to the emperor's conduct; he suspects me
of being the cause, and let it be understood that he had
proof of it. I think this is only a suspicion, for all my letters
have reached you, and if he had developed the writing he
would not have sent them to you. It is also quite impossible that he could decipher my letters to the King of
Sweden, but the baron warned me that I was much suspected and very inconvenient to them, and that often M de
Mercy requested him not to tell me the things he confided to
him. From that I judge they will seek all possible means
of injuring me with you, by inventing tales, though I ought
to hope and believe that my zeal and my devotion are too
well known to you to fear you would believe them. I venture, however, to ask you not to leave me in ignorance of
them, in order that I may refute them and continue to de-

serve the flattering confidence with which you have been so good as to honour me.

The news from Prussia is still good, M. C . . is ordered to communicate it to you. The King of Prussia wants to put himself at the head of his army. M de Mercy is enchanted with the emperor's reply, he boasted to M. de Breteuil that he was the author of it.

Count Fersen to Queen Marie-Antoinette.

March 6, 1792

I received yours of 2d yesterday. The details to which I referred Mr. C. were in the baron's papers which he sent you. As we no longer use the journals, none have been sent for two months; but we shall send them if there is need, notify M. Laporte to send you all he receives.

The emperor's reply is political galimatias, a lawyer's plea that says nothing, that is the only favourable way of looking at it. It cannot be reconciled with what he proposed to Berlin, — unless by supposing that he reserves to himself, in case he is forced to act, to make a subtle distinction in his conduct as head of the House of Austria and as head of the Empire, in that case, it is plain that he only wants to gain time to save' himself from invasion and put himself in the right. But if this is more bad faith, which is probable, his answer serves him marvellously well. As for me, I believe neither the one nor the other, I think he always wants to avoid acting, but fears to be forced into it by the other Powers, and that he consented to Prussia's proposal to raise their forces to fifty thousand men each, solely in the hope of excluding thereby the Northern Courts, by representing the Prussian and Austrian forces as more than sufficient; and if he does not succeed in that way, then he will still be so superior that they will find themselves

compelled to follow the course he points out. In this way
he expects to create in France a government which will
make that kingdom dependent upon him, take from it its
strength, and prevent it from ever again obtaining in Europe
the weight it once had.

But he does not see that with the influence of the Empress
of Russia, the good-will of the King of Prussia, and the ambition of the Duke of Brunswick, his game can be foiled; it
is then that the princes could be useful to you; for the
friendly powers would have the air of yielding to their en-
treaties, which would secretly emanate from you. The essential thing is to agree to bring the troops of the different
Powers to the frontiers of France, and I have written to
the King of Sweden, and to Russia and Spain, that I believe
everything ought to be sacrificed to obtain that agreement,
and that while the troops are marching there there will be
time enough to discuss the point of representing the non-
liberty of the king, and the question of where the congress
shall be held, — an assemblage which may then seem less
important, and possibly useless.

It is from this way of looking at the emperor's projects
that I have advised the baron not to be in a hurry, and to
specify in the promise to reimburse costs (which M. de
Mercy has asked for) that it will be done only after the
king is re-established in the plenitude of his authority such
as it was before the revolution.

You must warn Gog. that every time there is *beyond* the
cipher a number and a dash (for example, 49 —) that means
there is cipher up to the next full stop [.]; the rest means
nothing or will be in white ink. If there is $\underline{49}$, that is, the
dash *below* the number, the letter is for him. If *after* the
number there comes plain writing, then he will find white ink
between the lines. He must be warned of all this. When

you write to me, it will be better to do it in white ink between the lines of a cipher that means nothing; for they
might get the true cipher here. You must number each
letter carefully, that we may be sure none are lost. I am
certain they are not opened in Paris; they have not the
machine montée for that

Count Fersen to Queen Marie-Antoinette.

No. 3   March 9, 1792

We heard last night of the death of the emperor. This
news gives pleasure to some and pain to others, who fear the
delay it will cause in our affairs. As for me, I regard it
more as an advantage for you. The emperor is dead, but the
archduke of Austria is not, his power and his interest are
the same as ever. . . . The inclinations of the Archduke
Francis have always been favourable, and I know that he has
often blamed the feeble, slow, and undecided conduct of his
father He is a soldier in heart; more like Joseph than like
Leopold. This event will certainly increase the influence of
the King of Prussia, whom the Court of Vienna has strong
interest in pleasing in order to keep the imperial dignity, —
a circumstance which ought to be very favourable to you. I
think that a letter from you and from the king to the Archduke Francis would be very useful at this moment, the
attention would flatter him and warm his zeal for you.
After sharing his grief at the loss he has met with in a
father, and you in a brother, you might tell him that you
have not been left in ignorance of the feeling and interest
he has shown in your fate, and that you hope, from those
sentiments in him, that he will put more activity into the
prospects his father held out to you; and for that reason you
do not hesitate to give him the same confidence and to
repeat the request for the sending of a strong body of troops

to the frontier and the formation of a Congress at Aix-la-Chapelle or Cologne. You could tell him that you have been assured of the good disposition of the King of Prussia, and that you have long had unequivocal proofs of the interest of the Courts of Petersburg, Stockholm, and Madrid. You could end by making him feel that your position requires you to employ the greatest seciecy, and especially towards the princes, on account of the indiscretion of persons who surround them, and by asking for his good-will to the Baron de Breteuil, who has all your confidence. The letter cannot be written too soon. Send it by diligence, simply to my address, in a box which will contain cloth for a coat, some waistcoats, and new cravats — to make the thing look natural and avoid all suspicion.

I have not yet received the papers from Gog., the papers you mention, nor the letter for the Queen of Portugal; that is necessary, however Do not forget the matter of the money The better to avoid suspicion, it would be well to write at the same time a simple letter of compliments to the archduke, and send it by M. de Lessart, to which you might add something in the style of those gentry; reminding him in a few woids of what you have already written to his father, and how much you hope he may follow his steps and be as desirous to maintain peace between the two countries But you must manage that the two letters arrive at the same time, so that the archduke may not be uncertain as to your real meaning. You could inform M. de Mercy as to this, so that he may write to Vienna in consequence. In a conversation he had with the baron he spoke very well, and said · " We want no more declaiations; the emperor has at last changed his system ," then rising excitedly, and laying his hand on his sword he said: " *This* is what is wanted; the emperor is decided, and before long we shall have it." I would like to have witnessed such vivacity in M. de Mercy; it must have been a very extraordinary contrast to his usual self.

Baron Taube to Count Fersen.

STOCKHOLM, March 15, 1792.

The king orders me to direct you to make known to the King and Queen of France that in a private audience which the new minister of Prussia to this Court had with the king, H. M asked him what his master thought of the present state of France The minister replied: "The Queen of France is the sister of the emperor, my master fears that if power is recovered by the King of France the queen will favour her brother too much." "But," said the king, 'if France is eclipsed in the political balance of Europe, England will lay down the law to all the Powers." The Prussian minister assured him that if his master were satisfied that the queen would not give all her influence for the emperor he would at once sign a league with the other sovereigns to replace the King of France upon the throne. The king told him he was certain that the Queen of France, taught by these unhappy events, would employ her influence and authority solely in [*word of cipher illegible*] or for those who recovered for her husband and son the crown of France now usurped by the Assembly.

The King of Sweden wishes the Queen of France to know of this conversation, that she may understand the fears of Prussia, and take whatever measures she considers useful at the present conjuncture

Queen Marie-Antoinette to Count Fersen.

March 30, 1792

I have your letter of 27th. This is a very safe way, you can always write to me under this address, or that of M.

Broune, but you must put an *n* on your letters, and the first time put *n=*, to be more sure.

Ask Mme. Sullivan about the way she told Jarjayes I could receive . . . in a box of biscuits. I must know the name of the woman to whom it is addressed. But take care, Mr. C . . . knows nothing of this; he did not even wish her to see Jarjayes the last time.

What is the meaning of this new letter from Vienna in reply to the one by M. de Lessart? It seems to me as bad as the other. Every one here thinks it superb and excellent policy. It is certain that it will decide us to attack. They are awaiting only an answer to M. Dumouriez's letter. I have sent word of this to M. de Mercy. The plan is to attack by Savoie, and the country round Liège, they hope that as there are not many troops on that side they can do something. Turin was warned by me three weeks ago. It is essential to take precautions around Liège. They are sending to Deux-Ponts a M. Naiac, who lives in Vienna with Cardinal de Rohan; M. Chauvelin goes as minister to London.

I am much harassed now about finding a governor for my son. We have at last decided upon M. de Fleurian, but we do not yet know the moment when we shall make it known.

Mr. Crawford will talk to you of a way to write to me without cipher in Italian. Do not forget to send me the list of names. Our position continues dreadful, but less danger-ous since it is we who attack Austria. The ministers have just sanctioned the decree on passports.

Queen Marie-Antoinette to Count Fersen.

No. 4   April 15, 1792.

M. de Maulde starts for Vienna to-day, it seems to be the last mission to the king [of Hungary]; they are absolutely determined on war here. So much the better if that decides the Powers, for our position is no longer endurable. I have received yours of the 9th, there was no number, but I call it 2. I am uneasy about the return of M Gog. I am afraid he is watched, he must take great precautions. Adieu I cannot write more; I must give my letter.

Count Fersen to Queen Marie-Antoinette.

April 17, 1792.

You must already have heard the crushing news of the death of the King of Sweden. You lose in him a firm support, a good ally, and I a protector and friend. The loss is a cruel one.

The account that M. Simolin gave the baron of his negotiation in Vienna promises nothing more active from that Court than in the past. The same system is to be followed; and now that the King of Sweden is dead no one can be sure what course the Empress of Russia will take. In this uncertainty the surest means is to try to make France attack; a hostile step on your part is the only thing that will decide the Powers Still, if it could be delayed a month it would be better I will explain all this in detail in the box of biscuits.

I have spoken to Mme. Sullivan. The name of the the woman is Mme. Toscani, she is safe, and if you send her a box containing pieces of cloth or other things, as you did for Mr Crawford, she will pass it on Mme. Sullivan has said nothing about it to Mr. Crawford, he is so timid and cautious he would hesitate, and nothing would be done. That is why he did not wish her to see General Jarjayes; for otherwise he has no secrets from her, but tells her all.

Count Fersen to Baron Taube.

BRUSSELS, April 18, 1792

Since your crushing letter of the 29th I have heard nothing from you, my friend, the German post has doubtless been delayed by the bad roads. I cannot comfort myself for the dreadful loss we have met with. Every day my sorrow is renewed — the memory of kindness! that memory will never leave me, my gratitude can end only with my life. My God! shall I never again offer him my homage! You will feel the pleasure it would be to me to have his portrait, if I could.

The news we receive from Vienna is not good; there will be no more activity than under the late emperor, Simolin could do nothing. This disposition, and the present uncertainty about the empress, have led me to advise Their Majesties to incite the rebels to attack. Since the death of our king that is the only resource left to them by which to decide the Powers.

I have determined, my friend, not to return to Sweden at this moment. As I alone hold the thread of affairs, and all those of Their Majesties pass through me, I could not absent myself without their interests suffering, or, at any rate being wholly interrupted. If there is any such idea about me try to set it aside. . . .

Count Fersen to Queen Marie-Antoinette.

No 4   April 19, 1792

I received No. 4 yesterday. No. 3 is missing M. Gog. arrived this morning. He brings good news, though nothing certain until we receive something more positive from Berlin It seems they have at last determined to march. Baron Thugut told Breteuil under the deepest secrecy. I will send you the details Saturday in a box of biscuits. M. Gog. starts to-morrow ; he goes through France.

Queen Marie-Antoinette to Count Fersen

No 5   April 19, 1792

What follows is in the same cipher, but you can have it deciphered by another. Baron B. must tell M. de Mercy from me that I dare not write to him directly, or by a secretary, because I am horribly watched just now. Perhaps I shall never be able to write to you again   I will still try to find a way [*two lines missing*]. . . . The king desires that the King of England be secretly informed that the letter M. Chauvelin bears, though written by his own hand is at least not his own style. Adieu ; I will write to you in two days on the cover of the " Moniteur."

The ministers and the Jacobins will to-morrow make the king declare war against the house of Austria under pretext that by its treaties of last year it broke that of the alliance of 1756 [Treaty of Versailles [1]], and also that it has not replied categorically to the last despatch. The ministers hope that this step will create fear, and that negotiations will begin in three weeks. God grant it may not be so, and that vengeance may come at last for all the outrages endured in this country ! In what will be said in the declaration there is much complaint of the proceedings of Prussia, but no attack upon her.

Count Fersen to Queen Marie-Antoinette.

BRUSSELS, April 24, 1792.

I send you a despatch from Berlin which is important. It will give you an idea of what is taking place. In support of

---

[1] See history of this treaty in the " Memoirs of Cardinal de Bernis " in the present Historical Series of translations — TR.

this despatch comes the news that Baron Thugut told the baron that the King of Hungary [Archduke Francis] said he was weary of all that was happening in France and was determined to put an end to it and act, that he meant to march his troops in concert with the King of Prussia; that if the French attacked they must be kept amused for six weeks or two months till the armies could arrive; that whether they attacked or not, he was determined to attack them; and they must then be amused with appearances of peace until the moment when he was able to act. I do not know for what reason M. de Mercy does not agree to this letter, he has not spoken of it.

I received yesterday the news of the declaration of war by France, and I am very glad of it. It is the best and only thing that will decide the Powers The Empress of Russia has declared to Vienna her intention of taking an active part in the affairs of France, she says she wishes the restoration of the monarchy such as it was before the revolution. It was M. de Mercy who told me this

The news from Spain is not good, she will not act until the Kings of Hungary [the emperor] and Prussia have taken a course. The most useful thing she could do, and it agrees fairly well with her plans, would be to station a cordon of twenty thousand troops along the frontier, and furnish arms and ammunition to the Catholics and discontented persons in the southern provinces. This has already been asked and it ought to be insisted on '

I have as yet no news as to what concerns myself personally; I do not know if I shall be continued here or not. My father urges me to return to Sweden and abandon everything That is what I will never do, even if reduced to penury. I have enough property here to support me for some time by selling it. But if my father induces the Duke-

Regent to have the same will as himself, I may find myself embarrassed by the deprivation of my little revenue. As I am dependent on them for that, they may hope in that way to hold me, and even if the duke does not lend himself to it, I am afraid my father may try that method, but I am determined that nothing in the world shall induce me to abandon all at this moment.[1]

Count Fersen to Queen Marie-Antoinette.

No 8.   June 2, 1792.

Prussia goes right; she is the only one on whom you can rely. Vienna keeps to the project of dismembering France and of negotiating with the constitutionals. Spain is bad. I hope that England will be otherwise. The empress sacrifices your interests for Poland Our regent is certainly for you, but he can do nothing, or little. He means to send away the envoy they have sent to him, and that is why he has recalled his *chargé d'affaires* from Paris. He has urged the empress to do the same[2] Try to continue the war, and do not now leave Paris Have you sent me the blank signatures? — and to what address? Mme. Toscani [M. Crawford's housekeeper] will bring you my letters.

The first Prussian column will arrive July 9th The whole army will be there by August 9th. It will act on the Moselle and Meuse, the *émigrés* on the Philippesburg side, the Austrians on Brisgau. The Duke of Brunswick comes to Coblentz July 5. He will advance from there, mask the forts, and then with thirty-six thousand chosen troops, march straight to Paris. The empress sends fifteen thousand men

---

[1] See Appendix.

[2] The Duke-Regent of Sweden continued Count Fersen in the same confidential post in Brussels that he had held under Gustavus III But the Regent's intentions and sympathies were against the course of the latter, and he refused to co-operate with Russia in sending troops to France. —Tr

of whom three thousand are cavalry. They will disembark at Wismar and march through Germany. June 22d she sent thirty thousand men to Poland. [1]

The Vicomte de Caraman has returned within a week from Berlin He brings the positive assurance of the King of Prussia that he will listen to no negotiation or compromise; that he insists on the king being set free and making what Constitution he chooses. He wishes the king to know this, also that this resolution on his part cannot change, and the king can rely upon it. He furnishes the money for the troops he sends.

Queen Marie-Antoinette to Count Fersen. [2]

June 5, 1792

[*Plain writing*] I have received your letter No. 7, and I immediately withdrew your funds from the Boscaris company. There was no time to lose! the bankruptcy was declared yesterday and this morning the whole thing is public at the Bourse.

[*In white ink.*] Orders are given for Luckner's army to attack immediately, he opposes this, but the ministry insist The troops lack everything, and are in the greatest disorder.

[*Plain writing.*] You will send me word what I am to do with these funds. If I am master of them I can invest advantageously in the purchase of some fine domains of the clergy; that is, no matter what may be said, the best way of placing money. You can answer by the same channel by which I now write

---

[1] This letter is evidently of two dates, although it is printed as one letter in the French volume — TR

[2] Here begins a series of letters from the queen to Fersen, whom she addresses as M Rignon. They are partly in plain writing on the fictitious affairs of the supposed M. Rignon, with passages in cipher or in white ink interpersed The plain writing is not in the queen's hand, but probably in that of Goguelat. — TR

Your friends are fairly well. The loss they have met with is a great trouble to them. I do my best to comfort them, but they think the restoration of their fortune impossible. Give them, if you can, some consolation about this; they need it; their situation becomes daily more dreadful. Adieu; accept their compliments and the assurance of my entire devotion.

Queen Marie-Antoinette to Count Fersen.

June 7, 1792.

[*In white ink.*] The constitutionals have sent a man to Vienna; he will pass through Brussels. Warn M. de Mercy to treat him as if he had been announced and recommended by me, and negotiate with him on the lines of the memorial I sent him. We desire that he shall write to Vienna and announce his coming; recommend that they keep his journey secret, and that they hold to the plan made by the Courts of Vienna and Berlin, but say it is necessary to seem to enter into the views of the constitutionals, and, above all, let him think they do this in accordance with the wishes and requests of the queen; these measures are necessary.

It is not the Abbé Louis who goes; I do not know the name of the man who takes his place. Tell M. de Mercy that we cannot write to him, being too closely watched.

[*Plain writing.*] Here is the situation of your affairs with Boscaris and Chol, of whose failure I told you in my last letter. I am expecting news from La Rochelle to let you know how you stand with Daniel Gareché and Jacques Guibert. All I know is that their failure is not considerable. You would do better, as I have already told you, to buy the property of the clergy rather than trust your money to bankers. If you choose I will employ in that way the funds I receive for you next month. I have received your 7th and 8th.

Count Fersen to Queen Marie-Antoinette.

No. 9   June 11, 1792.

The King of Prussia wishes you to know that the Chevalier de Boufflers returns to Paris. He asked for orders, but as the king has a bad opinion of him he told him nothing, and the Chevalier knows nothing of his real intentions; therefore you are to put no faith in anything he may tell you, the king having changed in nothing. I think you would do well not to see Boufflers at all.

My God ! how your situation distresses me; my soul is keenly and sorrowfully affected   Try to stay in Paris, where they must come to your succour, the King of Prussia is decided about it, you can count on that.

The empress has asked Sweden for 6000 men; but money is needed for them. You have not told me whether you have sent the blank signatures, by whom and how.

The Sieur Bergstedt, chargé d'affaires of Sweden in Paris, to Count Fersen. Report of what took place at the Tuileries, June 20, 1792.

At four o'clock the Tuileries were invested by about 50,000 pikes; the cries were . "Down with Monsieur Veto, Madame Veto, and all their tribe !" etc, etc. The National Guard seemed determined to keep and defend the gates; no commander directed them. The royal gate was almost unguarded; three municipal officers required the twelve grenadiers who remained there to open it. The pikes then entered in floods. The king saw this influx, which was accompanied with horrible outcries. He ordered the door of his apartments to be closed; they opened those of the two first rooms; the third, that of the Swiss was defended. It was then that axes were employed. At the noise made by the breaking in of that door the king called for his hat, and entered the hall, ordering firmly that all doors.be opened, saying that he wished to show himself to the people and speak to them. As he said the words, the door, already battered, was driven in and a flood of pikes entered. A few faithful and courageous grenadiers pushed the king into the embrasure of the third window, telling him to trust to them and have no fear. "Fear!" said the king, "put your hand on my heart and feel if it beats more than usual." As he said those remarkable words, a man with a pike, presenting the point of his weapon called out, "Where is he, that I may kill him!"— "Wretch!" said an usher of the apartment, "there he is, your king; do you dare to look at him?" The pikes and the flood of men about him recoiled, seized with a sort of terror There was a moment's silence. The king tried to profit by it and speak, but another inundation of pikes arrived with such horrible cries that Jove's thunder itself could not have been heard. Nothing was heard but insults, curses, reproaches, threats. In the midst of this infernal scene Madame Élisabeth came to throw herself into the arms of the king, she was fortunately caught by the grenadiers, who were still guarding that one closed door; they pushed her behind them into the embrasure of the fourth window. There she remained three hours; the king the same time in his. The crowd flung a *bonnet rouge* to each of them and at the earnest entreaty of the grenadiers the king put his upon his head.

When the attack began the queen was with the dauphin in his apartment. At the first outcries she wished to go to the king; but already the intervening room was seized She cried out, "I wish to die at the king's feet!" They disobeyed her, and took her in spite of herself to the Council chamber where they made a rampart of the Council table, and a Monsieur Blegny went to call the grenadiers, who were still guarding a door now useless, inasmuch as the people were in all the rooms. Two hundred grenadiers followed him up a little staircase, they surrounded the table behind which were the queen and dauphin; and certainly it was providential that they took and occupied that position, for they were still moving to it when the apartment of the dauphin was seized through a door which the leader of the pikes seemed to know better than others, for very few of the servants of the household knew of it. Two troops of pikes entered the council chamber at the same moment by opposite doors. M Santerre, speaking in some sort in their name, harangued the queen. The queen, with supernatural courage, replied with an accent and majesty worthy of Maria Theresa. It was noticed that as she spoke the pikes drew back. Communication was then re-established between the room where the king was and that of the queen; by this manœuvre the pikes returned to the staircase, and some went down instead of re-entering. They succeeded by help of the grenadiers in bringing the king to where the queen was. The people cooled down, became pitying, some wept. The mayor, Pétion, harangued them, congratulated them on their "brave conduct," and then dismissed them.

Never was courage greater, grander, more dignified than that of the king, the queen, and Madame Élisabeth. The queen several times heard the people calling for her head, but her countenance never changed.

This date recalls a like event and foretells another — the scene, the actors, the means all changed.

Count Fersen to Queen Marie-Antoinette

No 10   June 23, 1792

The sending of Gog to Vienna was known at Coblentz on the day he arrived here, and the same day an express was sent from there to Petersburg to notify the empress. Bombelles writes it from there. There is certainly some one in your interior who writes everything to the princes

If Aranda [Spanish prime-minister] wants to have a direct correspondence with you, avoid it, he is false and wants to negotiate, and then you are lost   Our regent thinks rightly; he sends me letters of notification for you, with orders to send them to you without passing through your ministers, with whom we hold no communication. I fear that Spain, England, and the emperor [Francis II.] want to negotiate, we shall ward it off if possible. The emperor has the project of dismemberment, and if he does not obtain it from you, he will treat with the constitutionals and obtain it from them; you will then lose your authority without preventing the dismemberment. You must decide, if this becomes inevitable. What is your will in the matter? — There is perhaps one means of preventing it, namely: to give the King of Prussia a pledge in writing of reimbursement. He desires it, but he wants the king's signature. I still have one blank signature left, which I have not mentioned to the baron. Do you wish me to make use of it if it would be useful to us to secure the opposition of the King of Prussia to all dismemberment? Have you sent me other blank signatures, and how? It would be well if I had three more. Buy two pretty bonnets at the " charlotte de deuil ," send them to Mme Toscani, and tell her to sew the three papers to their foundations under the lining, and tell her to send them to M. Sullivan; she knows how   The signature can be written in black, or if necessary in white ink. In that case make a pencil mark where the name is. You could even (in both cases) have the shop bill written on one page of the sheet, for we only need the other page. Be sure that I shall use the signatures only if necessary and useful.

I have given your message to M. de Mercy, he understood it very well, and he has written to Vienna in consequence. In the affair where Gouvion was killed, Lafayette lost four hundred men, the peasants say, the Austrians one hundred and fourteen killed and wounded. I have warned Russia and Berlin of the sending of the Constitution, lest they be tempted to make bad use of it.

Queen Marie-Antoinette to Count Fersen.

June 23, 1792

[*White ink.*] Dumouriez starts to-morrow for Luckner's army; he promises to incite Brabant to insurrection. Saint-Huruge starts also for the same purpose.

[*Plain writing*] Here is the statement of sums I have have paid for you. I will send you that of your receipts as soon as I have made it out.

I think I have received all your letters. The last two are 8 and 9. The 9th was dated June 11th. I did not keep the date of the other.

Your friend is in the greatest danger. His illness makes frightful progress. The doctors can do nothing. If you want to see him you must hasten. Inform his relations of his unfortunate state. I have finished your affairs with him, and I have no further anxiety on that point. I will give you news of him assiduously.

Queen Marie-Antoinette to Count Fersen.

June 26, 1792.

[*Plain writing.*]   I have received your No. 10 and hasten to acknowledge it.   You will receive shortly all details relating to the purchase of the property of the clergy which I have made for you.   I confine myself to-day to putting your mind at ease about the investment of your *assignats ;* I have but few left, and in a few days I hope they will be as well invested as the others.

I am sorry not to be able to reassure you about your friend.   For three days however, the disease has made no progress, nevertheless, the symptoms continue alarming. He needs a crisis to bring him out of his present condition, and there is no appearance of that, this makes us despair. Inform all persons who have dealings with him of his situation, in order that they may take their precautions, time presses.   I shall keep you informed of the better or the worse of his state   Send punctually to the post.   Adieu.   Receive the friendship and compliments of all who interest you.

Count Fersen to Queen Marie-Antoinette.

No. 12   June 30, 1792

I received yesterday your letter of the 23d.   There is nothing to fear as long as Austria is not defeated   A hundred thousand Dumouriez could not incite this country [Austrian Low Countries] to rebellion, although it is well inclined to it.

Your position makes me ceaselessly anxious.   Your courage will be admired, and the firm conduct of the king will have an excellent effect.   I have already sent the account of the king's conversation with Pétion everywhere ; and I am going to send it to the "Gazette Universelle," it is worthy

of Louis XIV. The same tone should be continued, and
above all try not to be made to leave Paris. That is an
essential point. There it will be easy to reach you, and
that is the object of the Duke of Brunswick. He will precede his entry with a very strong manifesto in the name of
the Allied Powers, which will render all France and especially Paris responsible for the persons of the royal family.
He will then march straight to Paris, leaving the combined
armies on the frontier to mask the forts and prevent the
troops that are in them from acting elsewhere and opposing
his operations. The empress is marching thirteen thousand
men, and our regent consents to give her the eight thousand
she asked for. They are ready, and will march as soon as
we can get the money.

The Duke of Brunswick arrives at Coblentz on the 3d of
July; the Prussian division on the 8th. Seven thousand
men are to be detached at once for this country, and stationed at Luxembourg. Those who are here have committed
a folly in not attacking Luckner on his arrival. At present
he is too well posted and intrenched, there is every appearance that they will leave him there, until the other troops
arrive. They have committed another folly in letting sixty
chefs be taken before Maubeuge.

One M. Viette has passed through here; he told the
Vicomte de Caraman that he was sent by you to Coblentz on
a mission. He showed him a letter addressed to General
Schmidt, written, he said, with white ink between the lines.
He has no doubt made the same confidence to other persons.

I wrote you on the 25th, No 11, through Gog, and No. 10
through Mme. Toscani   Answer me about the blank signatures and the dismemberment. You ought to make Gog. write
to me every Sunday and Wednesday to give me details of
all that happens. When he writes "They say, but I do

not believe it" I shall know that the thing is certain. All letters written by this means arrive.

Queen Marie-Antoinette to Count Fersen.

July 3 1792

[*In cipher*] I have received yours of the 25th, No 11. I am much touched by it. Our position is dreadful, but do not be too anxious. I feel courage, I have in me something that tells me we shall soon be saved and happy. That one idea sustains me. The man I send is for M. de Mercy. I have written him very strongly to decide to speak. Act in a way to awe here *time presses*, there is no way to wait any longer. I will send the blank signatures in the way you requested.

Adieu ; when shall we see each other again in peace ?

Queen Marie-Antoinette to Count Fersen.

July 6, 1792.

[*In cipher.*] They brought me your last letter, written in white, after they had brought out the writing. This is the second time this has happened. We must take other measures to prevent this trickery. You will see the importance of this warning

A terrible catastrophe is expected on the 14th in all corners of Paris, especially at the Jacobins. They preach regicide ; sinister plans are being laid, but, being known, they may, perhaps, be foiled. The Jacobins from all the provinces are arriving here in crowds, there is not a day that I am not warned to be upon my guard, — sometimes by an officious person, sometimes by an intriguer. I am not left a moment of tranquillity

I have the three blank signatures, but I do not know how to send them, as the public coaches run no longer. Point out to me some other way.

Do not be too anxious on my account. Believe that courage always awes. The course we have just taken will give us, I hope, the time to wait; but six weeks are very long   I dare not write more. Adieu. Hasten, if you can, the succour promised for our deliverance.

[*In white ink*]   I exist still, but it is a miracle. The day of June 20th was dreadful. It is no longer I whom they chiefly want to destroy, they now want the life of my husband, and make no secret of it. He showed a firmness and strength which awed them for an instant, but the danger may return at any moment. Adieu; save yourself for us, and do not be too anxious about us.

Queen Marie-Antoinette to Count Fersen.

July 7, 1792

[*Plain writing.*]   I sent you, some days ago, a statement of your current debts. Herewith is a supplement which I received this morning from your London bankers.

[*In white ink*]   The different parties in the National Assembly united to-day. This union cannot be sincere on the part of the Jacobins; they are dissimulating to hide some project. We suppose one of their projects to be to make the king demand a suspension of arms and force him to negotiate a peace. You must give warning that all official action of that nature is not by the will of the king, and if he is forced by circumstances to manifest his will he will do so through the organ of M. de Breteuil. M. Crawford will receive before long the three blank signatures. warn him, so that he may open the package carefully. They are all written in white ink.

[*Plain writing.*]   I think you can do nothing better than invest here. Tranquillity is being restored, and all parties are uniting at this moment to carry out the Constitution.

Give me *carte blanche* and I am sure you can make good purchases and double your funds in two years. I have just bought the house we looked at together, rue de l'Université; it will cost me, all things included, 157,000 francs Adieu, my family are all well, and send their compliments; they desire ardently to see you again.

Count Fersen to Queen Marie-Antoinette.

BRUSSELS, July 10, 1792

M. Lasserez and M. Léonard have arrived and brought me your letters. I have no need to tell you that they give me great pleasure. Your courage is admirable, and the firmness of your husband has had a great effect. Both must be preserved to resist all efforts to make you leave Paris. It is very important that you remain there. *Nevertheless*, I am of M. de Mercy's opinion as to the one case in which you ought to leave it, but you must take care before you attempt it to be very sure of the courage and fidelity of those who contrive your escape, for if it fails you are lost beyond redemption, and I cannot think of it without a shudder.

They are hastening the operations as much as possible; in the first days of August the advance will begin. But to speak strongly at this moment without being ready to act at the moment of speaking would be a measure that would fail in its effect It would not awe, and might expose you still further.

From what you say about the sending of the blank signatures, I infer that you approved what I wrote to you, consequently, under circumstances more or less urgent, I shall make use (while awaiting the others) of the one I still have.

The conduct of Spain is shameful and blamed by all Europe. England does well. Our regent, in consequence of the de Staël intrigues, will not put himself forward. I try to foil Staël all I can, he sees much of M. de Verminac. We shall take care that the manifesto be the best possible, we are now busy with it   It makes the city of Paris responsible for the safety of the king and his family.

The horrible scene of June 20th has revolted all Europe and cost the revolution many of its partisans   Luckner and Lafayette seem to be abandoning this frontier and moving into the Bishoprics.   If the Austrians had shown a little more activity they could have carried off the Duc d'Orléans, and defeated Luckner's army at Courtrai.   The princes are to have an assembly of parliaments and peers at Manheim, a folly: we shall try to prevent it.   It is M. de Luxembourg who instigates all that.

Queen Marie-Antoinette to Count Fersen.

July 11, 1792

[*Plain writing.*]   I feel, my dear Rignon, what interest you have, relatively to your financial operations, in being *au courant* of passing events; so I shall do what depends on me to leave you nothing to desire in that respect.   Nevertheless, I ought to inform you that, my connections being of little extent and the circle in which I live being very narrow, I shall be but a poor resource.   But if I can be to you of little real utility, at least I can prove to you my zeal and good-will.

You have no doubt heard of the coming together of the different parties in the Assembly, of the step taken by the king to the Assembly, of the suspension of Pétion and Manuel by the department, of a few slight movements of the people to reinstate the mayor in his functions, and the wishes of part of the Assembly as to that.   That is the matter which chiefly occupies the Parisians to-day   It is said that Pétion will be reinstated, because there is a flaw in

the form of the suspension, so that the king will not confirm
it.   Others say that the king, alarmed at the power of the
mayor, disgusted with his pride, and convinced of his bad
intentions, will confirm the sentence of the department, but
I do not believe it.   The peace that Lamorette brought back
into the National Assembly only lasted a moment   Brissot
made a speech tending to inquire into the conduct of the
king since the beginning of the revolution and proposing to
suspend him, tending also to declare the nation in danger,
and the ministers responsible in a body ; declaring also that
they had not the confidence of the nation, and proposing a
decree of accusation against Chambon, etc   This incident
set every one to quarrelling again   The result was that the
six ministers were summoned, and required to render an
account within twenty-four hours of the state of the interior
of France, of the frontiers, and of the army.   They found
fault with them so harshly for four hours, and the ministers
felt so overweighted by the responsibility put upon them,
that they all resigned yesterday morning, and to-day the
king has no ministers.   The cowardice of the latter is generally blamed ; they had nothing to fear by following the line
of the Constitution.

People are uneasy at the approach of the anniversary of
the Federation.   It is feared that that religious and patriotic
fête may be the pretext of an attack upon the Tuileries.   The
ceremonial is not yet arranged   The royal family are to be
present at it   The number of Federals who will attend,
especially from the Southern provinces, is much smaller than
was expected.   Some are stopped by fear of being sent to
fight on the frontier ; others by work on the land.   The
greater number are from the neighbourhood ; it is thought
that all will pass off tranquilly.

The Duc d'Orléans has quitted the army in Flanders ; he

is now at Rince, he is held in such contempt among the troops that he was obliged to depart.   I will render you in a few days a summary of the business I have done for you since the first of the month.

[*In white ink.*]   The constitutionals, united under Lafayette and Luckner, want to carry the king off to Compiègne the day after the Federation, for this purpose the two generals are here.   The king is disposed to lend himself to this purpose; the queen opposes it   It is not known what will be the upshot of this great enterprise, which I am very far from approving.   Luckner takes the army of the Rhine, Lafayette that of Flanders; Biron and Dumouriez go to that of the centre

[*Plain writing.*]   Your banker in London is not very punctual in remitting to me your funds.   I wish you would write him a few words about it.   Adieu, my dear Rignon; I embrace you with all my heart.

Queen Marie-Antoinette to Count Fersen.

July 15, 1792

[*Plain writing.*]   Evil-minded people cause much anxiety as to the event of the Federation.   They announced the arrival of a multitude of brigands and a criminal enterprise on their part.   Perhaps you are agitated by the same fears; so I hasten to reassure you as to the fate of all in whom you are interested here.   M. Pétion is recalled to his functions by the National Assembly and the will of the people.   He has the public confidence which makes us hope that if any-one, by his personal influence can secure peace and successfully oppose the schemes of factious persons it is this magistrate, father of the people; it is thus that he is called by true patriots.

General Luckner arrived here on the night of the 13th.

He will appear to-morrow before the National Assembly. They say he has come to ask for an increase of 50,000 men to his army.

Paris is still in great agitation; they expect a great event which each party wants to turn to its own advantage; but I cannot explain myself further. A single day destroys calculations and changes circumstances. To keep you informed of events I ought to write to you twice a day.

We have here five or six thousand Federals, nearly all issuing from the club of the Jacobins. Some mean to stay here, others go to the camp at Soissons. We are expecting daily the armies of Marseille and Bordeaux The three regiments of the line which were guarding Paris are to start for the frontier, by virtue of a decree of the Assembly, in two or three days. There is much talk of sending away the Swiss Guard.

That, my dear Rignon, is about how things now are. I will write you to-morrow about your private affairs, to-day I have not the leisure. Adieu, I am wholly yours.

Send me word if you have received the gloves I sent you.

Count Fersen to Queen Marie-Antoinette.

No. 13.   BRUSSELS, July 18, 1792.

I have received all your letters and the three blank signatures, but the name comes out so feebly that I am not sure if I can make any use of them If you could find a safe means to send me others written in a stronger ink it would be well.

The princes have sent a memorial to all the Powers, in which they state that the king, by agreement with the constitutionals and deceived by them, is about to negotiate for a truce, etc, and begging them to pay no attention to it. They have sent this memorial to the baron asking his reply to it.

He was indignant and denied positively that such a thing had been done. He at once wrote to Count Schulemburg and the Duke of Brunswick that the princes were in error, and I have written it everywhere myself. M. de Calonne, to make it supposed that the baron was in agreement with such conduct, said : "You will see that the baron will not answer you" He advises many follies to the princes. M. de Lambert does well and tries to prevent them, and the Duke of Brunswick holds them back, but all this gives much trouble. . . .

They are working at the manifesto. I have written one which I gave to M de Limon, and he has given it to M. de Mercy, without his knowing that it is mine. It is very good, and such as they ought to desire. Nothing is promised to any one, no party is affronted, we are pledged to nothing, and Paris is made responsible for the king and family. They say that operations will begin on the 15th of August. Send me six copies of the " Cri de la douleur." I want to send them everywhere.

Queen Marie-Antoinette to Count Fersen.

July 21, 1791.

[*Plain writing.*] I send you to-day two pamphlets, two to Mme Sullivan, and two to Mr. Crawford. I am very glad that you were pleased with the gloves I sent you

All the members of the department of Paris have sent in their resignations A great number of the deputies of the right will do the same. M. Mathieu Montmorin has given his and gone to England. To-morrow they will definitely settle the fate of M. de Lafayette, it is generally thought he will be decreed accused.

The king, the queen, and Madame Élisabeth never appear in the garden without being insulted, in spite of the precautions taken to allow none but federals and persons who have tickets of service to enter the garden. The latter blame the federals, but it is more likely that the matter is an abuse of the cards rather than an abuse of their liberty by the federals. In addition, the rumour goes — but I warn you I do not believe a word of what I am going to tell you — that the Jacobins have more than ever a scheme to leave Paris with the king and go to the Southern provinces. For this purpose, it is said, they are bringing from the provinces numerous detachments of the National Guard drawn from all the *jacobinières;* eight hundred are to arrive to-morrow from Marseille. They say that in eight days this assemblage will be strong enough to execute that project. Others say that the Jacobins of the Assembly are awaiting the manifesto of the foreign Powers to take a course. It is expected this week; it is not known why it is delayed. If you know anything about its principal articles I wish you would let me know. On my side, I will keep you informed, as best I can, of what is going on here. Send me word if you have received all my letters.

All in whom you are interested here are well. I gave them news of you last evening; they heard them with pleasure and charged me to tell you so and urge you to write as often as you can. Adieu, my dear Rignon; I embrace you very tenderly.

Queen Marie-Antoinette to Count Fersen

July 24, 1792

[*In cipher.*] In the course of this week the Assembly will decree its removal to Blois and the suspension of the king. Every day produces a new scene: but always tending to the destruction of the king and his family; petitioners have said at the bar of the Assembly that if he is not deposed they will massacre him, and they have had the honours of the session paid to them. Tell M. de Mercy that the lives of the king and queen are in the greatest danger; that the delay of a day may produce incalculable evils, that the manifesto must be sent at once, that it is awaited with extreme impatience; that necesarily it will rally many persons round the king and secure his safety; otherwise, no one can answer for what may happen; the troop of assassins increases daily.

[*Plain writing.*] I have employed the rest of your funds, of which the above is an exact statement, in the purchase of two houses nearly new with good rentals. . . . These two houses can be let for ninety-five hundred francs; thus you see that your funds are not ill-invested.

Send me word if you have received the four preceeding numbers. Two days ago a letter was given to me from you, which I have sent to its address. You have probably received the six pamphlets you asked for.

Count Fersen to Queen Marie-Antoinette.

No. 14   BRUSSELS, July 26, 1792.

I have received your letter No. 4, and one of July 7 without number. I have already given warning that nothing is to be believed unless it comes through the Baron de Breteuil. You did very right not to let yourself be led away by Lafayette and the constitutionals. We have never ceased to hurry the manifesto and the operations. The latter will begin on the 2d or 3d of August. The manifesto is ready, and here is what M. de Bouillé, who has seen it, writes to M. de Breteuil: "They have followed your principles, and I venture to say ours, wholly in the manifesto and the general plan, in spite of the intrigues which I have witnessed, and at which I laughed, feeling certain, from what I knew, that they could not prevail." He is at Mayence, very well treated by the archduke and the king. — We have insisted that the manifesto shall be threatening, especially as regards responsibility for the persons of the royal family, and also that there shall be no question of the government and the Constitution — Schulemburg [Prussian minister] writes to the baron that the king will listen to no negotiation, and wants the liberty of the king.   They are printing a succinct statement of the reasons that make them go to war, which I send you; it is rather well done — Here is the baron's project for the ministry: *War*, La Galissonnière, who, he says, has furnished him with good ideas; *Navy*, du Moustier; the *Seals*, Barentin; *Foreign Affairs*, Bombelles; *Paris*, La Porte, and *Finances* to the Bishop of Pamiers, to avoid systems and have a man of order and firmness, with a finance council of six members.   Write me as soon as possible what you think of this   We have succeeded in excluding La Marck from affairs, and in preventing the emperor from sending him to reside with the Duke of Brunswick.   The King of Prussia would not have M. de Mercy at the conference; he attributes to him the slow, nerveless, and double conduct of the Court of Vienna   The *émigrés* are to be divided into three corps to act with the armies, but they will not be the advance guard as they had requested, and they will not be allowed to act independently.   I insisted strongly on that.   The princes will be with the King of Prussia, the Prince de Condé with Prince Hohenlohe, the Austrian, and M d'Egmont who commands the 3d corps with General Clerfayt.   Maréchal de Castries boasts of receiving communications direct from the king, he has even made the baron believe it.   He is a poor head in affairs.

Count Fersen to Queen Marie-Antoinette.

BRUSSELS, July 28, 1792

I have this moment received the declaration of the Duke of Brunswick [the manifesto], which is very good, it is the one given by M. de Limon, and it is he who sends it to me   To avoid suspicion I do not send it to you; but Mr. Crawford sends it to the English ambassador, Lord Kerry, and he will certainly show it to M. de Lambesc.

This is the critical moment and my soul trembles for it.   God preserve you all; that is my sole prayer.   If it is useful to hide yourself do not hesitate, I beg of you, to do so; it may be necessary, to give time to reach you.   In that case, there is a cellar in the Louvre, connected with the apartment of M. de Laporte.   I believe it to be safe and little known.   You could make use of it.

To-day the Duke of Brunswick puts his army in motion; it will take him eight to ten days to reach the frontier.   It is thought that the Austrians intend to make an attempt on Maubeuge.

Queen Marie-Antoinette to Count Fersen.

No. 7.   August 1, 1792

[*Plain writing.*]   I have received your No. 14 of July 26, with the printed paper inclosed.   I at once terminated the matter of which you wrote, and I now wait only for the necessary funds to fulfil my engagements, I think it would be best to send the money in specie as there is much to gain now by exchange on *assignats.*

I have not yet leased your houses.   The troubles in Paris are driving away the sort of people who would hire them. The murder of M. Desprémenil, the arrival of great numbers of suspicious strangers, and fear of the pillage of Paris are the principal causes of this exodus. Those who do not leave France go to Rouen and its environs. The event of the 30th has increased the uneasiness, irritated one half of the National Guard and discouraged the other. They are expecting a coming catastrophe; the emigration is doubling. Weak persons with pure intentions, those of uncertain courage and integrity hide themselves, the evil-intentioned alone show themselves with audacity. A crisis is needed, to bring the city out of the state of constriction in which it is, every one desires it, every one seeks it in the line of his own opinions; but no one dares calculate the results, fearing they may be to the profit of wretches. Whatever happens, the king and all honest men will not allow any attack on the Constitution; if that is overthrown they will perish with it.

Your friends are well and send you many compliments, desiring ardently to see you soon.

P. S. The package I sent to you by diligence bears the number 141, and each piece of stuff the following letters [*in cipher*]. White ink below.

[*In white ink.*] The king's life is evidently threatened, also that of the queen. The arrival of about six hundred Marseillais, and a quantity of other delegates from all the Jacobins increases our anxiety, which is, unhappily, but too well founded. They are taking precautions of all kinds for our safety, but assassins prowl round the palace incessantly, they excite the people, there is ill-will in one part of the National Guard, weakness and cowardice in the other. The resistance that can be opposed to the enterprises of those wretches is solely in a few persons determined to make a rampart of their bodies for the royal family, and in the regiment of the Swiss Guards. The affair which took place on the 30th, after a dinner in the Champs Élysées, between one hundred and eighty grenadiers of the élite of

the National Guard and the Marseille Federals, shows clearly
the cowardice of the National Guard and the little reliance
to be placed on that troop, which, in point of fact, imposes
only by its numbers   The one hundred and eighty grenadiers took to flight, two or three were killed and some
twenty wounded.   The Marseillais now police the Palais-
Royal and the garden of the Tuileries, which the Assembly
has ordered to be thrown open.   In the midst of such dangers it is difficult to concern ourselves with the choice of
ministers.   If we obtain one moment of tranquillity, I will
write you what is thought of those you propose.   For the
moment we can think only of escaping daggers and foiling
the conspirators who swarm about a throne so near to disap-
pearing   For a long time these wretches have taken no
pains to conceal their purpose of destroying the royal family.
At their last nocturnal meetings they differed only as to the
means to be employed   You must have judged from a preceding letter how important it is to gain even twenty-four
hours; I can only repeat it to-day, adding that if they do not
come, nothing but Providence can save the king and his
family.

[Those are the queen's last words to the world.   Before
they reached Fersen the 10th of August came and she was
lost forever to the sight of men.   The story of Count Fersen's subsequent efforts for her, in fact of all his hopes
and efforts for her, is one of cruel, unspeakable disappoint-
ment · the failure of Varennes, the cold indifference of
the emperor to his sister's fate, the dull diplomacy of the
Courts, each waiting on the others for the purpose of
doing nothing, the refusal of Louis XVI to leave Paris in
February, 1791, the death of the one true man, Gustavus III.,
the dastardly conduct of the Duke of Brunswick, the deser-

tion of Dumouriez by his army, — the failure of all these great efforts and many lesser ones, the victims left at last to die abandoned, was a crushing, hopeless grief to his knightly soul.

The close of his career carried on the fatality of its beginning. He seems never to have married, and to have lost in quick succession, soon after the queen's death, his dearest friends: his father, to whom he was deeply attached, his mother, sister, and his best friend, Baron Taube. For some years he lived a private life and travelled about Europe, always with a certain bitterness in his heart against Duke Charles, the Regent of Sweden, for his desertion of the King and Queen of France. In November, 1796, the young king's minority came to an end, and he soon after appointed his father's friend to be his ambassador at the Congress of Rastadt The French Republic refused to recognize Count Fersen, and the king then sent him to arrange his marriage with the granddaughter of the Grand-duke of Baden. This mission, however, did not prevent him from attending in a private capacity the conferences of the Congress.

In 1801 he was made Grand-Marshal of Sweden, and a year later, lieutenant-general In 1805, when the King of Sweden suddenly resolved to take an active part in the war against France, Count Fersen accompanied him through the campaign of that year in Swedish Pomerania. It is to his honour that he opposed the continuation of the war after it became useless through the peace made by Russia and Prussia, the king's allies. His letters to the king on this subject, a few of which have been published, show his attachment to the welfare of his country, but they offended the king, who ordered him to return to Sweden and remain there as chamberlain to the queen.

After the dethronement of Gustavus IV., the exclusion of

his descendants from the throne, and the accession of the
late regent as Charles XIII., the question of the succession
to the throne led to political dissensions and public riots.
Count Fersen was considered a partisan of the young son of
Gustavus IV., and on the occasion of a great public proces-
sion, which he was conducting as Grand Marshal of Sweden,
he was dragged from his carriage and murdered by the
populace, on the fatal date, to him, of June 20th in the year
1810, — nineteen years after the flight to Varennes.]

APPENDIX I.

———◆———

Count Fersen to Baron Taube

Aix-la-Chapelle, November 19, 1792.

My dear Friend, — What an epoch is this we live in ! it seems as if Providence were accumulating fatal blows to crush that good and most unfortunate family; my soul is torn in a thousand ways. You were already in despair, my friend, at the retreat of the Duke of Brunswick, well, you will be still more so when you learn that the Austrians have thought themselves obliged to abandon the Low Countries on the approach of Dumouriez and a mob of bandits, thieves, and rebels. It is a horror to think of; especially when we know it is to the weakness, imbecility, lack of energy in the government and Duke Albert, who commanded the army, that we owe this disaster — for the troops are excellent, they did prodigies of valour, but were badly led. The Wallons fought well, and were faithful until the moment when they saw that Brussels and the whole country was about to be abandoned, then only did the majority depart; after which fear seized every one, each thought only of saving himself, and everything was abandoned, cannon, magazines nothing was carried away, all was left to fall into the hands of the French.

The country was not in a bad state, there has been but one attempt at revolt, and that, a very slight one at Antwerp, was smothered by the burghers themselves ; no one, except the *canaille*, wanted the French; they have seen too much of the individual misery in France to wish to follow their example, but the Austrian government basely fled and abandoned them: it is horrifying. Imagine, my friend, that at Mons, when Duke Albert at last decided, but too late, to attack, General Beaulieu was sent with six thousand men to attack seventy thousand; he forced them to give way, but the rest of the Austrian army did not support him, and he was obliged to retreat to his position. I cannot begin to tell you the many little facts of this nature of which I have knowledge, briefly, the result of such multiplied follies is the retreat of the Austrians. Duke Albert has resigned the command, Generals Clerfayt and Beaulieu have accepted it, after much entreaty.

The princes and *émigrés* are at Liège in a deplorable condition, without money, without resources, in the greatest misery, without knowing whether the Powers will help them out of it or not. The whole of this neighbourhood is disaffected, and awaits the arrival of the French to declare itself. The French maxims of liberty and equality are gaining ground in the Electorates, in short, my friend, if the sovereigns do not feel their own interests, and league together to stop the evil by crushing it now, they will all be its victims. There will soon be neither kings nor nobles, and all countries will experience the horrors to which France is now a victim, to exist, and save enough to exist upon, a man must make himself a Jacobin. If you can procure the reading of my letters to the duke-regent you will see all the details of present events. We have no detailed news from Paris. They are busy with the king's trial, but there is reason to think he will not be executed, though certainly condemned. It is dreadful to me to write of such horrors, and I am cruelly tried.

I left Brussels on the 9th with Simolin and Crawford. We had our own horses and others that we hired; we reached Maestricht on the 11th with great difficulty, finding little to eat and nowhere to sleep. It was one long string of carriages and waggons the whole way, and never was there a more painful sight: those unfortunate French *émigrés* on foot, or in carts, along the whole road, with scarcely anything to eat, women of condition on foot, with their maids, or quite alone, carrying bundles in their arms or their babies! At Maestricht we had great trouble in getting any shelter; eleven thousand persons had arrived in three days. We remained four days, and on the 16th came here. We shall stay a short time and then, as MM. Metternich, Simolin, Mercy, and de Breteuil are going to Dusseldorf, I shall go too, so will Simolin; and I hope that Crawford will decide to settle there with us. Among my other troubles I fear that I shall soon have private embarrassments as to money. All my property in Paris is sold, or is to be; that which I have left in the Low Countries, in care of a gentleman, will probably be pillaged by the French. I could not bring away with me all that I had in Brussels, and I know not yet whether I can recover it or whether it is taken. You know, my friend, that I have never had one penny of salary, I desired none, the pleasure of serving my king and the King of France was ample compensation for my sacrifices ; but my position is becoming prolonged, my prospects are very uncertain, this removal has cost me enormously, and I have sacrificed much money on couriers, etc., etc , for which no one can repay me. God knows I regret nothing, and if, in the end, I can feel that I have been useful to them, I shall never regret anything, I vow myself willingly to all privations. I shall calculate, when I am rather more tranquil, what still remains to me, and then I shall see what I can do. I have made arrangements to have my letters sent to me from Brussels, but for the last few days none have reached me; that is still another privation and sorrow.

APPENDIX II.

The Archbishop of Tours to Count Fersen.

[*Extract of a letter from Paris*]   January 27, 1793

On the 21st, at half-past nine in the morning, the king came out of the Temple, escorted by four hundred cavalry and twelve hundred infantry.

He was driven, in the midst of profound silence, along the boulevards du Temple, Saint-Martin, and Saint-Honoré to the scaffold erected on the Place, formerly Louis XV., now called "Revolution," between the spot where the statue stood and the entrance to the Champs-Élysées.

On the back seat of the carriage and to left of the king, was his confessor, an Irish priest; on the front seat were two officers of the gendarmerie.

On reaching the foot of the scaffold, the king, with great coolness, allowed them to tie his hands; he then mounted with much courage.

He wished to speak to the people; but the noise of the drums stifled his voice. Nevertheless, those who were near the scaffold heard these words, said in a firm voice: "I pardon my enemies, and I desire that my death may be the salvation of France."

He drew his last breath at ten and three quarters; his fallen head was shown to the people. At the same moment the air resounded with cries of "Vive la nation! Vive la république Française!"

Several of the volunteers steeped their pikes in his blood; others their handkerchiefs.

His body and his head were brought and buried in the Madeleine.

The Archbishop of Tours has the honour, in conformity with the wish of Monsieur le Comte de Fersen, to send him the sad and horrible details of the atrocious crime, which would forever dishonour the French name were it not disavowed by those, in very great numbers, who are still worthy to bear it.

Letters from Paris are absolutely silent as to the rest of the royal family.

Sunday evening.

INDEX.

---

352   INDEX.

ÉLISABETH (Madame) de France, 93,
117, 175, 182, 240, 300, 325,
326.
EMIGRATION (the French), beginning
of it, 72; effect on the *émigrés* of the
king's death, 285.
ENGLAND (George III., King of), 10;
letter to King of Sweden promising
neutrality in affairs of France, 151,
155, 156, 190.
ENGLAND (Charlotte, Queen of), 10.
ESTAING (Amiral Comte d'), 22.

FAC-SIMILES of Marie Antoinette's writing, 223-227.
FAYETTE (Marie-Jean-Paul-Roch-Yves-
Gilbert-Motier, Marquis de la), 30, 81,
92-94, 115, 263-265.
FEDERATION (the Fête of) made ridiculous and indecent, 82, 83.
FERSEN (Frederick Axel, Field Marshal), letters of his son to him from
America, 21-64; the same on the
political aspects of France, 65-90;
on Count Axel's resolution to devote
himself to the King and Queen of
France, 84, 85; at and after the
King's attempt to escape, 114, 115.
FERSEN (Jean Axel, Count), his diary
and papers, 1; birth, parentage, and
education, 2, 3; extracts from diary,
3-12; visits Voltaire at Ferney, 5;
visit to Paris, the French Court,
5-9; visit to London, 10, 11; desires a military career, 11; second
visit to Paris, 12-14; the courtiers
jealous of the queen's regard for
him, his discretion, 13; desires to
aid the Americans in their struggle
for independence, 19; is appointed
aide-de-camp to the Comte de Rochambeau, 20; sails from Brest, May
4, 1780; letters to his father from
America, 21-64; return to France;
honours; Washington bestows the
Order of Cincinnatus upon him, 65;
confidential mission to the French
Court, 66-68; letters to his father
and King of Sweden on the political

aspects of France at the beginning of
the Revolution, 65-90; devotes himself in gratitude to the King and
Queen of France, 84, 85; memorial to
the king and queen as to their course
of action, 86-89; the king's adopted
course, 90; makes preparations for
the king and family to leave Paris,
96-114; the safe escape, 114, 115,
117; the stoppage at Varennes, 115;
Fersen's despair, 117; begins his
efforts to save the king and queen
by a confidential mission to Emperor
Leopold from Gustavus III.; gallant
proposal of Gustavus III., 119-139;
failure to rouse the emperor to action,
138; visits the princes and *émigrés*
at Coblentz, 140; efforts to obtain
an armed congress, 141; his correspondence with Queen Marie Antoinette begins, 144; his letters to and
from her, 164, 166, 168, 172, 173, 182,
198, 205, 218, 229, 236, 238, 309, 311,
313, 315, 316, 317, 318, 319, 321, 322,
323, 324, 327, 328, 329, 331, 332, 333,
334, 336, 337, 338, 339, 340, 342; letters to and from the King of Sweden,
151, 152, 153, 154, 160, 207, 233, 234,
305; letters to and from his friend,
Baron Taube, 91-96, 98, 99, 100, 102,
103, 110-112, 157, 161, 170, 232, 239,
315, 318, 347; memorial on the European position of the king and queen
addressed by Fersen to the queen,
186-198; diary from January 1, 1792,
to November 18, 1793, 242-303; Fersen goes to Paris to induce the king
and queen to escape, and fails, 244-
251; confidential remarks to him by
Louis XVI., 246, 305, 309; interviews
with the queen, 247-249; distress at
the death of the King of Sweden,
255; begins fresh efforts to save the
king and queen, 262 *et seq.*; receives
news of August 10, 1792, 263-264,
266, 267; flight of the Austrians
from Brussels after Jemmapes, 279-
282, 347-349; horror at the death of
Louis XVI., 283; renewed efforts to
save the queen, 284, 293, 294-297 *et seq,*

CPSIA information can be obtained at www.ICGtesting.com
Printed in the USA
LVOW132140270112

265900LV00016B/202/P